D0441632

Becoming a Candidate
Political Ambition and the Decision to Run for Office

Why does anyone make the move from politically minded citizen to candidate for public office? What factors contribute to the initial decision to run for office? What circumstances trigger and suppress political ambition over time? *Becoming a Candidate: Political Ambition and the Decision to Run for Office* explores the factors that drive political ambition at the earliest stages. Using data from a comprehensive survey of thousands of eligible candidates, Jennifer L. Lawless systematically investigates what compels certain citizens to pursue elective positions and others to recoil at the notion. She assesses personal factors, such as race, gender, and family dynamics, as well as professional circumstances and attitudes toward the political system to shed new light on the candidate emergence process. By developing a broader conception of political ambition, Lawless speaks to fundamental questions of electoral competition, political representation, and democratic legitimacy.

Jennifer L. Lawless is an Associate Professor of Government at American University, where she is also the Director of the Women & Politics Institute. She is the current editor of *Politics & Gender*. Her research focuses on political ambition, public opinion, and women and politics. Her articles have appeared in the *American Journal of Political Science*, *Journal of Politics*, *Perspectives on Politics*, *Political Research Quarterly*, *Legislative Studies Quarterly*, *Politics & Gender*, and *Women & Politics*. She is also the coauthor of *It Takes A Candidate: Why Women Don't Run for Office* (Cambridge 2005) and *It Still Takes A Candidate: Why Women Don't Run for Office* (Cambridge 2010) with Richard L. Fox. She is a recognized speaker on the subject of electoral politics, frequently discussing these issues on national and local television and radio. Her scholarly analysis and political commentary have been quoted in the *New York Times*, the *Wall Street Journal*, the *Washington Post*, and *USA Today*, among numerous other newspapers, as well as on the websites of CNN, MSNBC, and Fox News. In 2006, she sought the Democratic nomination for the U.S. House of Representatives in Rhode Island's 2nd congressional district.

List of Tables

List of Figures

Acknowledgments

In the spring of 2005, I entered the Democratic primary in Rhode Island's 2nd congressional district. And for 16 months, I loved every minute of campaigning my heart out. Well, maybe not every minute. I did not adore the 30 hours a week I spent on the phone asking people I had never met for more money than they could comfortably give. I was not a huge fan of smiling politely when, on what seemed like a daily basis, I heard that my hair was too long, my neckline too low, my heels too high (odd, considering that I was also "too short"), and my makeup too subtle to enter the hallowed halls of the U.S. House of Representatives. It would be untrue to say that I enjoyed the 48 hours of perpetual nausea and nerves leading up to the two televised debates (although the debates, themselves, were undoubtedly a high point of the campaign). And I can think of few activities more unpleasant than making the dreaded concession call on election night. But overall, my congressional campaign was the most fulfilling, most important, most life-changing event I have ever had the privilege to enjoy. The opportunities to connect with voters, learn about the issues and challenges people face, articulate and advocate for clear positions on a host of policies, and hold an incumbent accountable are rewarding in ways I cannot put into words.

I am always surprised, therefore, when people ask, "Why would you ever have run for office?" In fact, this question arose on the campaign trail quite frequently. "You seem like a nice person. Why would you ever want to go to Washington?" "You have great ideas. Why don't you work for an organization that can actually do something to implement them?" "Politics is completely corrupt and politicians get nothing done. You want to waste your time doing *that*?" Indeed, at least at the beginning of the campaign, the notion of a political science professor running for office because she cared about the issues, thought the incumbent was out of sync with his constituents, and believed she could win the race was so anathema to people's predispositions that rumors began to circulate that I was running for office so that I could acquire raw material for my next book.

Well, here's the book. It will become very apparent very early on that this book includes no personal stories, no anecdotes from my race, and no information I acquired on the campaign trail. As I said throughout the campaign, I ran for office because I believed that I would be a better voice in Congress. I had no interest in running to engage in participant observation that would bolster my research agenda or facilitate my tenure case. But even if the book sheds no light on my own experiences, I do hope that it provides some insight into the initial decision to run for office and the circumstances under which eligible candidates consider entering the electoral arena. After all, the past decade has been particularly tumultuous; we have seen the waging of two wars, acrimonious partisan rancor in Washington, one of the most unpopular and polarizing presidents in recent history, two shifts in congressional party control, and the government's ineffective handling of the Hurricane Katrina disaster. We have seen not only the election of the first black president of the United States, but also the ascension of Nancy Pelosi as the first female Speaker of the House, the emergence of Hillary Clinton as the first serious female presidential contender (not to mention the recipient of 18 million votes), and the nomination of Sarah Palin as the first female Republican vice presidential candidate. It is hard to imagine a more important time to study questions pertaining to candidate emergence, political ambition, electoral competition, and political accountability.

Even though this book has nothing to do with my own campaign experiences, there is one similarity between writing a book and running for Congress. The author and candidate are responsible for all the errors and missteps, but because of an amazing group of people who provide help and support along the way, those errors and missteps are often far fewer and farther between than would otherwise be the case. Such is certainly true of this book, so the list of thank-yous is long.

Richard Fox deserves the largest share of my gratitude. Ten years ago, we decided to administer – by ourselves – a multiwave national mail survey to 7,000 "eligible candidates." At the conclusion of a yearlong foray into data collection, we had signed, folded, sealed, and stamped almost 25,000 pieces of mail. We fed every envelope into the printer, by hand. We wrote a personal note on each letter, encouraging the recipient to complete the survey. We affixed an actual stamp to each piece of mail. And as proof of our insanity, we did it all over again seven years later so that we could have panel data. These national mail surveys serve as the basis not only for the two books Richard and I wrote together, but also for this book. It is not at all a stretch to say, therefore, that without Richard, there would be no book. But my appreciation extends far beyond the fact that he licks, seals, and stamps envelopes better than anyone I have ever met; is willing to travel across the country to engage in these endeavors; and can uncannily predict patterns of mail delivery. Richard has thoroughly read and insightfully commented on *everything* I have ever written, including this entire manuscript. He is an incredibly loyal friend despite also being the lucky target of more of my kvetching and melodrama than any person deserves. And he never makes me apologize for my tone.

I am also particularly grateful to Kathy Dolan, Walt Stone, and Linda Fowler, all of whom offered extensive and insightful comments from the inception of the 2001 Citizen Political Ambition Study through its completion. Scott Allard, Dave Brady, Dick Brody, Barbara Burrell, Mo Fiorina, Brian Frederick, Jim Gimpel, Sunshine Hillygus, Kent Jennings, Frances Lee, Cherie Maestas, Jane Mansbridge, Terry Moe, Karen O'Connor, Zoe Oxley, Kathryn Pearson, Kira Sanbonmatsu, Wendy Schiller, Keith Shaw, Sean Theriault, Sue Tolleson-Rinehart, and Darrell West provided feedback on pieces of the various book manuscripts and journal articles to come out of the project as well. And several students made important contributions. Thanks to Jinhee Chung, Sara Gentile, Shana Gotlieb, Ben Gray, Erik Kindschi, Nathan Kohlenberg, Marne Lenox, AnneMarie MacPherson, Ben Mishkin, and Teresa Tanzi.

From a practical standpoint, this endeavor would have been impossible without financial support from American University, Brown University, Cal State Fullerton, the Carrie Chapman Catt Center at Iowa State University, Stanford University, Union College, Hunt Alternatives Fund, and the Barbara Lee Foundation. In addition, Jonathan Ma and Eliana Vasquez provided invaluable assistance in assembling the initial sample and helping track the flow of mail. The second wave of the study could not have occurred without help from Dave Rangaviz. Sean Theriault and Dominique Tauzin stuffed more envelopes than any two people not conducting a national mail survey should ever have to stuff. I would also be remiss not to thank my former editor at Cambridge University Press,

Ed Parsons, and my current editor, Robert Dreesen, for help and support throughout the process.

It is no exaggeration to say that I managed to write this book and maintain some degree of sanity in the process because of the amazing staff at the Women & Politics Institute. I am grateful to Ava Lubell, Pamela Riis, Erica Best, Will Hubbard, Amanda Krause, Justyna Modzelewska, and Andy Reef for their incredible work ethic and dedication. Gail Baitinger demonstrated more concentration and diligence than I thought humanly possible as she tirelessly proofread the final version of the manuscript. My greatest share of gratitude goes to My-Lien Le, whose obsessive compulsive attention to detail allowed her to construct the index for the book in record time, and who shielded me from interruptions and annoyances during the writing process more effectively than I ever could have dreamed.

I would also like to thank my friends and colleagues from Brown University, where I began the book, and American University, where I finally finished it. In particular, Corey Brettschneider, Melani Cammett, Danny Hayes, Jan Leighley, and Wendy Schiller endured numerous complaint sessions about my progress (or lack thereof) and always managed to make me laugh, often at myself (although, truth be told, often at other people, too).

The final set of thank-yous is the most difficult to write because I do not even know where to begin. My parents, Margie and John Lawless, never waver in their support of anything I want to do. They told me, as a little girl, that I could be president of the United States. They accepted my decision to quit law school, work for a couple of years, earn virtually no money, and then pursue a Ph.D. They championed my decision to move across the country and spend four years at Stanford, even though that involved time zone issues and expensive plane tickets. They were the first to max out to my congressional campaign, even though they worried that people would be mean to me and I would cry a lot. They overlook the fact that I revert to the behavior of a fifteen-year-old whenever I spend more than three days at their house. And they always say yes, regardless of what I ask.

Adam Deitch and Nick Goldberg also deserve a share of thanks that is long overdue. When they agreed to put their lives on hold so that they could work for me when I ran for Congress, I could never have imagined how hard and smart they would work, how vital they would be for transforming me into a credible candidate, or what a critical source of friendship they would become. It is because of them that I never begin a sentence with "So, like, I think that ...," that I can call strangers and solicit financial contributions, that I speak in sound bites when offering political analysis, that I developed a far deeper sense of empathy, that I understand that walking 110 miles is not easy, that I drive especially carefully when the piña colada song is on the radio, and that I learned to appreciate the Black Eyed Peas.

It is no surprise, therefore, that it is my parents, as well as Adam and Nick, to whom I dedicate this book.

Mudslinging, Money-Grubbing, and Mayhem

Who Would Ever Run for Office?

Minneapolis FBI Agent Coleen Rowley rose to national prominence in 2002 when she exposed glaring gaps in pre–September 11 intelligence gathering and information sharing among U.S. law enforcement officials. Based on Rowley's iconic status (*Time* magazine named her one of its "Persons of the Year") and national security expertise, Democratic Party officials and members of Minnesota's congressional delegation encouraged her to throw her hat into the ring and challenge Congressman John Kline (R–MN) in 2004. Rowley turned down the invitation, explaining that she lacked the characteristics necessary to be a retail politician: "As a child, I only sold sixteen boxes of Girl Scout cookies. I was the lowest in the whole troop."[1] Yet two years later, something changed. Perhaps the Democrats' sustained recruitment efforts paid off. Maybe Rowley, who wanted to weigh in on issues of national security, was frustrated that President Bush did not name her to the Privacy and Civil Liberties Oversight Board.[2] Or it is possible that Rowley became more comfortable with the idea of being a candidate for public office. But with no additional experience or "skills" under her belt, and facing the same incumbent, Rowley announced her foray into electoral politics. The first-time candidate entered the 2006 congressional race and performed rather well; she garnered 40 percent of the vote.

[1] "FBI Whistleblower Says She Won't Run for Congress," Associated Press State and Local Wire, November 26, 2003.
[2] Beth Hawkins, "The Purity of Coleen Rowley," *Mother Jones*, March/April 2006. Accessed at http://motherjones.com/politics/2006/03/purity-coleen-rowley (March 6, 2011).

Party leaders did not recruit James Crabtree to run for office, and he lacked name recognition and notoriety, but he also sought an elective position in 2006. While serving in Iraq, Crabtree was among approximately one hundred marines from Travis County, Texas, who did not receive an absentee ballot in time to vote in the 2004 elections. When he returned to the United States in 2005, Crabtree investigated the situation and determined that the blame lay with County Clerk Dana DeBeauvoir.[3] Crabtree had never before considered a candidacy and admitted that "the last thing [he] expected to do was run for County Clerk."[4] But the anger he felt regarding his disenfranchisement, coupled with his belief that he was better suited for the job, propelled his decision to challenge DeBeauvoir when she sought reelection. Crabtree lost his first political bid, receiving 30 percent of the vote.

Robert F. Kennedy, Jr., also flirted with running for office in 2006, but unlike Coleen Rowley and James Crabtree, he ultimately decided against it. Eliot Spitzer's decision to run for governor of New York created an open race for attorney general. Despite a competitive field of Democratic candidates, party insiders and political analysts agreed that Kennedy's name recognition, political family ties, and reputation as an environmental crusader would have positioned him as the front-runner. Kennedy opted not to seek the Democratic nomination, though, explaining that he did not want to sacrifice time with his wife and six children.[5] He left the door open for a future run, however, stating that his political ambition would likely grow as his family circumstances changed: "I feel certain that I will run for office one day. But I think I need to wait a few years until my younger children get a little older."[6]

By virtue of even considering a run for public office, Coleen Rowley, James Crabtree, and Robert F. Kennedy, Jr., did something that never even crosses the minds of most citizens. Although the United States has 500,000 elective offices – most of which are situated at the local and state levels and meet only on a part-time basis – relatively limited

---

[3] "20 Year County Clerk Gets a GOP Challenge," *The Austin Chronicle*, October 20, 2006. Accessed at http://www.austinchronicle.com/gyrobase/Issue/print.html?oid=oid:412276 (March 6, 2011).

[4] Elizabeth Dunbar, "Amputee Iraq Veteran Seeks to Continue Service by Winning Election to Kentucky County Board," Associated Press, September 7, 2006.

[5] "RFK Jr. Rules Out Run for N.Y. Attorney General," *AllPolitics*, January 25, 2005. Accessed at http://www.cnn.com/2005/ALLPOLITICS/01/25/kennedy.newyork.ap/index.html (March 6, 2011).

[6] Jonathan Hicks, "Robert Kennedy Won't Run for State Attorney General," *New York Times*, January 25, 2005, page B1.

electoral competition pervades our political system. In 2010, thirty members of the U.S. House of Representatives faced no major-party challenger in the general election; more than fifty members found themselves with this luxury in 2006 and 2008. The lack of electoral competition in congressional primaries is even more striking. Since 1958, more than one-third of congressional incumbents have faced no primary opponent whatsoever (Lawless and Pearson 2008); an overwhelming majority of the others combat only nominal challengers. Roughly one-third of seats in all of the state legislatures across the country have gone uncontested since the 1990s.[7] The low level of competition is actually now so commonplace that, when she learned that only 29 percent of Connecticut's state legislators were running unopposed in 2010, Connecticut Secretary of State Susan Bysiewicz lauded her state's citizens for demonstrating "interest in the electoral process and running for office."[8] The lack of systematic election data at the local level makes it difficult to provide exact rates of electoral competition, but the number of uncontested seats on school boards and city councils is likely much higher (see Schleicher 2007).[9]

These dynamics are hardly surprising. For many people, running for office involves too much risk for too little reward. Considering a candidacy, after all, requires contemplating the courageous step of going before an electorate and opening oneself up to potential examination, scrutiny, loss of privacy, possible rejection, and disruption from regular routines and pursuits. It involves mulling over how to raise (sometimes

---

[7] For more information pertaining to state legislative competition in the 1990s, see Squire 2000. For levels of competition in the 2000s, see "Many State Legislative Races Are Uncontested," Associated Press, October 30, 2006. Accessed at http://www.msnbc.msn.com/id/15446775/ (July 3, 2010).

[8] Keith M. Phaneuf, "Competition for State Legislative Seats Reaches All-Time High," *Connecticut Mirror*, June 28, 2010. Accessed at http://www.ctmirror.org/story/6592/competition-state-legislative-seats-reaches-12-year-high (July 3, 2010).

[9] A Lexis-Nexis search of "uncontested local elections" provides a litany of cases from across the country in which no more than one candidate sought the local public office in question. In 2003, for example, 13 of the 19 races for the Onondaga County Legislature in New York went uncontested ("Forums to Address Voter Apathy," *The Post Standard*, April 1, 2004, page 6). In another example, Central County, California saw uncontested races for the Lafayette City Council, the Pleasant Hill Recreation and Park District, the Central Contra Costa Sanitary District, and the Mt. Diablo and Walnut Creek school boards. In addition, there were no candidates to file for the two open seats on the Canyon District school board (Cassandra Braun, "Some Regional Election Races Draw Little Candidate Interest," *Contra Costa Times*, October 21, 2004, page W01). Although there are certainly notable exceptions, these patterns are generally indicative of local electoral competition throughout the United States.

exorbitant) sums of money, navigate the media, and strike unappealing compromises. For high-level positions, candidates often need to engage in months of full-time campaigning, and success may mean indefinitely suspending one's career. At the local level, the political stakes may not be as high, but the decision to enter even a city council or school board race can involve holding oneself up before neighbors and community members (Shaw 2004; Golden 1996). And in many cases, the end does not justify the means, as the majority of Americans do not hold a favorable view of politicians and elected officials.[10] This position is summarized well by one of the eligible candidates I interviewed for this book – someone who decided unequivocally that he would never run for office: "No degree of civic duty or sense of obligation would lead a sane person to enter the trenches." Another put it a bit more colorfully: "Mudslinging, money-grubbing, mayhem. That's all it is. Why would anyone ever decide to get involved in that?"

Indeed, how can we explain the initial decision to run for office? What factors drive political ambition at the earliest stages and lead women and men to move from politically minded citizens to candidates for public office?[11] Why do accomplished, professional women and men consider entering the electoral arena, even when politics is often so poorly regarded? What personal and professional characteristics and traits foster a sense of political ambition? What circumstances serve to encourage and suppress that interest in running for office over time?

Despite the normative importance of understanding the process by which citizens become candidates and elected officials, and despite sixty years of research pertaining to political ambition and the candidate emergence process, we know very little about the initial decision to run, or not to run, for office. Certainly, case studies and historical analyses chronicle

---

[10] Pew Research Center for People and the Press, "Fewer Want Spending to Grow, But Most Cuts Remain Unpopular," February 10, 2011. Accessed at http://people-press.org/report/?pageid=1899 (March 7, 2011).

[11] Consistent with its traditional use in most political science research, my definition of *political ambition* is synonymous with the desire to acquire and hold political power through electoral means. Some scholars offer a broader conception of political ambition; it can manifest itself in forms other than running for office, such as serving as a community activist, organizing letter-writing campaigns and protests, or volunteering for candidates or issue advocacy groups (e.g., Burrell 1996). Because running for office is necessary to affect levels of electoral competition, political representation, and democratic legitimacy, I focus on the conventional definition of the term and examine the reasons that some citizens consider throwing their hats into the ring, whereas others do not.

officeholders' decisions to enter the electoral arena (e.g., Gaddie 2004; Witt, Paget, and Matthews 1994; Fowler and McClure 1989). Political biographies written by candidates and elected officials also shed light on the process by which they came to enter the political fray (e.g., Thompson 2010; Kennedy 2009; Palin 2009; Kunin 2008; Clinton 2003). But aside from a study focusing on potential candidates for Congress (Stone and Maisel 2003) and an investigation into gender differences in political ambition (Lawless and Fox 2010, 2005), no broad empirical work explores the dynamics underlying the initial decision to run for office.[12] Instead, and as I discuss more fully in Chapter 2, political scientists tend to focus on candidates and office holders – all of whom have already decided to run – and explore, retrospectively, the strategic nature of their political ambition. These studies provide insight into how a given political opportunity structure – such as an open seat, the partisan composition of the constituency, or term limits – affects individuals' decisions to enter specific races, seek higher office, or retire from politics altogether. But they are limited in the extent to which they aid in our understanding of whether or why certain people pursue elective positions in the first place, whereas others recoil at the notion. When we turn to the question of the process by which people gain or lose interest in running for office over time, we know even less.

This book offers the first broad, systematic exploration of the initial decision to run for office and how it evolves over time. I advance the central argument that if we are to understand fully the candidate emergence process, then we must broaden both our conception of political ambition and our examination of the factors that affect it. More specifically, it is essential to focus on *nascent political ambition* – the embryonic or potential interest in office seeking that precedes facing a particular political opportunity structure and deciding whether to enter a specific political contest. After all, if the notion of a candidacy has never even crossed an individual's mind, then he or she will never exhibit *expressive ambition* and actually run for office, regardless of the political opportunity structure he or she may face. It is vital also to consider and incorporate explicitly into our understanding of candidate emergence the concept of

---

[12] One exception is the 2005 article that Richard L. Fox and I published in the *American Journal of Political Science*. Although the arguments we put forward in that article are consistent with the central premises of this book, the article represents a far less nuanced account of the decision to run for office.

dynamic ambition – the process by which an individual gains or loses interest over time in running for office.

The central findings of this book reveal that substantial dividends yield from the study of political ambition when we do not limit our analyses to the decision making of political actors who are already fully immersed in electoral politics. Indeed, nascent ambition is influenced by factors such as minority status (both with regard to sex and race), family dynamics, professional circumstances, and a general sense of efficacy as a candidate, all of which fall outside the political opportunity structure on which most political ambition theory relies. Moreover, the data indicate that political ambition at the individual level fluctuates widely over time, long before eligible candidates face a political opportunity structure and well in advance of the realization of an actual candidacy. Achieving a full understanding of who will ultimately emerge as a candidate demands turning our attention to the earliest stages of the candidate emergence process and recognizing its dynamic nature.

To develop this broader conception of political ambition, I rely on data from the Citizen Political Ambition Panel Study. The panel consists of national surveys that Richard L. Fox and I conducted in 2001 and 2008 with "eligible candidates" – successful women and men who occupy the four professions that most often precede a career in politics. In-depth interviews with the eligible candidates complement the empirical analysis and add nuance to the findings. This study provides a significant method-ological advance in exploring candidate emergence and presents the first opportunity to examine broadly the process by which women and men decide to run, or not to run, for office. At its core, this book is about political ambition – who has it, how it is fostered, and how it evolves.

The Importance of Studying the Initial Decision to Run for Office

Because political scientists who study candidate emergence tend to focus on candidates and officeholders – all of whom have already demonstrated political ambition – we know relatively little about whether or why certain people pursue elective positions in the first place. Yet understanding this aspect of candidate emergence is of central importance for a number of reasons.

Foremost, electoral accountability is predicated on the notion that a large engaged group of citizens will develop and sustain an interest in seek-ing elective office. Indeed, democracy cannot function as intended if com-petent, politically interested citizens do not exhibit a sincere, sustained interest in running for office and a willingness to present a battle of ideas to the voters. This is particularly true in the candidate-centered electoral arena of the United States. As Gary Jacobson (2001, 57) notes, "Congressional election campaigns... are best understood as ventures undertaken by individual political entrepreneurs in a decentralized political marketplace." Competitive elections draw larger voter turnouts, encourage greater citizen political engagement, and heighten elected officials' responsiveness to their constituents (Barreto and Streb 2007). Because competition is a central criterion for evaluating the quality of elections, the viability of our electoral system and representative democracy is degraded when a broad group of citizens is not willing to enter the electoral arena, whether at the local, state, or federal level.

Studying the initial decision to run for office is particularly important for shedding light on questions of electoral accountability because career ladder politics tends to characterize candidate emergence in the United States. In most cases, the initial decision to run for office occurs at the local level; politicians often then opt to run for higher office (Jacobson 2001; Kazee 1994; Prinz 1993; Rohde 1979; Black 1972; Schlesinger 1966). Thus, the manner in which that initial ambition evolves sets the stage for climbing the political ladder and the quality of representation a public official provides. State legislators with ambition to seek higher office, for example, are more likely to monitor constituents' opinions than are those with no interest in one day running for higher office (Maestas 2003). Moreover, highly professionalized state legislatures populated with ambitious politicians tend to be more representative of statewide policy preferences than are their nonprofessional counterparts (Maestas 2000). Establishing a better understanding of policy making at all levels, as well as the extent to which policy makers will substantively represent their constituents, requires that we first examine the initial decision to run for office and how that ambition emerges, sustains itself, or dissipates.

When evaluating the health of democracy, however, it is necessary to assess not only the degree to which people are willing to engage the political system and run for office, but also the extent to which a diverse array of citizens is aware of and interested in pursuing the opportunity. As Sue Thomas (1998, 1) argues, "A government that is democratically organized cannot be truly legitimate if all its citizens... do not have a potential interest in and opportunity for serving their community and nation." Jane Mansbridge (1999, 651) elaborates:

> Easier communication with one's representative, awareness that one's interests are being represented with sensitivity, and knowledge that certain features of one's identity do not mark one as less able to govern all contribute

to making one feel more included in the polity. This feeling of inclusion in turn makes the polity democratically more legitimate in one's eyes.

In fact, political theorists have long ascribed symbolic or role model benefits to a more diverse body of elected officials (Amundsen 1971; Pitkin 1967; Bachrach 1967). In the case of gender, Barbara Burrell (1996, 151) captures the argument well:

> Women in public office stand as symbols for other women, both enhancing their identification with the system and their ability to have influence within it. This subjective sense of being involved and heard for women, in general, alone makes the election of women to public office important because, for so many years, they were excluded from power.[13]

Claudine Gay (2001, 589) summarizes a similar logic as applied to race:

> At the core . . . is the presumption that political interest and engagement are as much a response to the political environment and the opportunities it is perceived to present as they are a function of individual resources, such as education. Black congressional representation, by contributing to new political optimism, could prime the pump of minority voter participation and pull the black community into the political process.[14]

The presence of traditionally marginalized groups in positions of political power, in other words, conveys the political system's level of inclusiveness. Thus, the extent to which sex, race, and ethnicity affect candidate emergence bears directly on the citizenry's sense of inclusion.

The initial decision to run for office is also important because it is intertwined with fundamental issues of political representation. A compelling body of evidence suggests that particular sociodemographic groups are best able to represent the policy preferences of that group. In terms of women's substantive representation, for instance, women's presence in

---

[13] Several empirical studies corroborate this claim. Lonna Rae Atkeson and Nancy Carrillo (2007) find that as the percentage of a state's female legislators increases, so do female citizens' levels of external efficacy (see also Atkeson 2003). David Campbell and Christina Wolbrecht's (2006) cross-national study also uncovers a positive relationship between the presence of highly visible female politicians and adolescent girls' expectations of political engagement. On the other hand, Kathleen Dolan (2006) and Jennifer L. Lawless (2004a) find little empirical evidence – based on National Elections Studies data – to support the assumption that the presence of female candidates translates into any systematic change in women's political attitudes or behaviors. For a discussion of the difficulties involved in studying the potentially nuanced effects of symbolic representation, see Schwindt-Bayer and Mishler 2005.

[14] For a more elaborate discussion of symbolic representation regarding race and ethnicity, see Pantoja and Segura 2003; Gay 2002; Bobo and Gilliam 1990.

high-level elective office decreases the possibility that gender-salient issues will be overlooked. At both the national and state levels, male and female legislators' priorities and preferences differ. Based on an analysis of bill sponsorship and floor remarks in the 104th through 107th Congresses, Jessica C. Gerrity, Tracy Osborn, and Jeanette Morehouse Mendez (2007) find that women who replace men in the same district are more likely to focus on "women's issues," such as gender equity, day care, flextime, abortion, minimum wage increases, and the extension of the food stamp program (see also Burrell 1996).[15] Further, both Democratic and moderate Republican women in Congress are more likely than men to use their bill sponsorship and co-sponsorship activity to focus on "women's issues" (Swers 2002).[16]

In a similar vein, black and Latino representatives are most likely to represent the issue preferences of black and Latino constituents. Katrina Gamble's (2007) analysis of committee markup transcripts in the 107th Congress uncovers evidence that black members of Congress participate more in the markup process of "black-interest policies" – such as civil rights, urban development, unemployment, housing, and poverty – than do their white colleagues. These results withstand controls for the percentage of black constituents in the district, thereby suggesting that the race of the members, themselves, exerts an influence on the issues they prioritize. Michael Minta (2009) finds that legislator race and ethnicity also influence the propensity to intervene in agency policy making; black and Latino members of Congress are more likely than their white counterparts to attempt to affect agency oversight on policies that could

---

[15] For competing evidence, see Leslie Schwindt-Bayer and Renato Corbetta (2004), who argue that, controlling for party and constituency influences, member sex does not predict the "liberalness" of representatives' roll call behavior in the 103rd through 105th Congresses.

[16] Investigators have produced a wide array of empirical research that highlights the unique policy agenda women bring to elective office. For additional evidence of substantive representation at the congressional level, see Swers 1998; Paolino 1995. At the state level, see Thomas 1994; Berkman and O'Connor 1993; Carroll, Dodson, and Mandel 1991; Kathlene, Clarke, and Fox 1991; Thomas and Welch 1991; Saint-Germain 1989. And for a theoretical discussion of women's substantive representation, see Susan Moller Okin (1989), who argues that the presence of female legislators has finally allowed issues such as marital rape, domestic violence, and child custody – all of which have traditionally been deemed private matters – to receive public attention and debate. It is important to recognize, however, that with the growth of party polarization, fewer moderate Republican women serve in Congress. Accordingly, based on an analysis of roll call votes in the 108th and 109th Congresses, Brian Frederick (2009) finds that Republican women are ideologically indistinguishable from their male counterparts. This finding holds even when the analysis focuses strictly on "women's issues."

benefit black and Latino constituents. More broadly, many scholars find that electing more black and Latino legislators can result in greater substantive representation to black and Latino constituents at both the federal (e.g., Griffin and Newman 2007; Grose 2005; Canon 1999; Kerr and Miller 1997; Lublin 1997) and state legislative levels (Preuhs 2006; Haynie 2001).[17]

Because concerns surrounding electoral accountability, democratic legitimacy, and political representation are so fundamental, I situate my analysis on this foundation. This is particularly important given the candidate-centered political system in the United States. Political parties, after all, exert little control over who is nominated to run for office and provide only minimal financial and logistical support to candidates for most elective positions. Candidates, therefore, must raise money, build coalitions of support, create campaign organizations, and develop campaign strategies. In competitive electoral races, they often must engage in these endeavors twice – both at the primary stage and in the general election. Explicit linkages to political party organizations and platforms, as well as other support networks, are entirely the candidates' responsibility to develop. If we are to gauge prospects for the health of democracy in the United States, then we must assess the factors that lead eligible candidates to consider throwing their hats into the ring, as well as the reasons that their political ambition waxes and wanes.

Organization of the Book

Who runs for office? The pages that follow answer this question by reporting and analyzing the results of the Citizen Political Ambition Panel Study, a unique nationwide survey of almost 3,800 eligible candidates in

---

[17] Substantive representation applies beyond classifications of gender and race. Donald Haider-Markel's (2007) analysis of state legislative activities from 1992 through 2002, for example, reveals a similar pattern regarding gay and lesbian state legislators, who tend to be more likely to advocate for legislative outcomes that are favorable to the gay community. Researchers also find that openly gay legislators do relatively more to affect domestic partnership policies at the state level (Haider-Markel, Joslyn, and Kniss 2000). Similar findings also emerge from studies of representation among impoverished citizens. Greater political participation from the poor, for instance, has been associated with higher levels of welfare spending (Hill and Leighley 1992). Conversely, Frances Fox Piven and Richard Cloward (1997, 267) attribute "two decades of relative quiescence by the poor and working class" to one of the key reasons Congress managed to pass the 1996 welfare reform legislation that imposed time limits and work requirements on public assistance recipients.

2001, and a follow-up survey with more than 2,000 of them in 2008. I augment the data analysis with in-depth interviews of a representative sample of 300 of these respondents. The extensive interviews add depth to the broader empirical findings that emerge from the surveys.

Before turning to the data analysis, I establish the theoretical and historical underpinnings of my investigation of the initial decision to run for office. Chapter 2 evaluates the extant literature about the candidate emergence process and establishes the initial decision to run for office as a critical missing piece in developing a complete theory of political ambition. I also argue that, when focusing on the earliest stages of the candidate emergence process, it is critical to consider the manner in which political ambition fluctuates over time. Thus, I propose a two-stage conception of the process – considering a candidacy and deciding to enter an actual race – but incorporate into the early stage a dynamic component. The chapter concludes with a description of the Citizen Political Ambition Panel Study.

The empirical investigation of political ambition begins in Chapter 3, in which I document levels of nascent, dynamic, and expressive ambition among the eligible candidates in the study (more than 350 of whom actually ran for office). The data indicate that nascent political ambition is not static; rather, wide individual-level shifts in interest in running for office emerge between the two waves of the panel. Importantly, traditional gauges of the political opportunity structure, as well as standard gauges of political interest and activism, provide relatively little explanatory power when studying the initial decision to run for office.

The next four chapters test empirically a series of explanations for why some people consider entering the electoral arena and others do not. Each also sheds light on the extent to which these factors promote or suppress interest in running for office over time.

Chapter 4 examines minority status and offers an assessment of two key sociodemographic attributes that affect political ambition: sex and race. The results provide powerful evidence of a gender gap in political ambition and suggest that prospects for democratic legitimacy and political representation are far more precarious than scholars often assert. The data paint a more optimistic picture in terms of a racial divide (or the lack thereof) in interest in running for office. The intersectional analysis in the chapter, however, highlights the fact that women, regardless of race or ethnicity, are less likely than men to consider running for office and, accordingly, are less likely eventually to face the political opportunity structure to which most political ambition theory literature refers.

Most of the members of the candidate eligibility pool exist in the top tier of professional accomplishment and, in many cases, highly political environments. I argue in Chapter 5, however, that family dynamics across the life cycle exert a substantial influence on the initial decision to run for office, regardless of the political environments eligible candidates navigate. Early political exposure, for example, generates lasting effects that are independent and cannot be entirely compensated for by being politically active as an adult. Current family structures and responsibilities, on the other hand, as well as relatively dramatic life changes in these structures and responsibilities – such as marriage, divorce, having children move out of the house, or enduring health-related hardships within the family – do not account for the variation in the way interest in running for office ebbs and flows over time. This is not to suggest that current family dynamics play no role in influencing levels of ambition, though. Eligible candidates who receive encouragement to run from those who know them the best, such as their spouses, partners, and family members, are significantly more likely to consider entering the political sphere.

Chapter 6 moves beyond sociodemographic and family factors that influence the decision to run for office and focuses on eligible candidates' professional lives. The chapter uncovers varying levels of political ambition by profession, with lawyers and political activists significantly more likely than business leaders and educators to consider running for office. In exploring the causes of these professional differences, I argue that income, political proximity, and the qualifications and credentials that are often relevant to a political career vary across professional subcultures. Accordingly, although lawyers, business leaders, educators, and political activists are the most popular paths into the candidate eligibility pool, the politically relevant resources, connections, and skills acquired throughout the course of a career play a major role in considering a candidacy.

In Chapter 7, I shift the focus to the political environment and assess the intersection between political party and political ambition. The results reveal that, although party affiliation does not predict political ambition, the power of the parties as institutions is quite strong. Changes in attitudes toward party leaders and political institutions provide substantial leverage in accounting for individual-level changes in interest in running for office over time. That is, increased levels of cynicism over the course of the past decade – perhaps a result of public dismay over the war in Iraq; the aftermath of September 11, 2001; the failed government response to Hurricane Katrina; and perceptions of a paralyzed, polarized, gridlocked government – depress eligible candidates' ambition. Recruitment from party leaders, elected officials, and political activists, however, can exert a substantial positive impact on nascent ambition, even in cynical times.

Chapter 8, the final empirical chapter, turns to the second stage of the candidate emergence process and focuses on respondents who decided to throw their hats into the ring and actually seek elective office. The results indicate that it is vital to consider more than the political opportunity structure when assessing who will ultimately emerge as a candidate. Foremost, minority status, family dynamics, professional circumstances, and the political environment affect whether eligible candidates ever reach the second stage of the candidate emergence process and confront the decision to run for office. But many of the personal, professional, and political factors that affect whether an eligible candidate considers running for office also exert an additional influence on the likelihood of launching a campaign.

In the conclusion (Chapter 9), I summarize and assess the implications of the findings. The results culminate in substantiating empirically the theoretical distinction between nascent and expressive political ambition. To bypass nascent ambition and its dynamic nature, therefore, is to leave a critical void in our understanding of who comes to control the reins of all levels of government. The findings raise concerns about political representation and democratic legitimacy that examinations of expressive ambition overlook. I conclude the chapter by proposing a reasonable research agenda that will allow for a better understanding of the precandidacy stage of the candidate emergence process. If we are to gauge more accurately prospects for electoral accountability, democratic legitimacy, and political representation, then we must incorporate nascent and dynamic ambition into theories of candidate emergence.

The Decision to Run for Office

The Theoretical and Methodological Approach

In June 2008, fitness expert Richard Simmons testified before the House Education and Labor Committee about the ills of childhood obesity. In a passionate plea to the committee, Simmons asked the members to consider their shared responsibility for the epidemic and urged lawmakers to redouble their efforts to improve public schools' physical education and school exercise programs: "Our children today will not live as long as their parents. What have we done? What have we done to the kids of the United States of America? This is wrong! And I will dedicate the rest of my life [to this]!"[1] Then, to the committee's and the media's surprise, Simmons blurted out that dedicating the rest of his life to the issue might involve entering the electoral arena: "Chairperson George Miller, I just may run for office to help this really get through and not have one kid feel lousy about himself because he can't throw a ball!" Simmons, who had never before indicated any interest in running for office, followed up the hearings with a series of interviews in which he explained that if he concluded that seeking an elective position would be the most effective way to promote change, then that was the path he would take.[2]

Whereas Richard Simmons's articulation of his potential interest in running for office caught many people off guard, now-U.S. Senator Sheldon Whitehouse (D–RI) surprised no one when he announced that he

---

[1] "Richard Simmons Lobbies Against Obesity," *ABC 7 KGO San Francisco*, July 24, 2008. Accessed at http://abclocal.go.com/kgo/story?section=news/national_world&id= 6285036 (July 7, 2010).

[2] Lisa Desjardins, "Richard Simmons – Congressman?" CNN.com Political Ticker, July 24, 2008. Accessed at http://politicalticker.blogs.cnn.com/2008/07/24/richard-simmons-congressman/?fbid=mBjiEfZZZjj (July 7, 2010).

was considering challenging incumbent U.S. Senator Lincoln Chafee in 2006. In a comment he later described as "idiotic" and "stupid," White-house mused to a political reporter that he was "trained and basically bred" to run for office.[3] Indeed, the son of a diplomat (his father served as ambassador to Laos and Thailand) and a graduate of Yale University and the University of Virginia Law School, Whitehouse had been a fixture in Rhode Island politics for decades. He served first as an assistant attorney general, then as a U.S. attorney, and then won election as attorney general in 1998. Asked to characterize his interest in the 2006 Senate race, Whitehouse explained, "If you talk to somebody who is a musician and if they can't do it, life is not complete. This applies to anybody who cares deeply about doing something, whether it is driving NASCAR or performing surgery or caring for people in the ministry or tending bar." Not necessarily motivated by any one particular issue or policy, Sheldon Whitehouse had simply always had a passion for public service and an interest in running for office.

Together, these examples embody the central point I strive to make in this chapter. When we investigate political ambition and who runs for office, it is vital to step back and assess the early stages of the candidate emergence process. Despite their very different backgrounds, personalities, and political experiences, Richard Simmons and Sheldon Whitehouse both concluded that entering the electoral arena, or at least seriously considering a candidacy, might be the best way for them to fulfill their senses of civic responsibility. In Simmons's case, a particular issue drove his ambition. For Whitehouse, a politicized upbringing and proximity to politics likely contributed to his desire to serve in public office. In both cases, though, general interest in running for office preceded any discussion of a particular political opportunity, available seat, or winnable race. If we want to gain leverage over who ultimately emerges as a candidate, therefore, then we must examine the backgrounds, traits, and experiences that lead a broad sense of interest in running for office even to appear on an individual's radar screen.

This chapter sets the stage to examine the candidate emergence process and, subsequently, gauge prospects for electoral competition, democratic legitimacy, and political representation in U.S. political institutions. I begin with a brief overview of the extant literature pertaining to political ambition and argue that it overlooks the early stages of the process by

---

[3] Scott Mackay, "Trying for a Common Touch," *Providence Journal*, August 3, 2006, page A1.

which individuals first emerge as candidates for public office. To understand who runs for office and how that ambition evolves, I develop a two-stage candidate emergence process that accounts for several critical personal, familial, professional, and political characteristics and experiences. The chapter concludes with a description of the Citizen Political Ambition Panel Study, which allows me to generate a more inclusive theory of candidate emergence and the decision to run for office.

The Initial Decision to Run for Office: Developing a More Complete Theory of Political Ambition

Perhaps because of the numerous electoral opportunities in the United States, political scientists have long been interested in political ambition and the factors that motivate individuals to seek positions of political power. More than sixty years ago, Harold Lasswell (1948, 20) laid the groundwork for this type of investigation when he observed that the "conception of a 'political type' is that some personalities are power seekers, searching out the power institutions of the society . . . and devoting themselves to the capture and use of government." The early empirical research on political ambition promoted Lasswell's notion of the "political person." Accordingly, the quest to understand why people pursued political power, regardless of the level of office, focused on individuals' personal attributes, personalities, and motivations (Fishel 1971; Soule 1969; Barber 1965).

With the release of *Ambition and Politics* in 1966, however, Joseph Schlesinger fundamentally changed the manner by which scholars approach the study of political ambition. He put forward a rational choice paradigm to understand the decision to run for office. The rational choice framework conceptualizes political ambition as primarily a strategic response to a political opportunity structure. Aspiring candidates are more likely to seek office when they face favorable political and structural circumstances (Levine and Hyde 1977; Black 1972). More specifically, the number of open seats, term limits, levels of legislative professionalization, partisan composition of the constituency, and party congruence with constituents are among the factors individuals consider when seeking any elective position or deciding whether to run for higher office.[4] With the exception of general gauges of political interest,

---

[4] A substantial body of work that addresses political ambition falls within this rational choice paradigm. For the most recent scholarship pertaining to candidate emergence, see Maestas et al. 2006; Stone and Maisel 2003; Goodliffe 2001; Moncrief, Squire, and

financial security, and political experience, eligible candidates' characteristics are treated as relatively exogenous. That is, the literature tends to coalesce around the central premise that political ambition, itself, is a fixed attribute or inherent characteristic (Maestas et al. 2006). In other words, the "seats available and the hierarchy of positions for advancement give shape and definition to the political career" (Prinz 1993, 27).

Focusing on the political opportunity structure involved in running for a particular office has enabled scholars to generate broad theoretical claims regarding *expressive ambition* – that is, whether individuals will choose to enter specific political contests and, once they hold office, whether elected officials will maintain their current position (static ambition), run for higher office (progressive ambition), or choose to retire rather than seek reelection (discrete ambition). But by conceptualizing the decision to run for office as a simple cost–benefit analysis linked to a given political opportunity, political scientists have moved away from the early studies that shed light on the profile of the aspiring candidates who could ultimately throw their hats into the ring. Indeed, scholars have begun to demonstrate that a more complete understanding of candidate emergence demands expanding the rational choice paradigm in fundamental ways.

First, many political scientists – even some who work within the rational choice tradition – posit that the decision to run for office relies on a comprehensive set of considerations beyond a strict political opportunity structure. David Rohde's (1979) pathbreaking work on progressive ambition, for example, was among the first to acknowledge that elected officials assess the risks and value the rewards involved in seeking higher office differently, even when they face the same political context. More recently, Cherie D. Maestas and her colleagues (2006) provided convincing empirical evidence that when state legislators consider running for the U.S. House of Representatives, they employ a calculus that includes not only evaluating the political opportunity structure, but also a series of personal and institutional factors. Their examination of state legislators' decisions to seek higher office finds that a straight opportunity structure approach also overlooks the manner in which gender systematically intersects with progressive ambition (Fulton et al. 2006). Political ambition, therefore, is driven by more than the opportunity structure an individual faces.

Jewell 2001; Kazee 1994. For earlier assessments of political ambition, see Rohde 1979; Eulau and Prewitt 1973; Black 1972; Schlesinger 1966.

Second, a distinct, yet vitally important, phase of the development of political ambition occurs well before the actual decision to enter a specific race ever transpires. The rational choice paradigm assumes that, when faced with a favorable political opportunity structure (for example, a retiring incumbent or party congruence with the district), an eligible candidate will opt to enter a race. If the notion of a candidacy has never even crossed an individual's mind, though, then he or she will never be in a position to assess a specific political opportunity structure or identify the level of office in which he or she is most interested. Building on Lasswell's (1948) notion of a "political type," Richard L. Fox and I (2005) have argued that, to understand fully the decision dynamics involved in moving from "potential candidate" to "actual officeholder," it is necessary to assess *nascent ambition* – or general interest in considering a candidacy. In this initial step of the candidate emergence process, interest in seeking elective office is likely motivated not by the political opportunity structure, but by attitudinal dispositions and personal experiences that either facilitate or stunt the likelihood of even thinking about running for office.

Third, no existing theory of candidate emergence explicitly takes into account, or provides an understanding of, the process by which an individual may gain or lose political ambition. Certainly, aspects of the political opportunity structure can change; thus, implicitly, the rational choice paradigm allows for the possibility that someone might choose not to run for office at a particular time, but then opt to enter the electoral arena at another time. Here, though, the individual's ambition does not change; rather, the political opportunity structure changes. Even the scholars who focus on the manner in which individual characteristics do affect the decision to run for office tend to concentrate on fairly static sociodemographic factors and personal traits that do not change over the course of adulthood (e.g., Fulton et al. 2006; Maestas et al. 2006; Fox and Lawless 2005). Moreover, they rely on cross-sectional data at one snapshot in time. Yet not everyone who considers running for office maintains that level of political ambition over a lifetime. And individuals lacking the sociodemographic profile of a typical candidate can often be motivated to consider running for office by a change in circumstances. Essentially, personal and political attitudes and events likely constrain or promote political ambition through the life cycle. Summarized well by Ronald Keith Gaddie (2004, 199), "Efforts to craft theories of ambition and careers need to incorporate the notion that ambitions are not always fully conceptualized when a politician seeks office and that personal and political events will shape ambition through the career and the life."

Because nascent political ambition serves as a critical precursor to expressive ambition and the strategic factors associated with it, a more complete theoretical framework through which to study candidate emergence must include this earlier stage and its dynamic nature. Figure 2.1 depicts the conception of political ambition I employ throughout this book. Consistent with the rational choice paradigm, I view expressive ambition – the act of entering a specific race at a particular time – as a phenomenon driven largely by the political opportunity structure a potential candidate faces. The inclination to consider a candidacy, however, is far less proximate to a particular race than is expressive ambition. In this initial step of the candidate emergence process, I argue that interest in seeking elective office will be motivated by demographic characteristics, family dynamics, professional experiences, and political attitudes and dispositions that fall outside the realm of the opportunity structures to which most political ambition theory refers. Further, I argue that nascent ambition is far more fluid than current theories suggest. Changes in personal and professional experiences, perceptions of the political environment,

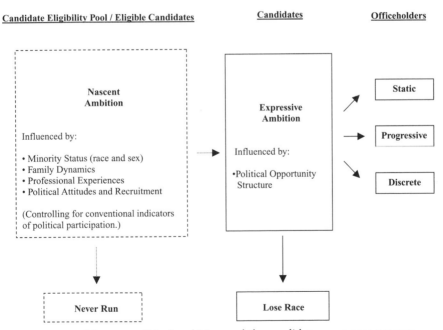

FIGURE 2.1 – Nascent political ambition and the candidate emergence process.

and attitudes about engaging the political system are among the series of factors that might make running for office occur to an eligible candidate at one time, but appear a completely remote endeavor at another (the dynamic component of nascent ambition is indicated by the box's dotted outline).

The chapters that follow address in detail the four central factors that fall outside the political opportunity structure, but that likely affect who considers running for office. In presenting an overview of my conception of ambition, however, it is important here to discuss – at least in the most general terms – the underlying logic of each expectation.

Minority Status: The vast majority of elected bodies in the United States continue to be dominated by white men. Men comprise 83 percent of members of the U.S. Congress, 88 percent of state governors, 93 percent of big-city mayors, and more than three-quarters of state legislators and statewide elected officials across the country. In terms of racial diversity, no African Americans currently serve in the U.S. Senate, and Deval Patrick (D–MA) is the only black governor. The proportions of black (9.5 percent) and Latino (5 percent) members of the House of Representatives are also lower than their population proportions of 13 percent and 15 percent, respectively (U.S. Census Bureau 2010). Racial minority representation is just as bleak at the state legislative level: 9 percent of state legislators are African American and 3 percent are Latino.[5]

If traditionally excluded groups are less likely to have role models to emulate, or have been socialized to believe that the political system is an arena in which their entry will not be embraced, then they may be less likely to consider running for office. Moreover, members of traditionally marginalized groups may also be less likely to possess other key ingredients that foster nascent ambition, such as a sense of efficacy in oneself as a candidate, a politicized upbringing, or the socioeconomic freedom to pursue a candidacy. This expectation is consistent with the research that finds that gender and race affect office holders and candidates' progressive ambition (Fulton et al. 2006; Moncrief, Squire, and Jewell 2001; Costantini 1990).

Family Dynamics: Political science scholarship uses the family unit as a medium through which to understand political participation. Studies of candidates and officeholders conclude that an "inherited" interest in

---

[5] These data are provided by the black and Latino caucuses of the state legislatures and are available on the National Conference of State Legislatures website, www.ncsl.org (July 18, 2010).

political affairs often accounts for the decision to enter politics, regardless of sociodemographic background or personality (see Flanigan and Zingale 2002). We have to look no further back than to the 2000 presidential election – which pitted Al Gore, the son of a former senator, against George W. Bush, the son of a former president – to see that history is rife with politicians from different generations of the same family. Family ties are also often evident among state legislators (Gaddie 2004) and even city council members (Prewitt 1970b). A politicized upbringing, therefore, can at a very early age plant the seeds from which nascent ambition grows.

Of course, a politicized upbringing is not the only way that family can play a role in candidate emergence, or the lack thereof. Broad examinations of political participation suggest that marital and parental status positively affect levels of political participation at the mass level (Verba, Schlozman, and Brady 1995). Over the course of the past decade, researchers have also provided evidence that these factors affect political ambition. Younger men and women, for example, often mention the trials and tribulations of maintaining the "balancing act" involved in reconciling a career and family with their political ambition (Gaddie 2004; see also Fulton et al. 2006; Theriault 1998). That said, younger people often also have more energy to enter politics (Gaddie 2004; Fowler and McClure 1989; Huckshorn and Spencer 1971; Swinerton 1968). Although little empirical evidence offers direction in terms of the degree to which family structures and placement in the life cycle affect political ambition, there is reason to believe that family dynamics make seeking elective office more viable at different points in an eligible candidate's life.

Professional Experiences: Certain professions serve as gateways to politics (Moncrief, Squire, and Jewell 2001). And there is broad acceptance of the notion that anyone who ultimately decides to seek office, especially high-level office, is competitive and driven. Clear indications of ambitious behavior in realms outside politics, therefore, can help predict who might consider running for office. More specifically, individuals who select high-prestige occupations and seek to rise to the top of their professions may be more likely to think about acquiring positions of political power or climbing the political career ladder (Hain and Pierson 1975).

Professional circumstances, however, likely affect political ambition beyond merely reflecting ambitious behavior. Eligible candidates' estimates of their feelings of efficacy, for example, are likely based on a relatively broad set of criteria, including whether they think they have sufficient knowledge, confidence, and skills to enter and thrive in the political sphere. This general sense of efficacy as a candidate, which can exert an impact on whether an individual considers entering the electoral arena, may derive from the income, political proximity, and politically relevant skills acquired in professional settings.

Political Attitudes and Recruitment: It is well established in the literature on political participation and attitude formation that presidential scandals, tumultuous social, economic, and political times, and reactions to political leaders directly influence citizens' trust in and cynicism toward government (e.g., Cook and Gronke 2005; Hetherington 2005; Citrin and Green 1986). In turn, levels of political trust and efficacy affect individuals' willingness to engage in political and community activities (e.g., Piven and Cloward 1997; Cohen and Dawson 1993). Running for office is, in many ways, the utmost form of political participation; thus, political trust and cynicism likely affect candidate emergence.

Because eligible candidates' attitudes toward and evaluations of the political system cannot be divorced from their party affiliation, though, it is likely that partisanship intersects with political ambition. Parties as institutions can also play a role in fostering interest in running for office because electoral gatekeepers tap their partisans to emerge as candidates. Even broad, general support for entering electoral politics can confer a sense of the legitimacy required to reach the point at which someone begins to assess the electoral environment. Women and men who receive encouragement to run for office from political actors are more likely to think seriously about a candidacy (see Jewell and Morehouse 2001; Aldrich 2000).

The evolution of political ambition at the individual level, therefore, is an intricate phenomenon, and many of these expectations are linked to one another. But together, these four broad factors represent a series of personal attitudes and characteristics – all of which fall outside the traditional political opportunity structure – that may influence the development of nascent political ambition.

It is important to note, however, that the linear depiction of candidate emergence presented in Figure 2.1 does not, necessarily, mean that the development of political ambition is a long and slow road. Certainly, that can be the case. Former President Bill Clinton (2004, 63), for instance, writes in his memoir that his *nascent ambition* emerged at an early age: "Sometime in my sixteenth year I decided I wanted to be in public life as an elected official.... I knew I could be great in public service." His *expressive ambition* surfaced at the age of twenty-seven, when Clinton sought a seat in the U.S. House of Representatives. In the aftermath of Watergate, and amid skyrocketing oil prices and gasoline rations,

Arkansas Democrats appeared well positioned to make gains in the 1974 congressional elections. But as Clinton (2004, 210) notes, "It became clear that no one in our area who could run a strong race was willing to do it." Therefore, he began to think about entering the race himself: "I was young, single, and willing to work all hours of the day and night. And even if I didn't win, if I made a good showing I didn't think it would hurt me in any future campaigns I might undertake." Although he lost his congressional bid, two years later, Clinton was elected attorney general of the state of Arkansas. And two years after that, he won the governorship.

But the process of moving from having no ambition to declaring a candidacy can also occur quite quickly; it can even be spurred by a single change in an eligible candidate's life. Consider Carolyn McCarthy, who now represents New York's 4th congressional district in the U.S. House of Representatives. McCarthy, a former nurse, spent most of her adult life uninterested in either local or national politics.[6] In 1993, however, her husband was killed and her son injured by a random act of gun violence on the Long Island Railroad commuter train. McCarthy began to lobby in support of an assault weapons ban bill in New York and emerged as a spokeswoman for families affected by gun violence. It was during this time that her *nascent ambition* took shape. Reflecting on her lobbying experiences, McCarthy recalls, "So many people shut the door in your face, and that probably made my final decision to run. It might have been the frustration meeting these politicians who give the impression that they don't care."[7] In 1996, McCarthy's member of Congress – Republican Daniel Frisa – voted to repeal a ban on nineteen types of assault weapons. McCarthy's *expressive ambition* came in the form of challenging Frisa in the general election. She garnered 57 percent of the vote and has won reelection handily for the past fourteen years.[8]

In short, the theoretical framework and findings presented in this book suggest that political ambition is a far more volatile commodity than prior research acknowledges, and that the initial decision to run for office is driven systematically by far more than a political opportunity structure.

---

[6] Dan Barry, "Long Island Widow's Story: Next Stop, Washington," *New York Times*, November 7, 1996, page B14.

[7] Laura Mansnerus, "In Person: From Private Anguish, a Public Figure Emerges," *New York Times*, March 21, 1999, Section 14NJ, page 4.

[8] McCarthy, who had been a lifelong Republican, originally planned to challenge Frisa in the Republican primary. When Republican Party officials told her that they wanted to avoid a divisive primary, the Democrats stepped in and encouraged her candidacy. Although McCarthy always caucused with the Democrats, she did not actually change her own party affiliation until 2003 (see Elisa Gootman, New York: Mineola: "McCarthy Quietly Changes Registration," *New York Times*, April 29, 2003, page B6).

And this is the case regardless of whether an eligible candidate opts to enter the electoral arena after a lifetime of political socialization or in response to a relatively short-term course of events.

The Citizen Political Ambition Panel Study

Despite the importance of exploring the ways in which people come to run for office, an empirical study is very difficult to execute. Perhaps most obviously, most people have never considered entering electoral politics as candidates. A 2002 Knowledge Networks survey revealed, for example, that 95 percent of the general population had never considered a candidacy. Fewer than 1 percent of the respondents had actually run for any elective position.[9] A broad mass population survey, therefore, cannot shed much light on the candidate emergence process; running for office is simply too rare an occurrence among the general public.

Even when we focus on an elite sample of eligible candidates, though, many undocumented considerations enter the decision to run for office, thereby causing a number of methodological and sample design issues to confront. Foremost, when an eligible candidate decides not to enter a race, the decision is often unknown, thereby making it hard to assemble a reasonable sample. In addition, many individuals who ultimately run for office may never have considered themselves eligible candidates prior to being recruited to run. It is difficult to construct a sample that accounts for local and state party organizations' widely varying recruitment efforts. Political concerns can also impede research attempts to identify eligible candidates. Sandy Maisel and Walter Stone (1998) recount, for instance, that some members of Congress attempted to persuade the National Science Foundation not to fund a study of eligible candidates for the House of Representatives. Members feared that the study might spur qualified challengers to enter races they would not otherwise have considered entering.

These methodological obstacles have generally meant that information pertaining to political ambition and the decision to run for office yielded

---

[9] To compare the candidate eligibility pool to the general population, I replicated many questions I asked the eligible candidates and administered, through Knowledge Networks, a stand-alone survey to a random sample of United States citizens. From August 23 to September 11, 2002, Knowledge Networks surveyed 2,859 adults. The general population data referenced here and throughout the remainder of this book are based on responses from the 1,104 women and 1,015 men who completed the survey (for a 74 percent response rate). For a complete description of the sample and sampling procedures, go to http://www.knowledgenetworks.com, or see Lawless 2004b.

from samples of actual candidates and officeholders.[10] Thus, with the exception of a study focusing on potential candidates for Congress, only some of whom had not previously held office (Stone and Maisel 2003), the datasets on which the extant literature on candidate emergence is based include candidates and elected officials, all of whom – by definition – exhibited political ambition when they entered their first political contest (e.g., Fulton et al. 2006; Maestas et al. 2006; Gaddie 2004; Berkman 1994; Canon 1993; Fowler and McClure 1989; Squire 1988). Because these studies focus on individuals who already sought or hold elected office, they are confined to politicians at a time in their lives following the formation and crystallization of political ambition. Women and men who may have held some level of interest in running for office, but who then lost it or never exercised it, fall out of the analyses.

The Citizen Political Ambition Panel Study provides the first research design aimed specifically at exploring the early stages of political ambition and the manner in which it changes over time. Richard L. Fox and I compiled a random, national sample of citizens who occupy the four professions and backgrounds that tend to yield the highest proportion of political candidates: law, business, education, and political activism.[11] In 2001, we administered by mail an elaborate survey to a national sample of 6,800 members of this "candidate eligibility pool" (Appendix A offers a detailed description of the sampling design). The survey asked respondents about their sociodemographic backgrounds, familial arrangements, political activism, political outlook, political experience, and willingness to run for office. We heard from 3,765 respondents (1,969 men and 1,796 women). After taking into account undeliverable surveys, this represents a 60 percent response rate, which is higher than that of similar elite sample mail surveys.[12] We supplemented the survey data with evidence gathered

---

[10] Linda Fowler (1993) provides an elaborate discussion of the theoretical, contextual, and empirical obstacles involved in uncovering the disincentives to seek public office (see also Rohde 1979).

[11] We disproportionately stratified by sex, so the sample includes roughly equal numbers of women and men, even though women comprise far less than 50 percent of the current eligibility pool. The central reason for this sampling decision was to allow for a fuller investigation of gender differences in political ambition (see Lawless and Fox 2010; 2005). Because the scope of this book transcends issues of gender and political ambition, each model I present throughout the remaining chapters not only controls for sex, but also discusses the extent to which the findings are driven, even in part, by the sex of the respondent.

[12] Walter Stone and Sandy Maisel's (2003) response rate for their survey of eligible candidates for Congress was 43 percent. In our pilot study, we achieved a 49 percent rate of response among members of the candidate eligibility pool in New York (Fox, Lawless, and Feeley 2001).

TABLE 2.1 *Demographic and Political Profile of the Candidate Eligibility Pool (in 2001)*

	Overall Sample	Lawyers	Business Leaders	Educators	Political Activists
Sex					
Men	53%	52%	58%	53%	50%
Women	47	48	42	47	50
Party Affiliation					
Democrat	46	49	21	53	52
Republican	30	29	55	19	23
Independent	21	20	21	24	20
Political Ideology					
Liberal	28	23	10	34	43
Moderate	52	62	59	51	34
Conservative	20	15	31	15	23
Race					
White	83	82	84	82	85
Black	10	11	5	9	12
Latino/Hispanic	5	5	9	7	2
Other	3	2	2	2	1
Level of Education					
No college degree	7	0	24	0	12
Bachelor's degree	21	0	48	11	38
Graduate degree	72	100	28	89	50
Household Income					
Less than $50,000	9	2	4	10	19
$50,001–$75,000	12	4	6	18	22
$75,001–$100,000	18	11	14	23	25
$100,001–$200,000	34	34	33	40	26
More than $200,000	27	48	44	9	8
Mean Age (Years)	48	45	50	50	51
N	3,572	1,138	667	936	831

Notes: Number of cases for each question varies slightly, as some respondents chose not to answer some demographic questions.

from 200 in-depth interviews with our survey respondents (for a full copy of the survey and the interview questionnaire, see Appendices B and D). The women and men who comprise the candidate eligibility pool have the professional, educational, financial, and political backgrounds typical of individuals who ultimately run for office (see Table 2.1).

In early 2008, following extensive Internet searches and phone calls, we obtained current address information for 2,976 members (82 percent) of the original sample of respondents who completed the questionnaire in 2001. We conducted a new survey that delved more deeply into political ambition, political proximity and exposure to politics, political recruitment, and eligible candidates' perceptions of themselves and the political arena (see Appendix C). The timing of the second survey carried the additional benefit of allowing for an assessment of changes in political ambition over the course of seven years that saw dramatic shifts in the political landscape. After employing standard mail survey protocol, we heard from 2,060 women and men, 2,036 of whom completed the questionnaire. This represents a 75 percent response rate for the second panel of the study. I supplemented the survey data with 100 telephone interviews with a random sample of the second-wave survey respondents.

The respondents who completed the 2008 survey are a representative subsample of the original eligibility pool. Controlling for sex, race, and profession, individuals who expressed some degree of political ambition in 2001 were no more likely to complete the 2008 survey than respondents who had never considered a candidacy. Similarly, eligible candidates who reported high levels of political interest, activism, or recruitment at the time of the 2001 survey were no more likely than those who did not to respond to the questionnaire. Moreover, no significant demographic or professional factors distinguish the 2001 and 2008 samples. The first column in Table 2.2 summarizes the profile of eligible candidates who completed the survey in 2001. The second and third columns in the table present demographics at two points in time for the subset of respondents who completed the 2008 survey. In terms of sex, race, level of education, household income, and age, the respondents who completed the second survey are a representative subset of the original respondents. They were slightly more liberal and Democratic in 2001 than was the overall sample, but these differences are minor.[13]

In presenting the central findings from the Citizen Political Ambition Panel Study, I rely on results from both waves of the survey. In most cases, I present the findings from the original data and sample to discuss

---

[13] The data presented in column 3, however, highlight that the profile of the eligibility pool changed, at least somewhat, between the two waves of the study. Household incomes, overall, increased. In addition, a significant portion of respondents increased their identification with the Democratic Party. Included in the partisan categories in 2008, however, are "independent leaners," who comprised 17 percent of "Democrats" and 11 percent of "Republicans." Considering that political ideology remained fairly constant, it is likely that the shift in party identification also reflects disillusionment with the Republican Party's face and name, as opposed to its ideological underpinnings, perhaps spurring a disproportionate share of independents to align with Democrats.

TABLE 2.2 *Comparison of Wave 1 and Wave 2 Respondents*

	Wave 1 Respondents in 2001 (%)	Wave 2 Respondents in 2001 (%)	Wave 2 Respondents in 2008 (%)
Sex			
Men	53	54	54
Women	47	46	46
Party Affiliation			
Democrat	46	49	60
Republican	30	28	32
Independent	21	21	8
Political Ideology			
Liberal	28	32	36
Moderate	52	50	44
Conservative	20	18	20
Race			
White	83	84	84
Black	10	9	9
Latino/Hispanic	5	5	5
Other	3	2	2
Level of Education			
No college degree	7	6	6
Bachelor's degree	21	17	17
Graduate degree	72	78	78
Household Income			
Less than $50,000	9	10	4
$50,001–$75,000	12	12	8
$75,001–$100,000	18	17	13
$100,001–$200,000	34	34	34
More than $200,000	27	29	40
Mean Age (Years)	48	48	54
N	3,572	2,036	2,036

Notes: The 2001 survey employed a three-point scale to measure party identification; in 2008, the survey used a seven-point scale. Included in the 2008
partisan categories are "independent leaners," who comprise 17 percent of
"Democrats" and 11 percent of "Republicans."

early political ambition and the decision to run for office. I incorporate
data from the 2008 survey to shed light on the extent to which ambition
is dynamic. Similar to the manner in which panel data play a critical
role in identifying and explaining changes in partisanship (Carsey and
Layman 2006; Goren 2005; Jennings and Markus 1984) and political

participation (Stoker and Jennings 1995), this panel allows me to document empirically the extent to which political ambition changes over time and examine what affects its evolution.[14]

Overall, the "eligibility pool approach" and sample allow for a nuanced examination of the manner in which women and men initially decide to run for all levels and types of political office, either now or in the future. And the approach is particularly suited to the question of the initial decision to run. The small group of scholars who examine eligible candidates' political ambition tend to employ the "reputational approach" (Stone and Maisel 2003; Kazee 1994). They compile a pool of eligible candidates by seeking out current officeholders and "political informants," many of whom are party leaders, convention delegates, county chairs, elected officials, and political and community activists. Researchers ask the informants to name prospective, viable candidates, typically for election to the House of Representatives. The prospects are then contacted and surveyed, as are many current officeholders who are positioned to run for higher office.

Although the reputational approach allows scholars to shed light on ambition to seek high-level office, as well as explore the specific dynamics that might spur a candidacy for a particular seat, it succumbs to several limitations when we turn to the initial decision to seek a political position. In most states, politics is a career ladder. Studies that focus on the decision to seek high-level office, therefore, are likely to identify as eligible candidates individuals for whom the initial decision to run has long since passed. Further, contacting only elected officials and informants for the names of eligible candidates restricts the sample to individuals who are currently deemed ready to run. Men and women who may be well positioned to consider a candidacy later in life are overlooked. Informants' personal biases can also influence the eligible candidates they name (Maisel and Stone 1998). This is particularly relevant when we turn to gender, race, and political ambition, as bias can result in too few women and racial minorities being identified, thereby prohibiting statistical comparisons among the subsamples in the pool.

---

[14] After all, cross-sectional data allow researchers to estimate only how particular circumstances and variables affect an individual's political ambition at one point in time. Panel data, which rely on individual outcomes at multiple points in time, allow for an examination of the factors that affect the propensity to gain or lose political ambition. Panel data carry methodological advantages as well. In addition to generating more accurate predictions with more efficient estimators and fewer multicollinearity problems, panel data also mitigate omitted variable biases (see Hsiao 2007; 2003).

Although the Citizen Political Ambition Panel Study represents a methodological breakthrough, it is important to acknowledge two specific limitations involved in employing the eligibility pool approach. First, the method means that we must forgo a nuanced analysis of the structural and contextual variables that might exert an impact on the decision to enter the electoral arena. If we focused on a single race or election, then the number of eligible candidates would be extremely small. We assembled a broad sample at the expense of analyzing the political opportunity and structural aspects of the decision calculus in any particular race or set of races. The absence of a specific office focus does mean, however, that we are limited in the extent to which we can assess the effects constituency demographics, incumbency, and other political opportunities exert on the inclination to consider a candidacy. Second, the approach relies on eligible candidates' perceptions of the political environment and their future candidacies, as opposed to more objective indicators of their electoral viability. Thus, the results might reflect a distorted version of reality. Because I am interested in the consideration process that members of the eligibility pool undergo, self-perceptions are perhaps as relevant as are objective assessments of the eligible candidates' likelihood of winning. After all, individuals often distort the probability of winning an election, but engage in behavior based on these distortions.

In short, what the approach sacrifices in precision and leverage in predicting who will enter a specific race at a specific time it makes up for in the broad-based nature of the sample. Because the strength of the research design is its ability to address considering a candidacy, Chapters 4 through 7 focus on this inclination and its dynamic nature. In Chapter 8, however, I do turn to the decision to enter an actual race, a more commonly studied phase of the candidate emergence process. No other study allows for as thorough an assessment of the critically important initial decision to run for office and the implications for democracy, electoral competition, and representation.

3

Political Ambition in the Candidate Eligibility Pool

The manner in which most elective positions in the United States are structured is geared to allow competent, politically interested individuals to step forward and serve as representatives of the people. In fact, more than two centuries ago, the founders worked to create a national legislature that allowed successful citizens to serve their nation for a few years. The notion of career politicians was not something they envisioned; it was something against which they warned. Weary of the power of hereditary succession and monarchical rule, for instance, Thomas Paine (1776) highlighted the ills of a ruling class:

> Men who look upon themselves born to reign, and others to obey, soon grow insolent. Selected from the rest of mankind, their minds are early poisoned by importance; and the world they act in differs so materially from the world at large, that they have but little opportunity of knowing its true interests, and when they succeed in the government are frequently the most ignorant and unfit of any throughout the dominions.

Alexander Hamilton (1787) also argued against career politicians, noting that "the natural cure for an ill-administration, in a popular or representative constitution, is a change of men." During the Constitutional Convention, Benjamin Franklin (1787) took the sentiment even further when he asserted that professional politicians were confined to an undesirable "state of servitude":

> It seems to have been imagined by some that the returning to the mass of the people was degrading the magistrate. This he thought was contrary to republican principles. In free Governments the rulers are the servants, and the people their superiors and sovereigns. For the former therefore to return among the latter was not to degrade but to promote them. And it would be

imposing an unreasonable burden on them...not allow them to become
again one of the Masters.

Since the time of the founding, therefore, the U.S. political system's success
has relied on a large number of civic-minded citizen legislators.

Certainly, over the course of the past 225 years, politics has become
increasingly professionalized. In the past fifty years alone, salaries and the
perquisites of office have made serving in the U.S. House of Representatives or the U.S. Senate a quite lucrative profession. In 1960, for example,
members of the U.S. Congress received an annual salary of $22,500. By
1985, the annual compensation had more than tripled; members received
$75,100 per year. When the 112th Congress convened in 2011, U.S. rep-
resentatives and senators earned salaries of $174,000.[1] Even accounting
for inflation and the buying power of the dollar, these salary increases
are rather substantial.

But Congress is somewhat of an anomaly. Most of the roughly 520,000
elective offices in the United States are situated at the local and state
levels (see Table 3.1). Each of the fifty state governments, for example,
elects a governor, as well as a series of statewide elected officials, such as
attorney general, comptroller, general treasurer, and secretary of state. An
additional 7,382 women and men occupy seats in state legislatures across
the country. And more than 1,000 others are elected to state boards, such
as the Public Utilities Commission in South Dakota, the Public Service
Commission in Tennessee, the Railroad Commission in Texas, and the
Commission of Public Lands in New Mexico. At the local level, literally
hundreds of thousands of women and men serve as mayors, city and
town council members, school board members, parks commissioners,
dog catchers, sheriffs, soil and water conservation directors, coroners,
auditors, sewage disposal authorities, tax collectors, and recorders of
deeds, to name just a handful of elective positions.

Many of these state and local positions pay only a token salary and
meet on a limited basis. The data presented in Table 3.2, for instance,
demonstrate that, at the state legislative level, serving as an elected official
is not intended to be a career. Consider the 424 state legislators in New
Hampshire; they receive only $200 for each two-year term, and they do
not receive any per diem pay for the days the legislature is in session. Most
of the forty-two states with part-time legislatures offer somewhat more
in terms of pay, but members, who must be available to serve for a few

[1] For more information on the salaries and perquisites members of Congress have received
over time, see Brudnick et al. (2010).

TABLE 3.1. *Governments in the United States*

	Number of Elective Bodies	Number of Elected Officials
Federal Government	1	
Executive branch		2
U.S. Senate		100
U.S. House of Representatives		435
State Government	50	
State legislatures		7,382
Statewide elected offices		10,036
State boards		1,331
Local Government		
Municipal governments	19,429	135,531
Town or township governments	16,504	126,958
County governments	3,034	58,818
School districts	13,506	95,000
Special districts	35,052	84,089
Total	87,576	519,682

Notes: Data on the breakdown of local governments are from the National League of Cities (2010), except the school district data, which were provided by the National Association of School Boards. State government elected officials data come from the National Conference of State Legislatures (2010a) and the Bureau of the Census (1992).

months each year, are still expected to maintain their professional careers (see Gray, Hanson, and Jacob 2000). The overwhelming majority of the 87,525 local governments across the country also operate on a part-time basis with limited, if any, compensation for their elected officials.

The sheer number of such positions indicates that U.S. citizens have always had ample opportunities to seek positions of political power, not necessarily because they want new careers, but rather, because they have a sense of civic engagement and responsibility. This chapter begins the analysis of who even considers seeking the vast number of elective offices in this country. Are eligible candidates interested in running for office? Do they set their sights on all levels of office? Do they concentrate their interests at the local level, where most elective positions are situated? Does their ambition sustain itself over time?

I employ the two-stage conception of candidate emergence presented in Chapter 2 as a framework through which to examine political ambition in the candidate eligibility pool and to begin to answer these questions. The central finding to emerge in this chapter is that roughly half the eligible candidates have at least considered running for office. Far fewer respondents have actually sought elective office. From the outset,

TABLE 3.2. *Structure of State Legislatures in the United States, 2010*

	Size	Annual Base Salary ($)	2010 Legislative Session
Alabama	140	0	January 12–April 22
Alaska	60	50,400	January 19–April 19
Arizona	90	24,000	January 11–April 29
Arkansas	135	15,362	February 8–March 4
California	120	95,291	January 12–August 31
Colorado	100	30,000	January 13–May 12
Connecticut	187	28,000	February 3–May 5
Delaware	62	41,680	January 12–June 30
Florida	160	29,697	March 2–April 30
Georgia	236	17,342	January 11–April 29
Hawaii	76	48,708	January 20–April 29
Idaho	105	16,116	January 11–March 29
Illinois	177	67,836	*meets all year*
Indiana	150	22,616	January 5–March 12
Iowa	150	25,000	January 11–March 30
Kansas	165	0	January 11–May 28
Kentucky	138	0	January 5–April 15
Louisiana	144	16,800	March 29–June 21
Maine	186	13,526	January 6–April 12
Maryland	188	43,500	January 13– April 12
Massachusetts	200	58,237	*meets all year*
Michigan	148	79,650	*meets all year*
Minnesota	201	31,141	February 4–May 16
Mississippi	174	10,000	January 5–May 3
Missouri	197	35,915	January 6– May 25
Montana	150	0	*no regular session in 2010*
Nebraska	49	12,000	January 6–April 14
Nevada	63	0	*no regular session in 2010*
New Hampshire	424	100	January 6–July 1
New Jersey	120	49,000	*meets all year*
New Mexico	112	0	January 19–February 18
New York	212	79,500	*meets all year*
North Carolina	170	13,951	May 12–July 15
North Dakota	141	0	*no regular session in 2010*
Ohio	132	60,584	*meets all year*
Oklahoma	149	38,400	February 1–May 28
Oregon	90	21,612	*no regular session in 2010*
Pennsylvania	253	78,315	*meets all year*
Rhode Island	113	13,089	January 5–June 11
South Carolina	170	10,400	January 12–June 3
South Dakota	105	6,000	January 12–March 30
Tennessee	132	19,009	January 12–June 10
Texas	181	7,200	*no regular session in 2010*
Utah	104	0	January 25–March 11
Vermont	180	0	January 5–May 12
Virginia	140	17,640	January 13–March 13
Washington	147	42,106	January 11–March 11
West Virginia	134	20,000	January 13–March 20
Wisconsin	132	49,943	*meets all year*
Wyoming	90	0	February 8–March 5

Notes: Data are compiled from the National Conference of State Legislatures (2010a, 2010b, 2010c).

therefore, the data substantiate the distinction between nascent and expressive political ambition. Moreover, they highlight the extent to which interest in running for office fluctuates over time; over the course of seven years, nearly 40 percent of the eligible candidates either gained or lost ambition. Because the analysis demonstrates that traditional gauges of the political opportunity structure tend not to account for nascent ambition or how that interest in running for office changes, this chapter sets the stage for the importance of turning to other explanations to predict who considers a candidacy.

Candidate Emergence from the Eligibility Pool

The pool of eligible candidates is comprised of successful individuals who are well positioned to seek public office. The most appropriate place to begin the analysis, therefore, is with an overview of candidate emergence through the lens of the two-stage process I outlined in Chapter 2. After all, developing a broader conception of political ambition is predicated on the distinction between considering a candidacy (nascent ambition) and actually running for office (expressive ambition). Moreover, we cannot begin to assess the extent to which personal, familial, professional, and political factors affect interest in running for office without first establishing eligible candidates' aggregate levels of political ambition.

Who Runs for Office? Eligible Candidates' Expressive Ambition
The bulk of the literature that examines political ambition focuses on the final stage of the candidate emergence process. That is, scholars investigate the decision to run for office by studying the candidates who throw their hats into the ring. Although my analysis zeroes in on the earlier stage of the process, the Citizen Political Ambition Study allows for an assessment of the entire candidate emergence process. More than 300 members of the sample had actually run for office by the time of the 2001 survey. An additional 54 respondents launched candidacies between the two waves of the study. Put somewhat differently, roughly 10 percent of the eligible candidates sought elective positions. Thus, we can begin with the later stages of the process to gain a handle on expressive ambition in the candidate eligibility pool.

As we might expect, the overwhelming majority of respondents who ran for office competed at the local level (see Table 3.3). Indeed, more than three-quarters of the women and men who launched a candidacy

TABLE 3.3. *Offices Sought and Won by Eligible Candidates*

	Level of Office Sought	Level of Office Won
Local	79%	69%
State	17	32
Federal	4	1
N	372	223

Notes: Results are based on the combined 2001 and 2008 survey data. The percentages for "Level of Office Sought" are based on the total number of actual candidates in the sample. Percentages in the "Level of Office Won" column are based on the number of candidates for each level of office.

sought a position on a school board, town or city council, or local board or commission. And they fared quite well. Overall, 60 percent of the eligible candidates who ran for office launched successful campaigns. As we can see from the second column in Table 3.3, levels of electoral success were greatest at the local level, where nearly seven of ten candidates won their races. But approximately one-third of the candidates who sought state-level positions also achieved victory on Election Day.

The fact that 10 percent of the respondents ran for office highlights the quality of this sample through which to study political ambition. Chapter 8 turns exclusively to the expressive ambition phase of the candidate emergence process. For the purposes of this chapter, however, I present the expressive ambition frequencies to underscore the importance of developing a broader conception of ambition. Ninety percent of respondents, after all, did not launch a candidacy. Certainly, some of these women and men chose not to run for office because they did not face a favorable political opportunity structure. Brian Forrest, a businessman from Kansas, for example, explained that he has not yet thrown his hat into the ring because he has "not yet figured out what's the most winnable seat."[2] He elaborated that the political opportunity structure is his main impediment:

> I think about running for office all the time. I get how politics works. I
> see the problems we're facing in the state. And I know I have the skills to

---

[2] To protect anonymity, I have changed the names and modified identifying references of the men and women who were surveyed and interviewed for this book. The backgrounds and credentials I describe, as well as the specific quotes I include, are taken directly from the surveys and interviews.

make things better. The question I'm facing right now is not whether I'll run for office, but when and for what position. I don't have control over those factors. I just need to wait and see what opens up for me.

But many of the eligible candidates did not "choose" not to run; rather, the notion of entering the electoral arena never occurred to them. Consider Ned Lawson, a high school principal in Florida. When I asked him if he had ever run for office, he laughed and said that the thought had never crossed his mind:

> I've never considered it. Never even for a nanosecond until right now. And that's how long it takes me to decide, "Nope, I never want to do that." Don't get me wrong – I'm really politically active, and I've served on several boards and commissions. It's just that running for office is all guts and no glory. That's not me.

April O'Neil, an attorney from Chicago, echoed this sentiment. She explained that the thought of running for office "exited her mind just as quickly as it entered it." Never before had she considered running for office and "never again will [she] think about it." Brian Crandall, a litigator in Sacramento, offered a similar view: "I can honestly say that I have never thought about running for office. It's up there on the list of things I'd never do, so why give it any thought?" Overall, 142 of the 300 individuals I interviewed never considered a candidacy. Thus, if we want to assess more broadly why so many eligible candidates never make it to the campaign trail, then rather than focus on the political opportunity structures of which so many are fully unaware, we must turn to the earlier stage of the candidate emergence process.

Who Considers Running for Office?
Eligible Candidates' Nascent Ambition

We can begin the investigation into the earlier stage of the candidate emergence process with an overall examination of nascent ambition. The survey asked members of the sample – directly – whether they ever considered running for office. From the outset, the data suggest that this sample of eligible candidates is well situated to enter electoral politics, as roughly half of them are cognizant of the possibility. Table 3.4, which presents responses to the general question about interest in running for office, indicates that more than 50 percent of the respondents acknowledge at least considering a candidacy; about one of every seven respondents has given running for office "serious" thought.

TABLE 3.4. *Nascent Ambition in the Candidate Eligibility Pool*

Have you ever considered running for office?	
Yes, I have seriously considered it.	15%
Yes, it has crossed my mind.	37
No, I have never thought about it.	49
Have you ever taken any of the following steps?	
Discussed running with community leaders	12
Investigated how to place your name on the ballot	10
Discussed running with party leaders	9
Discussed financial contributions with potential supporters	5
Took at least one of these steps	18
N	3,626

Notes: Results are based on the 2001 data. "Have you ever taken any of the following steps?" entries indicate the percentage of respondents who report engaging in each concrete step that tends to precede a candidacy. Numbers do not total 100 percent because respondents could have taken anywhere between zero and four steps.

This measure of whether a respondent ever considered a candidacy captures even the slightest inclination of running for office. Thus, the survey also included a battery of questions about whether respondents ever took any of the concrete steps that serve as precursors to seeking elective office. We asked the members of the sample whether they ever investigated how to place their name on the ballot, or ever discussed running with potential donors, party leaders, or community activists. Few respondents have taken multiple steps required to mount a political campaign, but 18 percent have engaged in at least one concrete activity that typically precedes launching a candidacy (see bottom of Table 3.4). Levels of interest in running for office, therefore, are still quite broad, even when we move beyond perceptual indicators. Moreover, taking any of the concrete steps correlates very strongly with reporting interest in running for office. Eighty percent of respondents who "seriously" considered running for office solicited financial contributions, investigated placing their name on the ballot, or discussed a potential candidacy with a party leader, elected official, or political activist. Only 19 percent of the women and men for whom running for office had "crossed their minds" reported engaging in any of these activities (difference significant at $p < 0.01$).

The survey data provide an opportunity not only to assess levels of nascent ambition, but also to investigate the levels of office in which potential candidates express interest. In many cases, politics is a career ladder; more than 70 percent of the members of the U.S. Congress, for instance, held office prior to running for the House or Senate (Malbin, Ornstein, and Mann 2008). To determine where eligible candidates focus their office-specific interests, the survey asked members of the sample to identify the first office they would seek, should they enter a political contest. It then presented them with a list of several local, state, and federal positions and asked whether they would ever consider running for any of those posts. These questions gauge broad interest in a series of potential positions a respondent could consider seeking; they are removed from any particular race at any particular time.

Many eligible candidates seem well aware of career-ladder politics; most respondents would get involved at the bottom rung of the political ladder (see Table 3.5). More specifically, nearly 70 percent of respondents select a local office – school board, city council, or mayor – as the first office for which they might run, whereas only 10 percent consider entering the political arena at the federal level. This does not mean, however, that the respondents are not interested in climbing the

TABLE 3.5. *Eligible Candidates' Elective Office Preferences*

	First Office Respondent Would Seek	Other Offices Respondent Would Consider
Local Office		
School board	37%	37%
Town, city, county council	26	35
Mayor	4	13
State Office	19	30
State legislator	2	9
Statewide office (e.g., attorney general)	1	10
Governor		
Federal Office	8	21
House of Representatives	2	16
Senate	0	4
President		
N	2,036	3,626

Notes: Results are based on the 2001 survey data. Entries in the "First Office Respondent Would Seek" column do not include respondents who said that they would never run for office, or who have already run for, and in some cases held, office. Entries in the "Other Offices Respondent Would Consider" column indicate the percentage of respondents in the full sample who said they would consider running for the specified position. Respondents who have already run for office often expressed interest in other positions. Percentages in the second column do not add up to 100 percent because respondents often expressed interest in more than one position.

political career ladder. Ellen Whitestone, an attorney who works right outside Philadelphia, summarized the views of several respondents who set their sights on running for office:

> I'm eager to get involved locally, run for some local position. But first – and I know this might sound pathetic – I'd like to get appointed to the Sidewalk Commission. It would be great experience and I'd also have a chance to solve some pressing neighborhood issues. Then, I could run for something local, build a base, and then consider the state legislature at some point down the road.

Bob Harrison, an educator in New Mexico, believes that "given how politics works – all the etiquette that's involved, all the unspoken rules – it'd be presumptuous to think about anything but local office at first. You pay your dues and then you get to run for something a bit more glamorous." James Bremer, the president of a government watchdog organization, arrived at the same conclusion: "You need to start local, work hard, and prove yourself before you can even think about moving up in the political world."

Although most of the eligible candidates (56 percent) state that, should they ultimately choose to run for office, they would be interested in a local-level position, 40 percent indicate interest in eventually running for a state-level position. Approximately one of every four respondents identified at least one federal-level position he or she would ultimately be interested in pursuing. If we consider "high-level office" to include federal positions as well as statewide offices, then 29 percent of respondents reported at least some degree of interest. These findings regarding elective office preferences reinforce the importance of homing in on the initial decision to run; most eligible candidates would opt to enter lower-level races before seeking entry into state-level or congressional races.

Predicting Nascent Ambition:
The Null Effects of the Political Opportunity Structure
Another way to assess the differences between the two stages of the candidate emergence process involves examining the extent to which the structural variables that most scholars find predict expressive ambition also affect nascent ambition. If nascent ambition is a precursor to expressive ambition, and if it taps into personal predispositions and circumstances that are relatively far removed from the political opportunity structure, then structural variables should not play a role in predicting whether a respondent has ever considered running for office.

Table 3.6 presents the logistic regression coefficients of a series of variables that tap into the political opportunity structure an eligible

TABLE 3.6. *Predicting Nascent Ambition: The (Null) Baseline Model (Logistic Regression Coefficients and Standard Errors)*

	Considered Running for Office
Electoral Features and Opportunities	
Size of the congressional delegation	− 0.01 (0.01)
Size of the state political opportunity structure	0.00 (0.00)
Size of the local political opportunity structure	0.00 (0.00)
Term limits	0.16 (0.09)
Part-time legislature	0.11 (0.10)
Legislative salary	0.00 (0.00)
Political Dynamics	
Democrat	0.18 (0.10)
Republican	0.04 (0.10)
Percent Democratic presidential vote share	− 0.01 (0.01)
Party congruence with the congressional delegation	0.09 (0.09)
Party congruence with the state legislature	− 0.07 (0.09)
Constant	0.59 (0.36)
Percent correctly predicted	54.7
Pseudo R-squared	0.01
N	3,319

Notes: Regression results are based on the 2001 data and the electoral features, opportunities, and political dynamics at that time. The reduced number of cases results from listwise deletion. The results are comparable for the 2008 data, but the sample size is smaller.

candidate might face. The equation controls for a state's electoral features and opportunities, such as the number of elected positions at the local, state, and federal levels, as well as the time commitment and compensation associated with them. I also include in the regression equation gauges of the political dynamics between an eligible candidate and where he or she lives; the respondent's party affiliation, the partisan leanings of the state, and the respondent's party congruence with the state, for example, have been shown to affect the decision to run for the state legislature and the U.S. Congress (see Chapter 2). Appendix F provides a complete description of all variables included in the multivariate analyses throughout this book.

This regression equation, which serves as the model of political ambition on which I build throughout the remainder of this book, reveals that gauges of the size and openness of the political opportunity structure, legislative professionalization, and a respondent's party congruence with elected officials in the state do not account for variation in whether he or she ever considered running for office. Several of these null findings may not be entirely surprising. The majority of individuals who considered running for office expressed interest at the local level. Thus, features of the state legislature or party congruence with state legislators or members of the congressional delegation are not, necessarily, the structural variables that would predict interest in running for local office. The total number of local governmental units by state, however, is also statistically insignificant. Further, if state-level structural variables played an important role affecting nascent ambition, then their influence should be evident, at least to some extent, when I restrict the analysis to respondents who reported a general interest in running for an office beyond the local level. Here, too, state-level measures of political opportunities, legislative professionalization, and party congruence with the legislature and/or congressional delegation do not affect a respondent's likelihood of expressing a general interest in a statewide or congressional position. Coupled with the lack of explanatory power conferred by the model, the structural variables' insignificance bolsters the importance of studying nascent ambition.

Dynamic Ambition in the Candidate Eligibility Pool

My broader conception of political ambition also involves a dynamic component; eligible candidates' general interest in office holding is not fixed, but rather, can wax and wane over time. Nancy Friedman, a New York attorney whom I interviewed, serves as a case in point. When her children were in school, Friedman thought that she might run for the school board. Then, as she built her law practice, she thought that a judgeship might be desirable. But now, at 61, she no longer has any interest in running for office: "The last time I considered running was a long, long time ago. My interests have changed, my life has changed. It's probably been twenty years since I thought running for office might be something on my horizon." Several of the respondents I interviewed shared similar stories. Tara Erickson, a New England attorney, thought about running for the zoning board when a series of ordinances affected the remodeling of her home and the expansion of the parking lot in her office complex:

> You feel dissatisfied about the way things are going and you think that maybe if you were in there, it would be different. But then you get married, have kids, have your elderly parents move in with you. It might sound

selfish, but you don't care enough about zoning ordinances anymore to get involved. At least that's what happened to me.

Edward Copeland's interest in running for office also changed over time. In the late 1990s, he "never would have thought about running for office." With a daughter in first grade and two sons who will be entering the public school system within the next few years, though, he "thinks all the time about running for the school board. It's the best way to improve the schools and take care of kids."

The panel data allow for a more systematic assessment of the extent to which political ambition at the individual level changes over time. In both 2001 and 2008, we included on the survey a question about interest in running for office at some point in the future. The data presented in the top half of Table 3.7 indicate that, in 2008, nearly 70 percent of respondents had at least some interest in the idea of a future candidacy.

TABLE 3.7. *Dynamic Ambition in the Candidate Eligibility Pool*

	Aggregate Levels of Political Ambition		Individual-Level Changes in Ambition	
	Frequency in Wave 1 (2001) (%)	Frequency in Wave 2 (2008) (%)	Gained Interest (%)	Lost Interest (%)
Interest in Running for Office in the Future:				
Definitely	3	3		
If the opportunity presented itself	17	15		
No interest now, but wouldn't rule it out forever	56	51		
Absolutely not	24	31		
Overall levels of change in ambition since 2001			15	23
Interested in:				
Local-level office	56	60	17	13
State-level office	40	38	12	14
Federal-level office	25	20	7	12

Notes: These data are based on the 1,810 respondents who answered the questions in both 2001 and 2008. Numbers do not add up to 100 percent for the levels of office in which respondents expressed interest because they could select multiple offices.

Indeed, nearly one in five eligible candidates expressed relatively strong interest in running for office, and half of the respondents were at least open to the idea. At the aggregate level, interest in running for office in 2008 was similar to interest in 2001, as were the levels of office in which respondents expressed interest.

More important, however, is the high degree of individual-level fluctuation in political ambition across the seven-year interval between the two waves of the panel. Although aggregate levels of future interest in office-seeking are similar across the two waves of the panel, the data highlight the dynamic nature of eligible candidates' general interest in running for office. Almost 40 percent of respondents moved along the continuum of interest in running for office in the future, with eligible candidates more likely to lose political ambition than to gain it. Further, shifts in political ambition were not driven by changes in attitudes about any one particular office or level of office. As the bottom half of Table 3.7 makes clear, movement in political ambition occurred across all levels of office. Depending on the level of office in question, as many as 30 percent of the respondents shifted interest and either gained or lost ambition. Here, the importance of panel data is particularly evident, as cross-sectional data at two points in time would not uncover these individual-level shifts.

All changes in interest in running for office are important to document, but particularly noteworthy are cases in which individuals move across the threshold of having little political ambition to expressing a fair degree of interest in running for office, or vice versa. Table 3.8 presents a simple cross-tabulation of respondents' interest in running for office in 2001 (at the time of the first wave of the study) with their interest in running in 2008; these data allow for an examination of where the shifts in political ambition occurred. The top row of the table, for instance, reveals that only one in four respondents who were definitely interested in running for office in 2001 remained certain in 2008 that they would run. Thirty-seven percent continued to have strong interest and thought that it was something they would like to do if the opportunity presented itself. Thirty-eight percent of the men and women who, seven years earlier, definitely planned to run for office at some point in the future no longer expressed a high degree of interest or ambition. On the other end of the spectrum, more than a quarter of respondents who had ruled out running as a possibility in the first wave of the study were willing at the time of the second wave to consider it, at least to some degree.

Although some random movement across categories of political ambition over the course of seven years is expected, we would not anticipate

TABLE 3.8. *Widespread Shifts in Political Ambition Over Time: Cross-Tabulation Results of Interest in a Future Candidacy in 2001 and 2008*

	Interest in Running for Office at Some Point in the Future (Wave 2 – 2008)			
	Definitely	If the Opportunity Presented Itself	No Interest Now, But Wouldn't Rule It Out Forever	Absolutely Not
Interest in Running for Office at Some Point in the Future (Wave 1 – 2001)				
Definitely (N = 57)	25 %	37	33	5
If the opportunity presented itself (N = 305)	7	43 %	42	8
No interest now, but wouldn't rule it out forever (N = 1,018)	1	11	67 %	21
Absolutely not (N = 430)	1	3	23	73 %

Notes: These data are based on the 1,810 respondents who answered the question in both 2001 and 2008. The data presented in each row indicate levels of interest in running for office in 2008 (Wave 2), broken down by the level of political ambition the respondent expressed in 2001 (Wave 1). Entries in shaded boxes represent the percentage of respondents in each category from 2001 whose future ambition remained static across the panel. Entries to the left of the shaded boxes in each row indicate an increase in ambition from 2001; entries to the right of the shaded boxes indicate a decrease in ambition from 2001.

such a high degree of change into and out of the two categories at the ends of the spectrum. Moreover, the respondents' actual behavior validates the substantial perceptual shifts in political ambition during this seven-year period. Twelve percent of the women and men in the candidate eligibility pool took at least one new concrete step between the two waves of the panel. Respondents whose ambition for a future candidacy increased over time were twice as likely to take at least one new concrete step as were those who reported no such increase (difference significant at $p < 0.01$).

The empirical findings, as well as the evidence from the interviews, suggest that ebbs and flows in interest in running for office precede the decision to enter an actual race at a given time. And a series of multiple regression analyses supports this conclusion. Table 3.9 presents three models, each of which tracks broad changes in political ambition between the two waves of the study. The first column reports ordered logistic regression coefficients for an equation that predicts change in ambition using a five-point scale. This ordinal measure of ambition allows for a maximum gain in ambition of $+2$ and a maximum loss in ambition of -2, based on the question that taps future interest in running for office.[3] The second and third columns in the table report the multinomial logistic regression coefficients predicting whether a respondent gained or lost ambition.

As was the case for predicting nascent ambition, I include in each model gauges of the political opportunity structure, as well as variables that measure changes in the political environment eligible candidates might have faced between the two waves of the study. Certainly, many aspects of the electoral environment – such as the size of the opportunity structure and levels of legislative professionalization – tend not to change over time. But eligible candidates often relocate, and shifting political dynamics and party strength in a state can also affect candidate emergence. Thus, I control for whether the respondent moved, became less ideologically congruent with the area in which he or she resides, or saw a change in the state's Democratic presidential vote share between the two waves of the study. I also control for the respondent's placement on the ambition scale in 2001 because that initial level of interest in running for office constrains, at least in part, the direction and degree of movement possible by 2008.

The regression results reveal that fluctuations in political ambition are far more complex than a mere reflection of changes in conventional indicators of the political opportunity structure. Indeed, none of the structural variables or the changes therein achieves conventional levels of statistical significance.[4] If we want to understand who will ultimately seek positions

---

[3] As reported in Tables 3.7 and 3.8, respondents could have scored between a 1 ("absolutely no interest in a future candidacy") and a 4 ("definitely plan to run in the future") on the ambition continuum at both points in time. Roughly one-third of the movement in ambition occurs between the middle two categories of the scale, though: "If the opportunity presented itself" and "No interest now, but wouldn't rule it out forever." Because these categories are perhaps not as distinct as the two endpoints of the ambition continuum, I err on the side of caution and perform the analysis with a dependent variable that collapses these middle two categories. The regression results are comparable when I employ a seven-point ordinal measure of changes in ambition.

[4] I also performed separate regression analyses predicting changes in ambition for the subsamples of respondents who expressed interest in local, state, and federal offices, including only the structural variables that would be expected to have an effect (i.e., the term limits variable for state-level office, but not local office; the Democratic presidential vote share for federal-level office, but not local office). In each of these cases, the structural variables failed to predict changes in interest in running for office.

TABLE 3.9. *Predicting Dynamic Ambition: The (Null) Baseline Model*

	Ordered Logit	Multinomial Logit	
	Change in Ambition (5-point scale)	Gained Interest in Running for Office	Lost Interest in Running for Office
Electoral Features and Opportunities			
Size of the congressional delegation	−0.00 (0.01)	−0.00 (.01)	0.01 (0.01)
Size of the state political opportunity structure	0.00 (0.00)	−0.01 (.01)	0.00 (0.00)
Size of the local political opportunity structure	0.00 (.00)	0.00 (.00)	0.00 (0.00)
Term limits	−0.18 (0.16)	−0.14 (0.20)	0.12 (0.18)
Part-time legislature	−0.18 (0.17)	0.11 (0.22)	0.28 (0.20)
Legislative salary	0.00 (.00)	0.00 (0.00)	0.00 (0.00)
Changes in Political Dynamics			
Democrat	0.04 (0.16)	0.29 (0.20)	0.13 (0.19)
Republican	−0.18 (0.17)	−0.08 (0.23)	−0.08 (0.20)
Change in party identification	−0.14 (0.11)	−0.03 (0.14)	−0.12 (0.13)
Increase in percent Democratic presidential vote share	−0.02 (0.04)	0.03 (0.04)	0.05 (0.04)
Moved	0.20 (0.18)	0.15 (0.21)	−0.29 (0.21)
Became incongruent with the political landscape	−0.18 (0.15)	−0.08 (0.19)	0.18 (0.17)
Baseline Level of Political Ambition (in Wave 1)	−1.13 (0.09)**	−0.75 (0.13)**	1.61 (0.12)**
(Threshold −2)	−9.26 (0.76)**		
(Threshold −1)	−4.19 (0.29)**		
(Threshold 0)	0.32 (0.26)		
(Threshold +1)	3.80 (0.51)**		
Constant		0.06 (0.34)	−4.49 (0.35)**
Pseudo R-squared	0.14	0.25	
N	1,548	1,548	

Notes: Regression results are based on data from respondents who completed both the 2001 and 2008 surveys. The reduced number of cases results from listwise deletion.
Significance levels: ** p < 0.01; * p < 0.05.

of political power, then we must recognize the dynamic nature of the early candidate emergence process and assess the factors that affect it.

Conclusion

The study of political ambition has largely been limited to the decision making of political actors who are already fully immersed in electoral politics. The methodological challenges involved in identifying and sampling a broad cross section of eligible candidates have deterred political scientists from investigating the critically important initial decision to run for office. The results presented in this chapter, however, highlight the prevalence of nascent ambition and its dynamic nature.

Studies that focus on the expressive ambition involved in entering state legislative or congressional races are incomplete because they do not take into account the selection process by which eligible candidates become actual candidates. After all, only about 10 percent of the respondents ever ran for office. But half the members of the candidate eligibility pool considered a candidacy, and more than two-thirds of the respondents are open to the idea of running for office at some point in the future. Examining the factors that affect broad interest in running for office, as well as circumstances that propel and suppress that interest, therefore, is critical if we seek to understand who ultimately emerges as a candidate. The next four chapters of the book investigate the influence that personal, familial, professional, and political factors exert on nascent ambition and the manner in which it increases and decreases over time.

4

Barack Obama and 18 Million Cracks in the Glass Ceiling

Sex, Race, and Political Ambition

On June 7, 2008, Hillary Clinton took to the podium for what would be her last speech as a presidential candidate. After thanking her supporters, volunteers, staff, and friends, she spoke very openly about what her candidacy meant for women's political progress: "You can be so proud that, from now on, it will be unremarkable for a woman to win primary state victories, unremarkable to have a woman in a close race to be our nominee, unremarkable to think that a woman can be the President of the United States. And that is truly remarkable."[1] Then, in what became perhaps the most famous lines of her campaign, then-Senator Clinton commented on the prospects of electing a woman president:

> If we can blast 50 women into space, we will someday launch a woman into the White House. Although we weren't able to shatter that highest, hardest glass ceiling this time, thanks to you, it's got about 18 million cracks in it. And the light is shining through like never before, filling us all with the hope and the sure knowledge that the path will be a little easier next time.... And all of you will know that because of your passion and hard work you helped pave the way for that day.

Nearly three months later, during her first speech as the Republican Party's vice presidential candidate, Sarah Palin uttered very similar words. She reminded her supporters at a Dayton, Ohio, rally that "Hillary left 18 million cracks in the highest, hardest glass ceiling in America. But

[1] "Transcript: Hillary Clinton Endorses Barack Obama," *New York Times*, June 7, 2008. Accessed at http://www.nytimes.com/2008/06/07/us/politics/07text-clinton.html?_r=1& pagewanted=all (August 19, 2010).

it turns out that the women of America aren't finished yet, and we can shatter that glass ceiling once and for all."[2]

Clinton's and Palin's candidacies made the 2008 presidential campaign historic, but the election of Barack Obama as the first black president of the United States was nothing short of monumental. On election night, in front of an audience of 125,000 people assembled in Grant Park in Chicago, then-President-Elect Obama reflected on the symbolism of his victory: "If there is anyone out there who still doubts that America is a place where all things are possible; who still wonders if the dream of our founders is alive in our time; who still questions the power of our democracy, tonight is your answer."[3] Sending a strong message about the importance of engaging the political system, regardless of race, class, sex, age, or ideology, Obama told the crowd about Ann Nixon Cooper, an elderly supporter from Atlanta:

> She was born just a generation past slavery...when someone like her couldn't vote for two reasons – because she was a woman and because of the color of her skin.... And this year, in this election, she touched her finger to a screen and cast her vote, because after 106 years in America, through the best of times and the darkest of hours, she knows how America can change.[4]

Indeed, throughout many of the interviews I conducted for this book in late 2008, both male and female eligible candidates across the country consistently reflected on the progress signified by the 2008 election cycle. Put simply by June Johnson, a Southern Republican lawyer, "Hillary Clinton and Barack Obama's experiences – the fact that she got as far as she did and the fact that he won – are major progress, plain and simple." In the words of Elaine Minor, a businesswoman from Philadelphia, "I now see, and more importantly, my children now see, that men and women of all races can achieve whatever they set their minds to do. And even when they don't win, they move the country forward in the process." David Rothstein, a Washington, DC, attorney echoed the sentiments of dozens of survey respondents: "The 2008 election made me proud – proud that a

---

[2] "Transcript: Palin's Speech in Dayton, Ohio," National Public Radio, August 29, 2008. Accessed at http://www.npr.org/templates/story/story.php?storyId=94118910 (August 19, 2010).

[3] Adam Nagourney, "Obama Elected President as Racial Barrier Falls," *New York Times*, November 6, 2008, page A1.

[4] "Transcript: Barack Obama's Victory Speech," National Public Radio, November 5, 2008. Accessed at http://www.npr.org/templates/story/story.php?storyId=96624326 (August 19, 2010).

woman could run a viable campaign and win presidential primaries across the country; proud that a black man could be elected president; and proud that my children will have such diverse role models." Summarized well by Hillary Clinton, the 2008 election "achieved milestones essential to our progress as a nation, part of our perpetual duty to form a more perfect union."[5]

Despite the diversity among the candidates in the 2008 race for the White House, elite-level politics remains a business dominated by white men. In fact, as of the 1970s, women occupied almost no major elective positions in U.S. political institutions. Ella Grasso, a Democrat from Connecticut, and Dixie Lee Ray, a Democrat from Washington, served as the only two women elected governor throughout the decade. Not until 1978 did Kansas Republican Nancy Kassebaum become the first woman elected to the Senate in her own right. Still, today, women's numeric underrepresentation is glaring. When the 112th Congress convened in January 2011, women held only 17 percent of the seats. They occupy the governor's mansion in only 6 of the 50 states, and they run City Hall in only 7 of the 100 largest cities across the country.[6]

For African Americans and Latinos, election to high-level office has also been slow-going. L. Douglas Wilder (D–VA) served as the first black governor elected in his own right, but that was not until 1989.[7] Only four African Americans have served in the U.S. Senate post-Reconstruction, three of whom were Democrats from Illinois.[8] Susanna Martinez (R–NM) serves as the only Latino/a governor in the United States; and although the first Hispanic governor served as early as 1875, only ten Latinos have ever held the position as the chief executive of a state.[9] Robert Menendez (D–NJ), who has served in the U.S. Senate since 2007, is only the sixth Latino ever to do so. Fewer than 15 percent of the members of the U.S.

---

[5] "Transcript: Hillary Clinton Endorses Barack Obama," *New York Times*, June 7, 2008. Accessed at http://www.nytimes.com/2008/06/07/us/politics/07text-clinton.html?_r=1& pagewanted=all (August 19, 2010).

[6] See Lawless and Fox (2010) for a detailed account of the numbers of women serving in all levels of elective office over time, as well as globally.

[7] P. B. S. Pinchback was the first African American governor; he was appointed governor of Louisiana and served for less than six weeks (from December 9, 1872 until January 13, 1873).

[8] Carol Moseley-Braun (1993–1998), Barack Obama (2005–2008), and Roland Burris (2008–2010) represented Illinois in the U.S. Senate. Edward William Brooke, a Republican from Massachusetts, was elected in 1966 and served from 1967 through 1979.

[9] These data are compiled by the National Governors Association and are available on its website, http://www.nga.org/ (September 24, 2010).

House of Representatives are black or Latino/a, as are only 12 percent of state legislators throughout the country.[10]

This chapter considers gender and race differences in political ambition as a driving force for the numeric underrepresentation of women, blacks, and Latinos.[11] Clearly, the roles that sex, race, and ethnicity play in politics are very complex. These indicators of minority status, after all, are linked to generations of cultural identities and political stereotypes. There is simply no way that one book, let alone one chapter in one book, can adequately address the extent to which minority status, exclusion, and political marginalization intersect with the candidate emergence process. This chapter can, however, paint a portrait of political ambition in the candidate eligibility pool by sex and race, as well as offer the first examination of the way they intersect in the candidate emergence process.[12]

My empirical assessment reveals that, despite similarities in levels of political participation, interest, and proximity, female eligible candidates are less politically ambitious than men. Not only are women less likely than men to consider running for office, but they are also less likely than men to express interest in high-level positions. When I turn to race, though, I find no such ambition gap. Black and Latino eligible candidates in this sample are at least as likely as their white counterparts to exhibit high levels of political participation and proximity. They are also as likely to report interest in running for office. The intersectional analysis adds a bit of texture to these broad findings; the gender gap in office-specific preferences is smaller among black and Latino respondents than among whites. Overall, however, the gender gap in political ambition is roughly the same size, regardless of race or ethnicity. This chapter, therefore, establishes one of the most critical findings of this book: a substantial winnowing process occurs in the candidate emergence process long before eligible candidates decide to run for particular offices at

---

[10] These data are provided by the black and Latino caucuses of the state legislatures and are available on the National Conference of State Legislatures website, www.ncsl.org (July 18, 2010).

[11] Because the number of Asian American and Native American respondents is so low, the empirical analyses cannot begin to shed light on these minority groups. Accordingly, the quantitative and qualitative data, as well as the literature reviewed in this chapter, focus on women, black, and Latino/a citizens.

[12] For a detailed, book-length treatment of gender and the manner in which it affects the initial decision to run for office, see *It Still Takes A Candidate: Why Women Don't Run for Office* (Lawless and Fox 2010). In that book, there is no treatment of race or the intersection between race and sex.

particular times. Politically interested and active women of varying racial and ethnic backgrounds are far less likely than men ever to make it to Election Day.

The Politics of Exclusion: Sex, Race, and the Conventional Explanations for Numeric Underrepresentation

Scholars have devoted the past few decades to gaining a better understanding of why so few women and members of racial minority groups occupy positions of political power in the United States. Much of the earliest research identified overt discrimination by voters and electoral gatekeepers as a critical impediment for women and minority candidates. Electoral gatekeepers all but prohibited women from running for office in the 1970s; and those women who did emerge as candidates often faced sexism and a hostile environment. Reflecting on the political arena for women in 1972, for example, U.S. Senator Barbara Boxer (1994, 73–4) recounts that being a woman was a "distinct, quantifiable disadvantage" (see also Witt, Paget, and Matthews 1994). The experiences of black candidates in the 1970s and 1980s were similar. Carol Swain (1995, 141) argues, for instance, that Alan Wheat and Ron Dellums, both of whom were black but were elected to the U.S. House of Representatives from majority-white districts, were discouraged from running in these districts. Black candidates were also discouraged from running for statewide office throughout these decades (Sonenshein 1990).[13]

In the contemporary electoral environment, however, the explanatory power of overt discrimination has been largely discarded. In terms of campaign fundraising receipts and vote totals, often considered the two most important indicators of electoral success, researchers find that women fare just as well as, if not better than, their male counterparts. More specifically, political scientists uncover no aggregate-level voter bias against female candidates for either the U.S. Senate (Smith and Fox 2001) or House of Representatives (Fox 2010; Lawless and Pearson 2008; Cook 1998; Dolan 1998). In terms of fundraising, at least at the congressional level, Richard L. Fox (2010) provides evidence of gender parity in campaign contributions. Summarized well by Kathleen Dolan (2004, 50),

---

[13] For the early analyses of sexism and gender bias in the electoral environment, see Rule 1981; Welch 1978; Diamond 1977; Githens and Prestage 1977. For evidence of racism and discrimination against minority candidates, see Swain 1995; Jones and Clemons 1993; Terkildsen 1993; Sonenshein 1990; Piliawsky 1989.

"Levels of bias are low enough to no longer provide significant impediments to women's chances of election."[14]

Research that focuses on the electoral fortunes of black candidates also uncovers little evidence of overt voter discrimination. Benjamin Highton's (2004) analysis of the 1996 and 1998 U.S. House elections reveals not only that white voters are no less likely to vote Democratic when the Democratic candidate is black, but also that they are no more likely to vote Democratic when the Republican candidate is black. Based on an analysis of precinct-level data, experimental data, and national exit poll data, Tasha Philpot and Hanes Walton (2007) uncover a similar result: black women are the strongest supporters of black female candidates, but experienced black female candidates attract both black and white voters, regardless of sex. And through an analysis of polling and election data for all black candidates for governor or U.S. senator from 1989 to 2006, Daniel Hopkins (2009) finds that, although African Americans running for office prior to 1996 performed nearly three percentage points worse than polling numbers predicted, the gap between polling and performance dissipated in the mid-1990s.[15]

In light of the growing contradiction between a political system that elects few women and minority candidates and a body of research that identifies the electoral environment as increasingly unbiased, political scientists have turned to institutional explanations to account for numeric underrepresentation. Most notably, they point to the incumbency

---

[14] The fact that women are just as likely as similarly situated men to win elections does not mean that pockets of bias do not exist, or that gender plays no role in electoral politics. Rather, female congressional candidates face more primary competition than do their male counterparts (Lawless and Pearson 2008), and they must raise more money to perform as well as men at the polls (Fiber and Fox 2005). In addition, geographic differences facilitate women's election in some congressional districts, but lessen their chances of success in others (Palmer and Simon 2008). Surveys of local party officials reveal that some electoral gatekeepers appear to continue to prefer male candidates (Sanbonmatsu 2006; Niven 1998). Examinations of campaigns show that gender stereotypes often still affect media coverage (Hayes 2011; Fowler and Lawless 2009; Lawless 2009; Rausch, Rozell, and Wilson 1999; Fox 1997; Kahn 1996). And voters continue to rely on stereotypical conceptions of women and men's traits, issue expertise, and policy positions (Lawless 2004b; Koch 2000; McDermott 1998; McDermott 1997).

[15] As was the case with sex, the mere fact that voters are willing to vote for minority candidates does not mean that racial stereotypes do not affect the experiences black and Latino candidates endure on the campaign trail. When white voters lack positive information about black candidates, for instance, they tend to allow stereotypes to fill the void (Hajnal 2007). Moreover, racialized campaigns can prime anti-black attitudes (Huber and Lapinski 2006; Mendelberg 2001; Valentino 1999; Citrin, Green, and Sears 1990).

advantage, which inhibits electoral opportunities for previously excluded groups, such as women and racial minorities (Palmer and Simon 2008; Nixon and Darcy 1996; Darcy, Welch, and Clark 1994; Studlar and Welch 1990; Welch and Karnig 1979). Not only do incumbents seek reelection in more than 75 percent of state legislative and congressional elections, but their reelection rates also consistently hover at 90 percent (Duerst-Lahti 1998, 19). In 2010, which was considered an anti-incumbency election cycle, only 37 members of the U.S. House of Representatives chose not to seek reelection (16 of whom stepped down to pursue a bid for higher office) and only 58 incumbents were defeated (4 in primaries and 54 in general elections).[16] In other words, 85 percent of incumbents seeking reelection won their races. The 2008 congressional election cycle saw even fewer open seats; only 31 incumbents (7 percent of the total House of Representatives membership) chose not to seek reelection. More than 90 percent of congressional incumbents also sought and won reelection in 2004 and 2006. As Keith Gaddie and Charles Bullock (2000, 1) conclude, "Open seats, not the defeat of incumbents, are the portal through which most legislators enter Congress." Under these circumstances, increasing the number of electoral opportunities for previously excluded groups, such as women, blacks, or Latinos, can be glacial.[17]

Other investigators point to "situational" factors as a prime explanation for the dearth of previously excluded groups in politics (Clark 1994; Welch 1978). An analysis of the professional occupations of members

---

[16] A Washington Post-ABC News poll conducted in April 2010 found that members of Congress faced the most anti-incumbent electorate since 1994. Less than one-third of all voters reported an inclination to support their current representative in the November 2010 general election. Dan Balz and Jon Cohen, "Poll Finds Americans in an Anti-Incumbent Mood as Election Nears," *Washington Post*, April 28, 2010. Accessed at http://www.washingtonpost.com/wp-dyn/content/article/2010/04/27/AR2010042705324.html (September 11, 2010).

[17] The power of institutional inertia, however, has been called into question. Certainly, incumbency continues to pose a serious obstacle, particularly at the federal level (Palmer and Simon 2008). But 21 states enacted state legislative term limits throughout the 1990s, and scholars uncovered no evidence that combating incumbency with term limits improved women's representation (Kousser 2005; see also Carroll and Jenkins 2003). In terms of electoral opportunities provided by term limits for blacks and Latinos, research suggests that term limits can increase representation in areas where the minority group's population is growing, but decrease the numbers of minority officeholders when the minority group's population shrinks (Casellas 2009; Cain and Kousser 2004). Based on these findings, although incumbency and the lack of open seats certainly pose barriers to women and minority groups' inclusion in politics, terms limits and increased electoral opportunities may present less of a workable solution than previously thought.

in the 111th Congress reveals that law, business, education, and politics are the four leading professions that precede congressional careers.[18] The same is true at the state legislative level (CAWP 2001).

Despite the fact that most candidates, regardless of sex or race, enter from these "pipeline" professions, far more men than women, and far more whites than blacks or Latinos, comprise them. Turning first to the field of law, the National Association for Law Placement Foundation (2010) found that women account for only 19 percent of the partners in the nation's major law firms; African Americans and Latinos each comprise roughly 2 percent of partners.[19] In the business world, white men overwhelmingly dominate the upper ranks. Only two companies (DuPont and Kraft Foods) included in the Dow Jones industrial average have female chief executive officers (CEOs), and only fifteen Fortune 500 companies have female CEOs (only one of whom is a woman of color).[20] Four black men and seven Latinos serve as Fortune 500 CEOs.[21] Gender segregation is also quite evident in higher education, especially on climbing the career ladder. Since 2003, women have comprised slightly more than half of all doctoral recipients, up from 12 percent in 1966 (Falkenheim and Feigener 2008). But the percentage of women among tenured college and university faculty is not appreciably higher than it was in the mid-1970s (Banerji 2006; Mason and Goulden 2002). Blacks and Latinos each hold only 5 percent of full-time faculty positions; among faculty members with tenure, 3 percent are black and 2 percent are Latino (Fields 2007). Obtaining the qualifications and economic autonomy required to pursue elective office, therefore, has been – and continues to be – much more readily available to white men.

---

[18] I drew this information from the *Almanac of American Politics* (Barone and Cohen 2008) and from the websites of members of the 111th Congress (see also Moncrief, Squire, and Jewell 2001; Dolan and Ford 1997).

[19] Although a growing number of women have been earning law degrees and moving into the legal profession, progress is slow. A decade ago, 13 percent of the partners in major law firms were women. For African Americans and Latinos, the gains have been equally marginal. Moreover, law school enrollments for blacks and Mexicans have decreased over the past decade; enrollments for non-Mexican Hispanics have seen slight increases (see Tamar Lewin, "Law School Admissions Lag Among Minorities," *New York Times*, January 6, 2010. Accessed at http://www.nytimes.com/2010/01/07/education/07law.html (September 11, 2010)).

[20] These data were gathered by Catalyst, a New York City based nonprofit research organization.

[21] Daryl C. Hannah, "First Black Woman Fortune 500 CEO," *DiversityInc*, May 22, 2009, Accessed at http://www.diversityinc.com/article/5879/First-BlackWoman-Fortune-500-CEO/ (September 11, 2010).

The central explanations that have emerged for gender and racial numeric underrepresentation in U.S. political institutions, therefore, tend to focus on voters' willingness (or lack thereof) to elect women and candidates of color, as well as the structural barriers that make it difficult for any previously marginalized group to enter the political arena.[22] Discrimination and structural obstacles certainly contribute, in varying degrees, to the gender and racial disparities in our political institutions over time. But the power of these explanations, even combined, is limited; neither focuses on the eligible candidates, themselves, or begins to tackle the fundamental question of whether women and racial minorities are as politically ambitious as white men to emerge as candidates.

Sex, Race, and Political Ambition: Existing Literature and Competing Expectations

The conventional assessment that emerges from the current explanations for gender and racial disparities in elective office is that, overall, we are on a positive course. To some degree, discriminatory attitudes and persistent stereotyping toward women and racial minorities in politics still exist. And overcoming institutional inertia is certainly complex and slow-going. But when women run for office, they fare at least as well as men. In most cases, black and Latino candidates also do not face aggregate-level bias at the polls. As women's presence in the candidate eligibility pool approaches men's, and as African Americans and Latinos continue to acquire the backgrounds and credentials most candidates possess, we should see the number of women and minority elected officials increase substantially. Completely missing from this prognosis, however, is an understanding of the gender and racial dynamics underlying the process

---

[22] Much of the research that focuses on electoral opportunities and the candidacies of racial minority groups also concentrates on electoral arrangements and redistricting (Canon 1999; Lublin 1997; Swain 1995; Darcy, Hadley, and Kirksey 1993). Of all black members to serve in the U.S. House of Representatives between 1970 and 1990, fewer than 5 percent came from majority white districts (Swain 1995). Moreover, the partisan composition of the black population – the overwhelming majority identify as Democrats – makes election in vast swaths of the country virtually impossible. The racial composition of electoral districts, coupled with the partisan distribution of the black population, therefore, serves as a structural impediment beyond incumbency that seriously hinders where and when black eligible candidates can successfully run for office. Further, an analysis of more than 7,000 cities reveals that district systems, as opposed to at-large systems, can lead to greater racial diversity among elected officials, as long as the underrepresented groups are highly concentrated and comprise a substantial portion of the population (Trounstine and Valdini 2008).

by which individuals move from the eligibility pool into elective office. Yet when we turn to the limited scholarship that focuses specifically on gender, race, and political ambition, it is clear that these ascriptive characteristics might affect the initial decision to run for office.

In terms of gender, Richard L. Fox and I (2010) provide a book-length assessment of why women do not run for office. We argue that the most fundamental barriers to women's representation derive from the patterns of traditional gender socialization to which scholars have long referred, but had previously been limited in studying empirically.[23] More specifically, even in the current era, the primary institutions of social and cultural life in the United States continue to impress on women and men that traditional gender roles – embodied by heterosexual marriage, in which women assume the majority of household labor and child care responsibilities – constitute a normal, appropriate, and desirable set of life circumstances (see also Freedman 2002; Jennings and Farah 1981; Fowlkes, Perkins, and Tolleson Rinehart 1979). Not only do women continue to bear the responsibility for a majority of household tasks and child care, but they also face a more complicated balancing of these responsibilities with their professions than do men. A masculinized ethos in many public and private institutional settings reinforces traditional gender roles. Political organizations and institutions that have always been controlled by men continue to operate with a gendered lens that promotes men's participation in the political arena and does not sufficiently encourage women to break down barriers in traditionally masculine spheres and environments (e.g., Enloe 2004; Flammang 1997; Carroll 1994). Further, whereas men are taught to be confident, assertive, and self-promoting, cultural attitudes toward women as political leaders continue to leave an imprint suggesting to women – even if only subtly – that it is often inappropriate or undesirable to possess these characteristics. Traditional gender socialization, in

---

[23] When we wrote the first edition of our book (2005), none of the sixteen published academic books that concentrated predominantly on political ambition focused on gender. A search of scholarly journals in the disciplines of political science, sociology, and psychology revealed a similar pattern. The only national study of the interaction between gender and political ambition appeared in 1982, when Virginia Sapiro reported that female delegates to the 1972 national party conventions were less politically ambitious than their male counterparts. Over the course of the three decades since Sapiro's article appeared, ten articles have investigated gender and the candidate emergence process. Eight of these articles are based on samples of actual candidates and officeholders, all of whom, by definition, exhibited political ambition when they entered political contests. The two articles that focus on individuals who have not yet run for office rely on data from the single-state investigation that served as the pilot study for our 2005 book.

short, creates a set of circumstances in which the greater complexities of women's lives, both in terms of how society perceives them and the manner in which they perceive themselves as eligible candidates, depress their political ambition.

Our previous work pertaining to gender and the decision to run for office goes a long way in establishing and shedding light on the reasons for the gender gap in political ambition. Nowhere in the book, however, do we even begin to scratch the surface of the interplay between race and sex. We do not examine whether white women and women of color are equally likely to possess the levels of political participation, interest, and proximity that serve as key ingredients to foster interest in running for office; we offer no analysis of the extent to which women from various racial backgrounds exhibit comparable levels of political ambition; and we provide no assessment of whether women from different racial backgrounds express interest in the same elective offices.

The lack of research on race and ambition extends beyond assessments of the intersectionality between race and gender, though. In fact, almost no research specifically addresses race or ethnicity in the candidate emergence process at all. The one study that does focus on race and ambition is a study of black elected officials from Michigan in the 1970s, in which Pauline Terrelonge Stone (1980) concludes that black elected officials may be less ambitious than politicians of other races. Of course, the study, which lacks a comparison group of other races, focuses on individuals who have all exhibited ambition by virtue of running for and winning elective office. Further, every black governor and U.S. senator, as well as the overwhelming majority of black members of the U.S. House of Representatives, was elected after the 1970s; Stone's study, therefore, is limited in what it can say about political ambition among members of racial minority groups in the contemporary environment.

The literature on political participation, which sheds substantial light on race differences in levels of political activism, generates competing hypotheses when we turn to political ambition. On one hand, we might expect members of racial minority groups to exhibit higher levels of political ambition than whites. After all, since the 1970s, investigators find that, after taking into account socioeconomic status, African Americans participate at higher rates than whites.[24] This increased level of activism

---

[24] Early research on race and political participation uncovered lower levels of political activism by blacks. Scholars explained the race gap by focusing on racial differences in the ingredients that foster political activism, such as income, education, and occupational

might result from the fact that members of disadvantaged groups are more likely to form group attachments that result in a strong group consciousness. A large body of research suggests not only that voters tend to support candidates who elicit group identification, but also that this tactic can stimulate voter turnout and political activism.[25] On the other hand, members of racial minority groups might demonstrate lower levels of interest in running for office than whites. Both personal accounts (Cose 1994) and detailed empirical studies (Hochschild 1995) reveal that middle-class blacks often feel more alienated from and angry toward the social and political systems in which they live. This alienation can result in disinterest in running for office and joining the system from which an eligible candidate feels alienated (e.g., Gay 2001; but see Stokes 2003).

If we expect both women and men across races and ethnicities to operate as strategic politicians, then we should also expect eligible candidates to incorporate their experiences and perceptions – which cannot be divorced from patterns of traditional gender socialization or race – into their political decision making. Minority status should play a role in the probabilities eligible candidates accord to the costs and benefits associated with considering a candidacy and ultimately throwing their hats into the ring.

Similarities in Political Participation, Proximity, and Interest: An Overview by Sex and Race

Running for public office represents the ultimate act of political participation; it signals an individual's willingness to put himself or herself before the voters and vie to become a member of an elected body. Citizens with relatively high levels of political activism, interest, and proximity to the political arena, therefore, are most likely to emerge as candidates. Thus, it is important to begin the analysis of gender, race, and political ambition with an overview of whether women and men, as well as

status (Matthews and Prothro 1966; Orum 1966). This socioeconomic explanation for lower black participation was soon discarded, however, as it became clear that, controlling for these measures, African Americans actually participated at higher rates than whites (Olsen 1970).

[25] For analyses of group consciousness among Latinos, see Masuoka 2008; Sanchez 2006; Stokes-Brown 2006; Stokes 2003. For studies of group consciousness among African Americans, see Gay 2001; Bobo and Gilliam 1990; Hamilton 1986; Guterbock and London 1983; Abney and Hutcheson 1981; Shingles 1981; Abney 1974. And for group consciousness pertaining to women's vote choice, see Burns, Schlozman, and Verba 2001; Smith and Fox 2001; Plutzer and Zipp 1996; Chaney and Sinclair 1994.

whether whites, blacks, and Latinos/as, in the candidate eligibility pool are equally likely to engage the political system and gain firsthand exposure to politics.

Let us turn first to levels of political participation. Figure 4.1 presents the percentages of women and men who participated in various political activities over the course of the past year. Not only are the respondents very politically active, but men and women are also roughly equally likely to engage in all types of political participation. These comparable rates of participation between women and men in the candidate eligibility pool are largely consistent with patterns of political participation at the mass level. In every presidential election since 1980, and in all congressional elections since 1986, women have voted in equal or higher proportions than men (CAWP 2008). Women also sign petitions, attend public meetings and rallies, and write to elected government officials at rates similar to those of men (Conway, Ahern, and Steuernagel 2004).[26]

Figure 4.2 breaks down the political participation data by race. Again, the members of the sample – whether white, black, or Latino/a – are far more politically active than the general public, from contributing money to campaigns to contacting elected officials to volunteering their time for political causes. Consistent with the participation literature, black respondents, on six of the eight measures, are statistically more likely than their white and Latino/a counterparts to have engaged in that type of participation. Only in terms of paying dues to an interest group do white respondents have a statistically significant (albeit substantively small) advantage. The data presented in Figure 4.2 also reveal that, at least in terms of writing letters to newspapers and attending political meetings, Latino/a members of the sample are somewhat less politically active than their white counterparts. We should be cautious in making too much of these differences, though, because of the size of the Latino subsample.

The 2008 survey data move beyond typical measures of political participation and allow for an examination of more nuanced gauges of exposure to politics and the electoral arena. More specifically, we included in the second-wave survey a series of questions pertaining to respondents' direct

[26] For examples of some of the earlier studies of gender and political participation that found men more likely than women to participate in politics, see Campbell, Converse, Miller and Stokes 1960; Lane 1959. For a discussion of the manner in which increased educational and occupational opportunities have afforded women the characteristics that correlate positively with the propensity to engage the political system, see Verba, Schlozman, and Brady 1995; Teixeira 1992; Conway 1991; Dolbeare and Stone 1990; Bergmann 1986; Baxter and Lansing 1983.

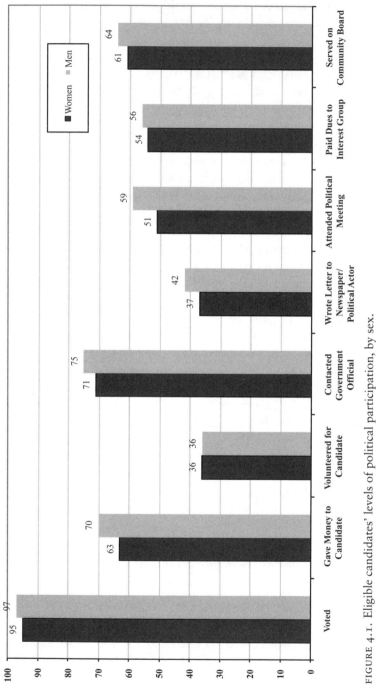

FIGURE 4.1. Eligible candidates' levels of political participation, by sex.

Notes: Results are based on the 2001 survey data. Bars indicate the percentage of respondents who engaged in each activity over the course of the past year. Voting refers to the most recent presidential election. Levels of political activity might be somewhat inflated because they are based on respondents' self-reports, but there is no reason to expect levels of inflation to correlate with respondent sex. Sample sizes: for women, N = 1,676; for men, N = 1,885.

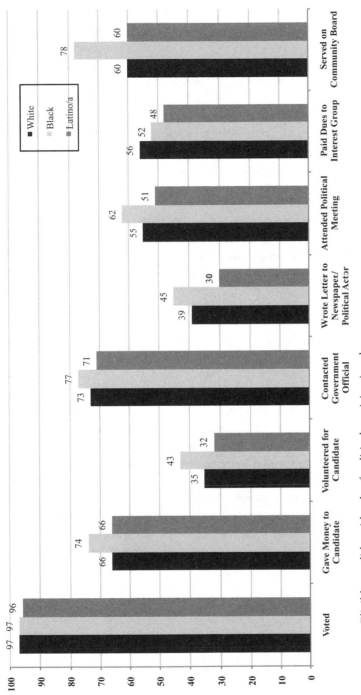

FIGURE 4.2. Eligible candidates' levels of political participation, by race.

Notes: Results are based on the 2001 survey data. Bars indicate the percentage of respondents who engaged in each activity over the course of the past year. Voting refers to the most recent presidential election. Levels of political activity might be somewhat inflated because they are based on respondents' self-reports, but there is no reason to expect levels of inflation to correlate with respondent race. Sample sizes: for whites, N = 2,907; for blacks, N = 335; for Latinos, N = 175.

contact with and observation of elected officials. The findings are similar to the participation results (see Figure 4.3). On three of the four measures of political proximity, no gender or race differences emerge from the data. More than half of the women and men in the pool of eligible candidates, regardless of race, interact with elected officials professionally or socially.

Despite the general similarities across sex and race regarding levels of political activism and proximity, three noteworthy differences merit acknowledgment. Statistically, women are less likely than men to have contributed money to a campaign. Again, this finding is consistent with political behavior in the general population. In 2008, for example, women comprised 44 percent of Barack Obama's donor base and 28 percent of John McCain's.[27] Men are also statistically more likely than women to attend political meetings or interact with elected officials as part of their job, although the substantive differences are quite small. Finally, black respondents are 15 percent more likely than white respondents, and 27 percent more likely than Latinos, to have had an elected official as a family member or friend. Although the gaps in these participatory acts are not striking, these differences could certainly carry implications for running for office. Both checkbook activism and networking with other politically minded citizens, especially family members and friends, might confer to eligible candidates the name recognition and familiarity that attract the recruitment often needed to spur on candidacies.

The slight advantage men appear to have in political participation and proximity, however, is offset by women's slightly higher levels of political interest. Forty-three percent of women in the candidate eligibility pool follow national politics and current events "closely" or "very closely," compared with 33 percent of men (difference significant at $p < 0.01$). An 8-percentage-point gender gap emerges when we turn to local politics: 49 percent of women, versus 41 percent of men, report following the news in their community "closely" or "very closely" (difference significant at $p < 0.01$). No differences across racial lines characterize political interest.[28]

---

[27] Open Secrets provides detailed donor demographic information for the 2008 presidential election, as well as election data from 1976 through 2008. These statistics can be accessed at http://www.opensecrets.org/pres08/donordemCID_compare.php?cycle= 2008 (July 15, 2009).

[28] Eligible candidates' daily media habits also reflect high levels of political interest, regardless of sex or race. Roughly three-quarters of respondents read a print or online newspaper every day; more than 50 percent watch the local television news on a daily basis; 17 percent tune into talk radio seven days a week; and 16 percent report watching CNN or MSNBC each day.

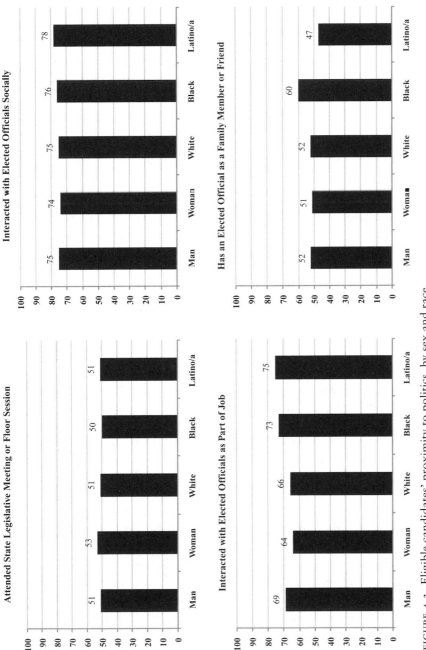

FIGURE 4.3. Eligible candidates' proximity to politics, by sex and race.
Notes: Results are based on the 2008 survey data. The only statistically significant gender difference is interacting with elected officials as part of their job ($p < 0.05$). The only statistically significant race difference is having an elected official as a family member or friend ($p < 0.05$). Sample sizes: for women, $N = 872$; for men, $N = 1,021$; for whites, $N = 1,593$; for blacks, $N = 157$; for Latinos, $N = 102$.

Overall, if heightened levels of political activity, proximity, and interest situate members of the eligibility pool to emerge as actual candidates, then the data presented in Figures 4.1, 4.2, and 4.3 suggest that the members of the sample are very well positioned. Certainly, there are some differences in eligible candidates' levels of political activism, proximity, and interest. But for the most part, the women look a lot like the men; and the small racial differences in political activism that emerge indicate that blacks are a bit better situated than the rest of the respondents. Minority status, in other words, is not a detriment – within the candidate eligibility pool – to being well situated and politically well connected to run for office.

Sex, Race, and Interest in Running for Office

Despite the similar political experiences and levels of activism among men and women, as well as across races, substantial differences emerge when we turn to nascent ambition. Most notably, the data presented in Figure 4.4 indicate that 59 percent of men, compared with 43 percent of women, have considered running for office. Indeed, men are nearly twice as likely as women to report having "seriously considered" a candidacy; women are approximately 40 percent more likely than men never to have thought about running for office (differences significant at $p < 0.01$). Although the proportion of respondents who considered running differs by profession, with lawyers and political activists most likely to have considered a candidacy, the gender differential is statistically significant at $p < 0.01$ within each subgroup (see Chapter 6 for an analysis of professional differences and political ambition).

Not all minority status classifications depress levels of political ambition, though. When we turn to race, the bivariate analysis reveals that, similar to the manner in which black respondents are somewhat more politically active than their white and Latino counterparts, they are also more politically ambitious. They are 25 percent more likely than white respondents and 50 percent more likely than Latinos to report having seriously considered running for office (differences significant at $p < 0.01$). Black respondents are also the subgroup least likely never to have thought about launching a candidacy.

The gender gap within each racial group, however, is substantial. The disparity is largest among white respondents; women are 17 percentage points more likely than men never to have considered running for office (58 percent of women, compared with 41 percent of men, never considered a candidacy; difference significant at $p < 0.05$). But black and Latino

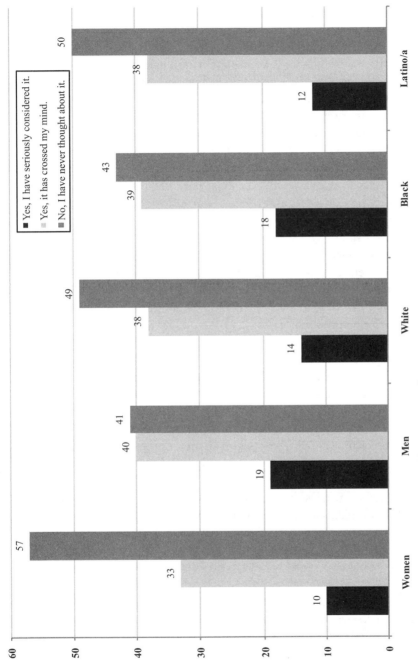

FIGURE 4.4. Interest in running for office, by sex and race.

Notes: Results are based on the 2001 survey data. The gender gap in political ambition is statistically significant at p < 0.01. In terms of race, the only statistically significant finding is that black respondents are more likely than whites and Latinos to have seriously considered running for office and less likely never to have thought about running (p < 0.05). Sample sizes: for women, N = 1,676; for men, N = 1,885; for whites, N = 2,907; for blacks, N = 335; for Latinos, N = 175.

men are also significantly more likely than their female counterparts to consider running for office; a 14-percentage-point gender gap in ambition emerges in each of these subsamples (significant at $p < 0.05$).

Importantly, sex remains a significant predictor of considering a candidacy even after controlling for race and many of the traditional correlates of political behavior. Table 4.1 presents the logistic regression coefficients of two models that predict nascent ambition. In the first model, I include indicators of minority status; basic gauges of political knowledge, interest, efficacy, and conventional participation; and the electoral features and political dynamics presented in Chapter 3. In the second model, I supplement these explanatory variables with interaction terms between eligible candidates' sex and race. As expected, when levels of political interest, political knowledge, and political participation increase, so does the inclination to consider a candidacy. But regardless of these factors, women are substantially less likely than men to consider running for office. More specifically, the logistic regression coefficients translate to mean that women are 15.4 percentage points less likely than men, all else being equal, to have the notion of running for office ever appear on their radar screens (men have a 0.59 probability of considering a candidacy; women's predicted probability is 0.44).[29]

The regression equations also shed light on the racial disparities at the bivariate level. The coefficients on race, in and of themselves, fail to achieve statistical significance in both models. Further, the statistically insignificant interactions between sex and race indicate that the gender gap in political ambition not only persists across racial lines, but also exerts the same relative effect for white, black, and Latino/a respondents.[30] The racial differences in nascent ambition that emerged in the bivariate analysis, therefore, are driven by black respondents' higher levels of political participation.

Not only are women less likely than men to consider running for office in general, but the data reveal that women are also less likely than men

---

[29] Predicted probabilities calculated here and throughout the remainder of the book represent the independent effect exerted by a statistically significant variable as I vary its value from its minimum to its maximum, holding all other variables at their sample means and modes.

[30] Regression analyses with interaction terms between the significant background variables and the sex of the respondent indicate that these traditional correlates of political ambition do not exert differential impacts on men and women. The same is true for race. None of the interaction terms achieves conventional levels of statistical significance. Further, when interaction terms are included, the principal components' coefficients, magnitudes, and levels of significance remain unchanged.

TABLE 4.1. *Who Considers Running for Office? Effects of Race and Sex on Predicting Nascent Ambition (Logistic Regression Coefficients and Standard Errors)*

	Considered Running for Office (Model 1)	Considered Running for Office (Model 2)
Minority Status		
Sex (female)	−0.62 (0.08)**	−.69 (0.09)**
Black	0.02 (0.14)	−.20 (0.19)
Latino/a	0.05 (0.18)	−.12 (0.24)
Sex * Black	−	0.45 (0.27)
Sex * Latino/a	−	0.45 (0.37)
Indicators of Political Engagement		
Political knowledge	0.12 (0.08)*	0.12 (0.05)*
Political interest	0.15 (0.03)**	0.15 (0.03)**
Political efficacy	0.01 (0.04)	0.02 (0.04)
Political participation	0.30 (0.02)**	0.30 (0.02)**
Electoral Features and Opportunities		
Size of the congressional delegation	−0.01 (0.01)	−0.01 (0.01)
Size of the state political opportunity structure	0.00 (0.00)	0.00 (0.00)
Size of the local political opportunity structure	0.00 (0.00)	0.00 (0.00)
Term limits	0.16 (0.10)	0.16 (0.10)
Part-time legislature	0.16 (0.12)	0.16 (0.12)
Legislative salary	0.00 (0.00)	0.00 (0.00)
Political Dynamics		
Democrat	−0.01 (0.11)	−0.01 (0.11)
Republican	−0.11 (0.12)	−0.12 (0.12)
Percent Democratic presidential vote share	−0.00 (0.01)	−0.00 (0.01)
Party congruence with the congressional delegation	0.00 (0.10)	0.00 (0.10)
Party congruence with the state legislature	−0.11 (0.10)	−0.12 (0.10)
Constant	−2.16 (0.45)**	−2.14 (0.45)**
Percent correctly predicted	68.5	68.0
Pseudo R-squared	0.24	0.24
N	3,193	3,193

Notes: Regression results are based on the 2001 data and the electoral features, opportunities, and political dynamics at that time. The reduced number of cases results from listwise deletion. The results are comparable for the 2008 data, but because the sample is smaller, I present the 2001 data. Significance levels: * $p < 0.05$; ** $p < 0.01$.

to consider running for high-level elective offices. As I discussed in Chapter 3, most respondents who are willing to consider running for office at some point in the future would get involved at the bottom rung of the ladder. But women are particularly likely to exhibit this preference. Seventy-six percent of the women, compared with 60 percent of the men, select a local office – school board, city council, or mayor – as the first office for which they might run (gender difference significant at $p < 0.01$). The gender gap in interest reverses itself with increases in the stature of the level of office. Men are significantly more likely than women to identify a state office (25 percent of men, compared with 18 percent of women) or federal office (15 percent of men, compared with only 6 percent of women) as their first choice (gender differences significant at $p < 0.01$). The gender gap in ambition for high-level office is wider when we consider that more women than men are unwilling to enter any electoral contest. Thirty-one percent of women, but only 23 percent of men, stated unequivocally that they have ruled out any consideration of a future run for office.

The magnitude of the gender gap in interest in high-level office is even greater when we turn to the positions in which respondents might ever be interested in seeking. Table 4.2 presents the percentages of eligible candidates who would entertain a candidacy for nine elective offices. The data presented in the first two columns indicate that whereas men are about as likely as women to consider running at the local level, women are significantly more likely than men to dismiss the possibility of ever running for a state or federal position. In fact, if we consider "high-level office" to include federal positions as well as statewide offices (i.e., governor, attorney general), then men are 59 percent more likely than women to express interest (22 percent of women, compared with 35 percent of men; gender difference significant at $p < 0.01$).[31]

Although women of all races are markedly less likely than men to consider running for office, the gender gap in office-specific preferences is not entirely consistent across racial lines. These differences, however, may be driven, at least in part, by the smaller sample sizes of black and Latino/a respondents. The magnitude of the gender gap in interest in

---

[31] In multiple regression analyses that predict interest in high-level office, the coefficient on sex remains negative and statistically significant even after controlling for political engagement, electoral features and opportunities, and political factors (as gauged in Table 4.1). The substantive significance of the coefficient is quite large as well. Women are 16.8 percentage points less likely than men, all else equal, to express interest in high-level office. Neither the coefficient on black nor Latino/a achieves conventional levels of statistical significance, and in this fully specified model, interaction terms between race and sex are also insignificant.

TABLE 4.2. *Differences in Eligible Candidates' Elective Office Preferences, by Sex and Race*

	Total Sample		White		Black		Latino/a	
Question: If you were going to run for office – either now or in the future – what position(s) would you ever be interested in seeking?								
	Women Men		*Women* Men		*Women* Men		*Women* Men	
Local Office								
School board	41%*	37%	41%**	36%	42%	39%	28%	32%
Town, city, county council	36	37	36	36	35	38	27	31
Mayor	11**	17	10**	16	13†	20	14	18
State Office								
State legislator	27**	36	27**	37	21†	29	19	24
Statewide office	11	10	10	11	9	9	8	8
Governor	6*	13	5**	13	7	11	11	15
Federal Office								
U.S. House	15**	28	14**	27	20	26	25	30
Senate	12**	21	11**	20	17†	23	22	20
President	3*	5	3**	5	4	5	4	5
N	1,653	1,870	1,374	1,514	161	170	64	111

Notes: Results are based on the 2001 survey data. Entries indicate the percentage of respondents who said they would consider running for the specified position. Percentages do not add up to 100 percent because respondents often expressed interest in more than one position. The N for each race does not add up to the total N because several respondents did not identify their race on the questionnaire. Significance levels of chi-square test comparing women and men: * $p < 0.05$; ** $p < 0.01$; † $p < 0.10$.

many offices is comparable in size across race, even if not statistically significant.

The general finding pertaining to the gender gap in high-level office interest among eligible candidates is consistent with research pertaining to officeholders. Evidence suggests that once women enter electoral politics, they are less likely than men to climb the political career ladder (Fulton et al. 2006; Lawless and Theriault 2005). In fact, school boards, which are the offices with the highest ratio of women officeholders (estimated at about 40 percent), are not typically used by politicians who harbor ambition to launch political careers for higher levels of office (Deckman 2007; see also Hess 2002; Bullock et al. 1999). The gender disparity in progressive ambition could be a result of differences in the reasons men and women enter politics in the first place. Timothy Bledsoe and Mary

Herring's (1990, 221) study of city council members concludes that men are more likely than women to be "self-motivated – guided by political ambition." By contrast, women tend to be more motivated by community issues (Fox 1997; Astin and Leland 1991).[32]

Evidence from the interviews, however, points to an additional reason that women may be less likely than men to exhibit ambition for high-level offices: perceptions of sexism and bias. The 2008 survey included a battery of questions in which respondents were asked whether they believe women still face significant gender bias in the electoral arena when they run for high-level office. Eighty-seven percent of female respondents and 76 percent of male respondents agreed that the electoral environment was more difficult for women than for men. Similarly, despite the fact that women who actually run for office raise just as much money as their male opponents, eligible candidates did not perceive the electoral environment this way. Sixty-four percent of women and 38 percent of men contended that it is more difficult for women than for men to raise money for a political campaign. In fact, 12 percent of women stated outright that they were not qualified to run for office simply because they were the "wrong" sex. In addition, even though the women and men were geographically matched, women were approximately 25 percent more likely than men to judge their congressional elections as "highly competitive."

Certainly, these perceptions are linked to patterns of traditional socialization that play a substantial role in depressing women's political ambition (Lawless and Fox 2010). But they might also be linked to the 2008 election cycle; the power of Hillary Clinton's loss, in other words, should not be underestimated. Maria Lane, a professor at a large university in New England, argued that Hillary Clinton's campaign sent a strong signal to women across the country: "If she couldn't win the White House – and she had more resources and connections than any other woman ever will – then that sends a pretty clear message. Women should focus on lower offices if they want to succeed and make a difference. Otherwise, they'll never get a seat at any table."

Even though they have risen to the top ranks within often male-dominated professions, and despite the fact that they come from the management and leadership positions that tend to position candidates for the highest public offices, women of all races are far less likely than

---

[32] Richard L. Fox and Zoe Oxley (2003) find an interaction between candidate sex and office type in state executive elections. Women are less likely to run for offices that are inconsistent with their stereotypical strengths, and high-level offices are more likely to fall into that category.

men to consider running for office, and white women are particularly unlikely to express interest in entering the upper echelons of the political arena. The data suggest, however, that it may be the case that women are less likely to set their sights on the highest elected offices not because they are not interested in statewide or federal positions, but rather, because they have come to believe that they cannot succeed in pursuing such an endeavor. The notion of running for high-level office, therefore, never even crosses their minds.

Sex, Race, and Changes in Interest in Running for Office: Predicting Dynamic Ambition

Despite the dramatic events that occurred between the two waves of the panel – the waging of two world wars, hyperpartisan gridlock in Washington, the Hurricane Katrina disaster, the highly unpopular presidency of George W. Bush, Nancy Pelosi's selection as Speaker of the House of Representatives, and Hillary Clinton's and Barack Obama's campaigns for president – the gender gap in considering a candidacy in 2008 was essentially unchanged from 2001. When I include in the analysis the 163 respondents whose first consideration of running for office occurred between the two waves of the study, the gender gap in political ambition is 17 percentage points. That is, overall, 47 percent of women, compared with 64 percent of men, reported that the idea of running for office had at least "crossed their mind." Hillary Clinton's loss might have signaled to many women that attaining high-level office might be more difficult than they previously envisioned, but the data do not indicate that her run or her loss affected nascent ambition in the candidate eligibility pool. In a similar vein, Barack Obama's victory represented a milestone for African Americans and the political system. Yet black respondents' levels of political ambition in 2001 and 2008 were roughly the same.

More broadly, the multiple regression results presented in Table 4.3 reveal that neither an eligible candidate's sex nor his or her race predicts gains or losses in ambition across the two waves of the study. The statistically insignificant regression coefficients indicate that, controlling for structural variables and political factors, women and men of all races are just as likely as one another to report shifts in interest in running for office over time.[33]

---

[33] When I supplement the regression equation with interaction terms between each of the variables with sex and race, none achieves statistical significance. Thus, the same factors drive the shifts in interest in running for office for both women and men, and across races.

TABLE 4.3. *Changing Interest in Running for Office: Effects of Race and Sex on Predicting Dynamic Ambition (Ordered Logistic Regression Coefficients and Standard Errors)*

	Change in Ambition (5-point scale)
Minority Status	
Sex (female)	0.01 (0.13)
Black	0.44 (0.25)
Latino/a	0.14 (0.28)
Indicators of Political Engagement	
Political knowledge	0.14 (0.07)*
Increase in political interest	0.09 (0.05)
Increase in political efficacy	0.10 (0.06)
Increase in political participation	0.08 (0.04)*
Electoral Features and Opportunities	
Size of the congressional delegation	− 0.00 (0.01)
Size of the state political opportunity structure	− 0.00 (0.00)
Size of the local political opportunity structure	0.00 (0.00)
Term limits	− 0.20 (0.16)
Part-time legislature	− 0.18 (0.18)
Legislative salary	0.00 (0.00)
Political Dynamics	
Democrat	− 0.02 (0.17)
Republican	− 0.10 (0.18)
Change in party identification	− 0.12 (0.11)
Increase in Democratic presidential vote share	− 0.01 (0.04)
Moved	0.18 (0.19)
Became incongruent with the political landscape	− 0.15 (0.15)
Baseline level of political ambition (in Wave 1)	− 1.12 (0.09)**
(Threshold − 2)	− 8.77 (0.78)**
(Threshold − 1)	− 3.76 (0.35)**
(Threshold 0)	0.79 (0.33)*
(Threshold + 1)	4.26 (0.55)**
Pseudo R-squared	0.16
N	1,441

Notes: The reduced number of cases results from listwise deletion. Significance levels: * $p < 0.05$; ** $p < 0.01$.

Conclusion

In April 2007, five Democratic state legislators served on the host committee for a fundraiser to elect Catherine Ceips, a Republican seeking an open seat in the South Carolina State Senate, a Republican with whom these Democratic representatives had little in common, policywise. The Democrats crossed party lines because Democratic Senator Linda Short chose not to seek reelection. As the only female state senator, Short's departure from the institution would mean a 100 percent male governing body. Anne Parks, a Democratic representative, explained that her support for Ceips was "because of the gender, because there won't be a woman in the Senate. I think we need some female representation."[34] Ceips lost her race, and the South Carolina State Senate has been all male since January 2008. Although the remaining 49 states have at least two women serving in their state senates, Hawaii, Massachusetts, Oklahoma, Rhode Island, and Wyoming have no female Republican senators; the West Virginia state senate has no female Democrats (CAWP 2010h). Thus, despite the high-profile candidacies of Hillary Clinton and Sarah Palin in 2008, as well as the incessant media attention received by, among others, House Minority Leader Nancy Pelosi and Congresswoman Michele Bachmann (R–MN), women remain an anomaly in elective office.

The data presented in this chapter suggest that this pattern will persist into the foreseeable future. Women and men in the candidate eligibility pool may be similarly situated in terms of their professional success and levels of political participation, proximity, and interest. But women of all races exhibit significantly lower levels of interest in entering electoral politics than do their male counterparts. Moreover, when women do express interest in running for office, they are more likely than men to focus their political ambition at the local level. The conventional indicators of political ambition, such as political participation, proximity, and interest, as well as structural variables that tap into the political environment in which eligible candidates might emerge, do not account for the gender differences in the likelihood of considering a candidacy.

When we focus on race and the manner in which minority status affects political ambition, however, the story is a bit more complicated. Given the racial and ethnic composition of U.S. elected officials, coupled with studies that reveal no widespread discrimination against black and Latino candidates, we might expect racial differences in political ambition to account for some of the numeric underrepresentation of racial minorities. Yet within the candidate eligibility pool, such is not the case. Granted, these results might be an artifact of the professional and socioeconomic

---

[34] "Women Cross Lines for Candidate: Chester's Short Isn't Seeking Re-Election; Some Want to Keep a Female in the Senate," *The Herald*, distributed by McClatchey-Tribune Business News, April 2, 2007.

status required to make it into this sample of the candidate eligibility pool. But it is from these professions that most candidates, regardless of race, tend to emerge.

The next three chapters add texture and specificity to the question of who runs for office, and in doing so, shed additional light on the manner in which sex and race affect the candidate emergence process.

5

You Could Be President Someday!

Early Socialization, the Role of Family, and Political Ambition

I've seen how a person can really have an impact on what's going on around you. You couldn't leave my dinner table without the sense that you had an obligation . . . to try to impact your world. . . . Eating was almost incidental to the discussion, whether it be my mother's teaching career or what was going on in our state or the nation or the world.

> – Beau Biden, Attorney General of Delaware and son of Vice President Joe Biden[1]

When you are around politics, you realize there is nothing that special about being a politician or a policy maker. When you are in that environment, when you are younger and exposed to it, you look at it and say, "I could do that."

> – Lisa Murkowski, U.S. Senator and daughter of former Alaska Governor and U.S. Senator Frank Murkowski[2]

As a teenager and young adult . . . I knew there was this wonderful man in office and moving up higher who was concerned with the working person. And his grassroots ability was phenomenal. He knew a lot of people all over the state and that is what I intend to do in each of the 100 counties here in North Carolina.

> – Kay Hagan, U.S. Senator and niece of former Florida Governor and U.S. Senator Lawton Chiles[3]

---

[1] Shannon Canton, "Family Business," *Delaware Today*, July 2003. Accessed at http://www.delawaretoday.com/Delaware-Today/September-2008/The-Biden-Archive-Family-Business/ (October 22, 2010).

[2] Carl Hulse, "On Capitol Hill, a Family Business Thrives," *New York Times*, December 20, 2008, page A4.

[3] Bill Rufty, "Lawton Chiles' Niece Runs for U.S. Senate," *The Ledger*, November 11, 2007, page B2.

Although it may be rare to grow up in families as political as those of Beau Biden, Lisa Murkowski, or Kay Hagan, family dynamics play a substantial role in politics. We need to look no further than the typical campaign ad, website, or political acceptance or resignation speech for examples of politicians invoking the influence and importance of their families in their political decision making.[4] Yet even though politicians rely on their families – in terms of the civic duty they attribute to their parents for instilling in them, and the support for which they regularly thank their spouses and children – we know little about whether and to what extent family dynamics systematically affect candidate emergence. After all, most of what we know about the role of family dynamics in politics yields from studies of candidates and elected officials, all of whom managed to enter the electoral arena, regardless of their family circumstances, structures, roles, and responsibilities.

This chapter presents an analysis of the role of family in the candidate emergence process. I begin with an assessment of the manner in which eligible candidates' early political socialization affects their levels of interest in running for office as adults. The results are striking: a politicized upbringing lays the foundation for political ambition, regardless of the political exposure and experiences an individual acquires in adulthood. I then turn to family structures and roles in eligible candidates' current households. Somewhat surprisingly, most of the empirical measures of family structures and responsibilities, as well as changes in these roles and responsibilities over time, do not affect interest in running for office. Evidence from the interviews, however, suggests that they do add complexity to the decision to run (or not to run) for office, especially for women. Ultimately, though, a supportive family mitigates the difficulty involved in reconciling family roles with political ambition and serves as an important predictor of interest in running for office. From childhood through adulthood, therefore, living among politically engaged family members foments and sustains eligible candidates' interest in entering the electoral arena.

In the Genes: The Lifelong Effects of a Politicized Upbringing

A cursory glance at some of the most high-profile political races in 2010 reveals several examples of second-generation political ambition. Andrew

---

[4] For recent examinations of the manner in which candidates incorporate family roles and dynamics into their campaigns, see Druckman, Kifer, and Parkin 2009; Brader 2006; Iyengar and McGrady 2006.

Cuomo was elected governor of New York, a position held by his father Mario from 1983 through 1994. Former U.S. Senator Lincoln Chafee, the son of former U.S. Senator John Chafee, was elected governor of Rhode Island. Robin Carnahan sought the U.S. Senate seat previously held by her mother in Missouri. Senate Majority Leader Harry Reid's son, Rory, battled to win the governorship in Nevada. And Rand Paul, whose father serves in the U.S. House of Representatives from Texas, was elected to the U.S. Senate from Kentucky.[5]

Although it may be somewhat uncommon to "inherit" the political ambition and opportunities of these candidates and elected officials, more modest levels of political interest are often passed on within the family unit (Flanigan and Zingale 2002). Consider, for instance, the case of former Florida Governor Charlie Crist, who recounts his first political memory as distributing campaign literature for his father, a member of the Pinellas County School Board in Florida in the 1960s: "I just liked it. I liked the interaction with people and thought it was a lot of fun."[6] Crist quickly threw himself into another campaign: his own race for seventh grade homeroom representative. He won that election, stayed active in student government, and ultimately served as class president during his senior year at St. Petersburg High School. After graduating from college and law school, Crist served as the state director for U.S. Senator Connie Mack, won a Florida State Senate seat shortly thereafter, was elected commissioner of education in 2000, attorney general in 2002, and governor in 2006.[7]

In another example of the manner in which early political exposure can foment and cement political ambition, Gabriel Bonder ran for (and won) a seat on the Milford, Connecticut, Board of Education when he was only 20 years old. The son of Nancy Seltzer – a member of the Planning and Zoning Board – Bonder remembers a childhood of accompanying his mother to political meetings. Seltzer's colleagues recall her son "watch[ing] us at meetings all the time and ask[ing]

---

[5] Missouri Governor Mel Carnahan (1993–2000) sought the U.S. Senate seat in 2000. Three weeks before Election Day, he was killed in a plane crash. His wife, Jean, finished the campaign on his behalf and when Mel Carnahan won (it was too late to remove him from the ballot), the governor appointed Mrs. Carnahan to fill the seat until a special election that would take place in November 2002. Jean Carnahan ran for reelection in 2002, but lost to Jim Talent.

[6] Carlos Moncada, "Governor Known as Likeable," *Tampa Tribune*, November 19, 2006, page 1.

[7] "Meet Charlie," Charlie Crist for U.S. Senate, accessed at http://www.charliecrist.com/about-charlie (October 22, 2010).

questions."[8] Raised with a sense of civic duty and the notion that elective office is a way to fulfill that obligation, Bonder concluded that running for the board of education was the best way to exercise his passion.

A similar pattern emerged in many of the interviews I conducted with eligible candidates. Ted Martin, an educator in Florida, has been politically active since elementary school, in large part because of his mother's political behavior. He recalled, "I grew up really poor with a working mom. We had no assets, but she always told me that freedom was my biggest asset, and that it was my responsibility to get involved in the community, in politics, to give back. That really stayed with me." Shana Mills, a social sciences professor who frequently attends demonstrations and rallies promoting social justice, also attributed her political interest and activism to her very political family: "Cesar Chavez and Martin Luther King were a big part of my life at home. Their pictures were on the walls. They were my role models." Put simply by Tony Arriaga, a litigator from Chicago, "My parents took me with them on Election Day from the time I could walk. They took me to political meetings and fundraisers from as far back as I can remember. And they always told me that their parents did the same. I guess that politics in my family is in the genes."

More generally, political scientists Paul Allen Beck and M. Kent Jennings (1982, 98) find that highly politicized parents often create a family environment "charged with positive civic orientations ... thus endowing their children with the motivation prerequisites for later [political] participation." Recent studies suggest that adolescents who discuss politics and current events with their parents also develop higher levels of political knowledge and demonstrate a greater propensity to vote, attend community meetings, and engage the political system through signing petitions, participating in boycotts, or contributing money (McIntosh, Hart, and Youniss 2007; Andolina et al. 2003).[9]

---

[8] Bill McDonald, "Milford Student Eyes School Board Seat," *Connecticut Post Online*, June 21, 2007.

[9] Alva Myrdal (1968) offered some of the earliest attempts to urge social scientists to consider the role of family when explaining individual-level behavior. The family unit as a tool of analysis in American political science scholarship has since been employed as a mechanism through which to understand political socialization (Hess et al. 2006; Owen and Dennis 1988; Jennings and Markus 1984; Jennings and Niemi 1981; Almond and Verba 1963) and political participation and issue preferences (Burns, Schlozman, and Verba 2001; Renshon 1975; Niemi 1974). More recently, scholars have also begun to explore the extent to which political attitudes and behaviors are the result not only

Involvement in political associations, campaigns, community service, and school elections also affects levels of political interest and activism (Hart et al. 2007; Fox, Lawless, and Feeley 2001; Verba, Schlozman, and Brady 1995). Further, greater exposure to civics education in high school and college can result in long-term gains in political efficacy and interest, both of which heighten levels of political activism (Pasek et al. 2008). Minnesota State Senator Ellen Anderson, for instance, was first inspired to run for office by late-U.S. Senator Paul Wellstone, who was Anderson's political science professor at Carleton College in 1980.[10] After graduating from college, she earned a law degree and was a practicing attorney when Wellstone offered her a position as director of research for his first U.S. Senate campaign in 1990. Reflecting on the campaign, Anderson recalls:

> It was a transformative experience for me, because I was kind of like a lot of young people at that time... just really cynical about politics. But I really believed in Paul and what he stood for.... So when he got into the U.S. Senate, it really opened my eyes and made me think that running for office is a noble cause. And it's the first time it ever occurred to me – like a light bulb going off in my mind – "Oh, I could do that."

Two years later, Anderson sought and won a seat in the Minnesota State Senate, where she has championed renewable energy legislation, as well as the Employers Nursing Mothers Accommodations Requirement Bill, which, among other things, exempts breastfeeding from the crime of indecent exposure.

The early political socialization process can clearly instill in many individuals the belief that they have the power to take part in the democratic process. Thus, a thorough examination of the role that family plays in the candidate emergence process must begin with an assessment of the patterns of political socialization to which the women and men in the candidate eligibility pool were exposed. We can begin to answer this question by examining how often respondents recall discussing politics with their parents, whether they ever received encouragement to run for office from their parents, and whether either of their parents ever ran for office.

The top half of Table 5.1 reveals that respondents were raised in relatively political households. Not only do more than one-third of the

---

of environmental and socialized factors, but also genetic factors passed on from one generation to the next (Alford, Funk, and Hibbing 2008, 2005; Beckwith and Morris 2008).

[10] Todd Messelt, "Profiling the Legislature: Senator Ellen Anderson," *The Legal Ledger*, St. Paul, September 17, 2007.

TABLE 5.1. *Eligible Candidates' Political Socialization Patterns*

Politics at Home	
Parents were "very concerned" about politics when the respondent was growing up	35%
Parents spoke to respondent about politics when he/she was growing up	71
Parents suggested that respondent run for office	40
Parent(s) ran for office	14
Politics at School	
Students in respondent's high school were "very concerned" about politics	16
Students in respondent's college were "very concerned" about politics	40
Respondent ran for office in high school or college	55
N	3,538

Notes: Results are based on the 2001 survey data. Number of cases varies slightly, as some respondents omitted answers to some questions.

eligible candidates remember their parents being "very concerned" about politics and current events, but roughly 7 of 10 respondents also grew up in households in which political discussions regularly occurred.[11] Moreover, 40 percent of the respondents received parental enticements to seek political office at some point in the future (perhaps because 16 percent of the women and 13 percent of the men came from families in which a parent actually sought public office).[12] More than half of the women and men ran for office as high school and college students (see the bottom of Table 5.1).

Although we should be careful when drawing broad conclusions from these data because they rely on retrospective assessments of family dynamics, the power of a politicized upbringing is clear when we turn to the manner in which a political household correlates with respondents' interest in running for office. Table 5.2 presents the bivariate relationship between the frequency with which a respondent's parents suggested that

[11] In the general population, 51 percent of women and 54 percent of men state that they discussed politics at least occasionally in their childhood homes (Knowledge Networks 2002).

[12] Although the majority of eligible candidates were raised in relatively politicized homes, some notable gender differences emerged. Women were 15 percent less likely than men to have their parents encourage them to run for office. They were nearly 20 percent less likely to have their fathers speak with them about politics. See Lawless and Fox (2010) for an elaborate discussion of gender differences in the political socialization process.

TABLE 5.2. *The Lasting Imprint of Early Encouragement to Run for Office*

	Ran for Office in High School or College	Considered Running for Office as an Adult	"Seriously" Considered Running for Office as an Adult
When you were growing up, how often did your parents tell you that you should run for office someday?			
Frequently	76%	71%	28%
Occasionally	72	70	19
Seldom	63	62	14
Never	47	42	12
N	3,509	3,491	3,491

Notes: Results are based on the 2001 survey data. Entries indicate the percentage of respondents who had run for student government, considered running for office, or seriously considered running for office as an adult. In each case, the chi-square test comparing individuals who ran or considered running with those who did not achieved statistical significance at $p < 0.01$.

he or she run for office and the respondent's political ambition. The data presented in the first column are to be expected; respondents whose parents encouraged them to run for office when they were growing up were far more likely to seek elective positions in student government. More specifically, fewer than half of the eligible candidates who grew up without receiving the suggestion to run for office threw their hats into the ring as high school or college students. More than three-quarters of the respondents who "frequently" received encouragement from their parents to run for office, however, pursued student government positions.

The data presented in the second and third columns of Table 5.2 indicate that parental encouragement for a candidacy during childhood and adolescence transcends student government. Eligible candidates who reported growing up in a household in which their parents frequently suggested that they run for office were approximately 70 percent more likely to consider running for office as adults, and more than twice as likely to consider "seriously" such an endeavor than were respondents who never received parental encouragement to enter politics (differences significant at $p < 0.01$).

The relationship between a politicized upbringing and political ambition as an adult also came through very clearly in the interviews. Jennifer Starr, a lawyer from North Carolina, serves as a good example. When asked about her initial interest in pursuing public office, she referred to her childhood: "I remember, when I was a little girl, talking to my parents

about becoming president of the town where we lived. They told me that
the person in charge of the town is called the mayor. So, I decided that I
wanted to be mayor. Even now – thirty years later – it's something that
still appeals to me." John Hayes, a political activist from Oregon, also
linked his interest in politics to his political childhood:

> When other kids used to play board games with their families after dinner,
> our family used to play "Name the Presidents." By the time we were 10 or
> 11, my sister and I could recite every president – in order. And when that
> became too easy, we moved on to the U.S. Senate. Other kids aspired to be
> celebrities; we wanted to be politicians.

Tom Harborside, a Virginia CEO, grew up in a very political household
and ran for the student council in high school. These experiences triggered
his thoughts of running for office as an adult. After he ran for class president, Mr. Harborside thought, "Maybe someday I'll run for president of
the United States."

The regression results presented in Table 5.3 confirm the pattern that
emerged at the bivariate level and in the interviews: political discussions
and exposure to politics in childhood significantly increase the propensity
to consider running for office as an adult. I modeled whether a respondent ever considered running for office, supplementing the minority status, electoral features, and political dynamics variables (as discussed in
Chapters 3 and 4) with indicators of a politicized upbringing. The results
reveal that early political exposure generates lasting effects that are independent and cannot be entirely compensated for by being politically active
as an adult. In fact, growing up in a "political household" – one in which
political discussions regularly occurred and respondents received regular
encouragement to run for office – is the third most important predictor
of considering a candidacy in adulthood.

The joint effect of the various indicators of a politicized upbringing is
even more striking. Together, these variables exert three times the effect
of sex on considering a candidacy; growing up in a political home, therefore, can more than compensate for the disadvantage women face in
developing nascent ambition.[13] But even among members of the sample

---

[13] Sex remains a significant predictor of considering a candidacy, with women less likely
than men to have considered running. But a politicized upbringing nearly doubles both
women and men's likelihood of considering a run for office, which is one way to close the
gender gap in political ambition. A woman whose parents never suggested that she run
for office and never talked about politics in the home has a 0.37 probability of considering
a candidacy. Frequent political discussions and regular parental encouragement to run
for office in childhood increase a woman's likelihood of considering a candidacy to

TABLE 5.3. *Impact of a Politicized Upbringing on Considering a Candidacy (Logistic Regression Coefficients, Standard Errors, and Change in Probabilities)*

	Coefficient (and Standard Error)	Maximum Change in Probability (percentage points)
Politicized Upbringing Indicators		
"Political" household index	0.25 (0.04)**	31.0
Parent ran for office	0.41 (0.12)**	10.0
Ran for office as a student	0.47 (0.08)**	11.5
Minority Status		
Sex (female)	−0.63 (0.08)**	15.5
Black	−0.08 (0.15)	−
Latino/a	0.00 (0.19)	−
Indicators of Political Engagement		
Political knowledge	0.15 (0.05)**	10.8
Political interest	0.17 (0.03)**	34.0
Political efficacy	0.02 (0.04)	−
Political participation	0.29 (0.02)**	56.8
Electoral Features and Opportunities		
Size of the congressional delegation	−0.01 (0.01)	−
Size of the state political opportunity structure	0.00 (0.00)	−
Size of the local political opportunity structure	0.00 (0.00)	−
Term limits	0.19 (0.10)	−
Part-time legislature	0.14 (0.12)	−
Legislative salary	0.00 (0.00)	−
Political Dynamics		
Democrat	0.03 (0.12)	−
Republican	−0.12 (0.12)	−
Percent Democratic presidential vote share	−0.00 (0.01)	−
Party congruence with the congressional delegation	−0.02 (0.10)	−
Party congruence with the state legislature	−0.11 (0.11)	
Constant	−3.55 (0.50)**	
Percent correctly predicted	70.1	
Pseudo R-squared	0.28	
N	3,142	

Notes: Regression results are based on the 2001 data and the electoral features, opportunities, and political dynamics at that time. These probabilities were calculated by setting all continuous independent variables not under consideration to their means and dummy variables not under consideration to their modes. The change in probability reflects the independent effect a statistically significant variable exerts as we vary its value from its minimum to maximum (i.e., the change in probability for "Ran for Office as a Student" reflects the fact that a respondent who ran for office as a student is 11.5 percentage points more likely than a respondent who did not run, all else equal, to consider running for office). The results are comparable for the 2008 data, but the sample size is smaller. Significance levels: * $p < 0.05$; ** $p < 0.01$.

who express the utmost levels of political interest as adults, growing up in a household in which politics was discussed and running for office was encouraged boosts the likelihood of considering a candidacy by 26 percentage points. Experience running in a high school or college student body election increases the likelihood by an additional 11.5 percentage points.

The role of a politicized upbringing in the development of nascent political ambition suggests that specific experiences that might seem far removed from the decision to enter electoral politics do, in fact, influence the likelihood of considering a candidacy. And the magnitude of the effect of these preprofessional experiences is dramatic. Because politicized upbringings do not fall within the rubric of political opportunity structures, most studies of political ambition tend to overlook their lasting impact.

The Influence of Family Structures and Roles on Political Ambition

Broad examinations of political participation suggest that age, marital status, and parental status positively affect levels of political participation at the mass level (e.g., Wolfinger and Wolfinger 2008; Verba, Schlozman, and Brady 1995). Over the course of the past decade, researchers have also provided evidence that these factors affect political ambition. Younger eligible candidates are often better able to endure the rigors of a campaign and engage in the activities necessary for networking and fundraising (Gaddie 2004; see also Fowler and McClure 1989).[14] In fact, among office-holding national political convention delegates, younger delegates are more likely than delegates over the age of 55 to express interest in seeking higher office at some point in the future (Gaddie 2004, 25).

It is also often the case that women and men who are married with children are motivated or inspired to run for office because of their family circumstances. Jim Webb, a Vietnam War veteran who served as an assistant secretary of defense and Navy secretary under Ronald Reagan, considered the U.S. invasion of Iraq in 2003 "an incredible strategic blunder of historic proportions." It was not until his son was deployed to Iraq with the Marines, however, that Mr. Webb decided to enter the 2006

0.72. If either parent ever ran for office, then a woman's probability of thinking about launching her own run for office in adulthood further increases to 0.80.

[14] For earlier research pertaining to the manner in which family structures and arrangements affect political participation, see Huckshorn and Spencer 1971; Swinerton 1968.

U.S. Senate race in Virginia and fight to change the policy. Campaigning in desert boots given to him by his son, Webb often reminded voters, "If half of the United States Congress had to wake up and worry about a loved one, I think we'd have a different policy."[15] When Cindy Sheehan's son, Casey, was killed in Iraq in 2004, she, too, entered the political arena. Best known for calling for the impeachment of President George W. Bush, Sheehan challenged then-Speaker of the House Nancy Pelosi – whom Ms. Sheehan argued had the power to prevent votes on war funding bills and to demand a timetable for withdrawing troops from Iraq – for her congressional seat in 2008.[16]

Family circumstances can motivate candidacies for lower levels of office as well. Harriet Woods, who eventually became lieutenant governor of Missouri, began her foray into the political arena when she complained to the city council of University City, Missouri, that the noise generated by cars riding over a manhole cover outside her home disturbed her children's naps. When the council ignored her complaint, Woods first initiated a petition drive to close the street to through traffic; she then sought (and won) a seat on the council herself.[17] Mario Obledo, a political aide to a former mayor of San Antonio, Texas, launched a bid for a city council seat because of San Antonio's growing traffic problems. His two-year-old daughter had a medical condition that required the family to make regular trips to Houston for hospitalization and treatment. It was through caring for his daughter that Mr. Obledo became aware of the need for more green space and a light rail, both of which would help families navigate the city and "bridge the gap between developers and the community."[18] Gloria Sanchez, one of Obledo's opponents, also attributed her decision to run to her child. When her son became a police officer, Sanchez became increasingly interested in crime and criminal justice. Perhaps most importantly, she sought to ensure that the police

---

[15] Michael Sluss, "Webb Makes Iraq Focus of the Campaign," *Roanoke Times*, October 15, 2006. Jim Webb defeated Republican incumbent George Allen with 49.6 percent of the vote. Virginia State Board of Elections, accessed at http://www.sbe.virginia.gov/ElectionResults/2006/Nov/htm/index.htm (October 29, 2010).

[16] Josh Harkinson, "Pushing Pelosi," *Mother Jones*, January 31, 2008. Pelosi won reelection with 72 percent of the vote (see http://www.cnn.com/ELECTION/2008/results/individual/#CAH08).

[17] Patricia Sullivan, "Harriet Woods; Inspired Creation of Emily's List," *Washington Post*, February 10, 2007, page B04.

[18] Joseph S. Stroud and Laura E. Jesse, "District 8 Has Two More Council Candidates," *San Antonio Express News*, February 20, 2007, page B3.

force expanded, "not only to protect residents, but to protect each other."[19]

On the other hand, women and men often also mention the trials and tribulations of maintaining the "balancing act" involved in reconciling a career, a family, and political aspirations (Gaddie 2004; see also Fulton et al. 2006).[20] Susan Molinari (R–NY), for example, was a rising star in the Republican Party when she announced her decision to leave the House of Representatives in 1996. She accepted a position as an anchor of a CBS news program so that she could spend more time with her daughter, Ruby.[21] When she was first elected in 1990, Molinari had no children. Scott Muschany, a former state representative from Missouri, decided not to seek reelection in 2008 because he wanted to spend more time with his wife and children: "In several years, I'll have an opportunity to run for office again, but I'll never have an opportunity to raise these boys again."[22] Aware that there are certainly conditions under which we might be dubious of the "family explanation" offered by outgoing elected officials, Mr. Muschany elaborated, "There's no scandal as far as I'm aware of. My wife and I just decided it wasn't the right time to continue."

Family considerations often also play a role in the decision not to seek higher office. In an interview with *Roll Call*, for instance, Bobby Harrell, the Speaker of the House in the South Carolina Assembly, explained that he chose not to run for the open U.S. Senate seat in 2004 because of his eleven year-old daughter, Charlotte: "She asked me if I was going to run. . . . I thought she would enjoy it because it would be like my current job, just on a grander scale. I said to her, 'I don't know, sweetheart. What should I do?'" When Charlotte replied, "Daddy, please don't do it. I don't see enough of you now," Harrell decided not to throw his hat into the ring.[23] State Senator Kirk Dillard decided not to enter the race for the U.S. Senate in Illinois in 2004 for similar reasons. With two daughters – ages

---

[19] Ibid.

[20] A study of members of the candidate eligibility pool in New York, for example, found some, though not overwhelming, evidence that traditional family structures decrease the likelihood of running for all levels of office (Fox and Lawless 2003; see also Conway, Ahern, and Steuernagel 2004; Sapiro 1982).

[21] "Molinari to Resign from Congress for CBS," *AllPolitics*, May 28, 1997. For more on members of Congress who choose to retire from the House of Representatives because the "family-unfriendly" schedule of Congress makes it difficult to balance career and familial responsibilities, see Theriault 1998.

[22] "Missouri State Representative Withdraws Candidacy for Reelection," *Associated Press State and Local Wire*, May 20, 2008.

[23] Louis Jacobson, "When Top Recruits Don't Run, It's Usually A Lifestyle Decision," *Roll Call*, December 7, 2005.

3 and 10 months – Dillard concluded that "family comes first over politics, especially with young children. . . . Given a vote between being a dad and a U.S. senator, I would vote to be a dad any time."[24] Put simply by former Congresswoman Jane Harman, "The schedule is the pits. There is absolutely no way to be a full-time parent and serve in Congress."[25]

Family considerations affect political decisions at the state and local levels, too. Multnomah County Commissioner Serena Cruz, for example, opted not to run for chair of the Commission when her term expired in 2006 because even though this enclave of Portland, Oregon, "need[ed] new leadership," Cruz decided to focus on starting a family:

> When I was 30 and thinking about running for office, and I hadn't met my husband yet, I always assumed I'd have a family. Years pass by really quickly. I'm a political person, but this is a situation where I don't want to end up on the other side of 40 regretting not giving this the best chance I could.[26]

Greensboro, North Carolina, councilwoman Laura Wiley chose not to run for a State House seat because "being away from home for extended periods" made her "heartsick."[27]

The manner in which family roles and responsibilities appear both to motivate and depress political ambition among actual candidates and elected officials emerged as a pattern among women and men in the candidate eligibility pool. Table 5.4 presents eligible candidates' interest in running for office broken down by a series of family structures and roles. The data in the top half of the table reveal that marriage, parental status, and plans to begin a family in the future do not systematically influence interest in running for office. Roughly half the eligible candidates have considered running for office, regardless of whether they are married, parents, have young children, or hope to become parents at some point in the future.

The bottom half of the table, however, suggests that – at the bivariate level – the responsibilities that often accompany marriage and parenthood do correlate with political ambition. As we might expect, eligible candidates who are responsible for the majority of the household tasks

[24] "Report: Dillard Decides Not to Run for U.S. Senate," *Associated Press State and Local Wire*, July 22, 2004.
[25] Dana Wilkie, "Harman, Prototypical Politicians of the 90s, Juggles Family, Career," *Copley News Service*, April 9, 1998.
[26] Kimberly A. C. Wilson, "Commissioner Won't Run for Top County Job," *The Oregonian*, May 18, 2005.
[27] Sue Schultz, "Wiley Withdraws from North Carolina House Race," *News and Record*, May 12, 2004, page B1.

TABLE 5.4. *Bivariate Relationship Between Family Structures and Roles and Considering a Candidacy*

	Considered Running for Office (%)
Family Structures	
Not married	49
Married	52
No children	49
Has children	52
Does not have children living at home	50*
Has children living at home	54
Does not have children under age 6 living at home	51
Has children under age 6 living at home	55
Does not plan to start a family or have more children in the future	52
Plans to start a family or have more children in the future	55
Family Roles	
Responsible for the majority of the household tasks	44**
Equal division of labor in the household	51
Spouse/partner responsible for the majority of the household tasks	60
Responsible for the majority of the child care	47**
Equal division of labor regarding child care responsibilities	53
Spouse/partner responsible for the majority of the child care	59
N	3,574

Notes: Results are based on the 2001 survey data because of the greater number of cases. The 2008 results are comparable. Number of cases varies slightly, as some respondents omitted answers to some questions. The household tasks data do not include respondents who are not married or living with a partner; the child care arrangements data do not include respondents who do not have children. Levels of significance for chi-square tests comparing interest in running for office by family structures and roles: * $p < 0.05$; ** $p < 0.01$ (the asterisk indicating statistical significance appears next to the first category listed for each family structure or role).

are approximately 27 percent less likely than those whose spouse is the primary caretaker of the home to have considered running for office. A similar finding emerges with respect to child care responsibilities. Eligible candidates who are responsible for the bulk of the child care are significantly less likely than those who shoulder less than a majority of it to consider a candidacy.

Throughout the course of the interviews, several respondents elaborated on the difficulties involved in integrating politics into their daily lives. Dominique Beaulieu, for example, assessed her situation this way: "When I was single, I often worked on campaigns, and was much more politically active. With young kids, this whole side of me has been put on hold. I'd like to resume working in politics when the kids are older. Right now, I can only handle being a lawyer and a mother." Nick Hansen, a litigator from Albuquerque, also dismissed the idea of running for office because of his parental responsibilities, which he acknowledged already shirking:

> I'm a partner in my law firm. I can barely manage to get to school plays and soccer games. It seems like every free minute I think I'm going to have winds up getting spent on some crisis at work, some trial we didn't expect to make it to the courtroom, some client whose circumstances are way more difficult to deal with than we anticipated. What kind of husband and father would I be if I took on anything else right now? I barely see my family as it is.

Tracy Ball, the director of a state environmental organization, reflected on her typical day and laughed at the possibility of finding the time even to consider a candidacy: "I am so tired after spending a day in the office then coming home to take care of whining, sniffling kids and having to cook dinner. I can't even imagine going to a town council meeting or a PTA meeting, never mind running a campaign for state senate." Rachel Anderson voiced a similar view. She explained that, with a full-time job as the vice president of a major corporation and two young children, "Even thinking about running for office – from a practical standpoint – is out of the question."

It is important to recognize, however, that even though women and men might both discuss the difficulties associated with balancing family and professional responsibilities with politics, the structures and roles, themselves, are deeply linked to sex. Certainly, many of the barriers to women's advancement in formerly male fields are changing drastically, as identified in Chapter 4. Correspondingly, the conception of a rigid set of sex roles has dissipated with the increasing number of two-career families (Coltrane 2000). Yet surveys of two-income households continue to find that women spend twice as many hours as men working on household tasks, such as cleaning and laundry. Married women also continue to perform significantly more of the cooking and child care than do their spouses, even when they are the primary breadwinners in a family.[28]

---

[28] For evidence of the gendered division of household labor and child care responsibilities over the course of the past twenty years, see McGlen et al. 2005; Burns, Schlozman.

When women do enter the public sphere, they often face what political communications scholar Kathleen Hall Jamieson calls the "double bind." She explains that "the history of western culture is riddled with evidence of traps for women that have forcefully curtailed their options" (1995, 4). Women who venture out of the "proper sphere" often find themselves in a "catch-22": if they achieve professional success, then they have likely neglected their "womanly" duties; if they fail professionally, then they were wrong to attempt entering the public domain in the first place. Liane Sorenson, the president of the Women's Legislative Network of the National Conference of State Legislatures and a member of the Delaware State Senate, summarized the implications of the double bind: "If a male lawmaker leaves a meeting to watch his son play soccer, everyone says he's a wonderful father. But if a woman does it, you'll hear she's not managing her responsibilities."[29] The essence of the bind is that professional women are constantly judged not only by how they manage their careers, but also by how well they perform the duties of a wife and mother. To be successful public citizens, women must also be successful private citizens. Thus, it is not surprising that political scientist Sue Thomas (2002) finds that female state legislators continue to be primarily responsible for housework and child care even after they are elected to public office.

The "double bind" clearly transcends into the candidate eligibility pool and serves as a dilemma that women who are well positioned to run for public office today must reconcile. The top portion of Table 5.5 reveals that women with professional careers continue to be significantly more likely than men not to have traditional family arrangements. Women are about twice as likely as men to be single; they are also almost twice as likely to be separated or divorced. Further, women are nearly 20 percent less likely than men to have children.[30] There are no gender differences in these components of family structures within the general population (Knowledge Networks 2002). Female eligible candidates' family structures might reflect that being a wife or mother can serve as an impediment to professional achievement, a goal that women in the sample

---

and Verba 2001; Galinsky and Bond 1996; Apter 1993; Blumstein and Schwartz 1991; Hochschild 1989.

[29] Sonji Jacobs, "Politicians Who Are Moms Must Juggle Priorities," *Atlanta Journal-Constitution*, May 16, 2004, page 1D.

[30] Based on data from the 1970s, Susan J. Carroll and Wendy Strimling (1983) and Marcia Manning Lee (1976) uncover similar gender differences in candidates and legislators' family structures. The past three decades, therefore, have seen little change in the sociodemographic attributes of well-situated eligible candidates.

already attained. The gendered demands and expectations of the professions in which many eligible candidates work may also make women in the candidate eligibility pool less likely than men to enter into traditional family arrangements (see also Alejano-Steele 1997).

Women who are married and who do have children, however, tend to exhibit traditional gender role orientations. The survey asked respondents whether they or their partners are responsible for the majority of household and child care responsibilities. The bottom half of Table 5.5 reveals a gendered division of labor. In families in which both adults are working (generally in high-level careers), women are twelve times more likely than men to bear responsibility for the majority of household tasks, and about ten times more likely to be the primary child care provider. These differences in family responsibilities are not merely a matter of

TABLE 5.5. *Eligible Candidates' Current Family Structures and Responsibilities*

	Women (%)	Men (%)
Marital Status		
Single	15**	8
Married or living with partner	70**	86
Separated or divorced	12**	6
Parental Status		
Have children	66**	84
Children living at home	38**	49
Children under age 6 living at home	14	15
Household Responsibilities		
Responsible for majority of household tasks	48**	4
Equal division of labor	40**	33
Spouse/partner responsible for majority of household tasks	11**	61
Child Care Responsibilities		
Responsible for majority of child care	42**	4
Equal division of child care	25**	26
Spouse/partner responsible for majority of child care	6**	46
N	1,659	1,875

Notes: Results are based on the 2001 survey data. Household responsibilities figures are based on the subsample of respondents who are married or living with a partner. Child care arrangements figures are based on the subsample of respondents who have children (numbers do not total 100 percent because 26 percent of women and 24 percent of men had grown children, live-in help, day care providers, etc.). Significance levels of chi-square test comparing women and men: * $p < 0.05$; ** $p < 0.01$.

gendered perceptions. Both sexes fully recognize this organization of labor. More than 60 percent of men acknowledge that their spouses are responsible for a majority of household tasks, whereas fewer than 5 percent of women make the same claim. Summarized well by Barbara Kim, a New York executive:

> Women are busier than men, especially professional women, because once we get home from work, we have a whole second shift to do. The housework, taking care of the children. And we're more attached to our families, so the time we do have, we want to spend with our spouses and children.... For men, there are fewer outside of the job responsibilities and family time is just not as important.

Regardless of the advances women have made entering the workforce and achieving professional success, both women and men identify the prevalence of traditional household roles and responsibilities.[31]

Indeed, the qualitative evidence from the interviews sheds substantial light on the manner in which family structures and responsibilities affect candidate emergence. Of the 150 women I interviewed, 82 stated that children made seeking office a much more difficult endeavor for women than for men. In the 150 interviews with men, only seven respondents raised the issue of children serving as an impediment to running for office. For the most part, men do not express concerns about reconciling their careers or family roles with the decision to run for office.

Multiple regression analysis of the extent to which traditional family structures affect political ambition, therefore, must evaluate simultaneously the gender gap in interest in running for office. Table 5.6 replicates the model of considering a candidacy to which I have been adding throughout the book, but also includes gauges of family structures and responsibilities. The regression results indicate that family dynamics are not statistically significant predictors of considering a run for office. This result holds when I interact the sex of the respondent with the family structure and role variables. Thus, family structures and roles, in and of themselves, do not systematically affect interest in running for office. Rather, the bivariate findings that emerged in Table 5.3 are driven by sex; women – regardless of their family structures and roles – remain less likely than their male counterparts to consider running for office. Because women also report responsibility for the majority of the household tasks

---

[31] For a detailed analysis of eligible candidates' perceptions of why traditional gender roles define their households, see Lawless and Fox 2010.

TABLE 5.6. *Impact of Family Structures and Roles on Political Ambition: Predicting Whether Respondent Ever Considered Running for Office (Logistic Regression Coefficients and Standard Errors)*

Sex (female)	−0.77**
	(0.10)
Married	0.05
	(0.15)
Children	−0.19
	(0.13)
Children under age 6 living at home	0.19
	(0.14)
Responsible for majority of household tasks	−0.02
	(0.10)
Responsible for majority of child care	0.11
	(0.15)
Pseudo R-squared	0.30
Percent correctly predicted	70.7
N	2,992

Notes: Results are based on the 2001 survey data. The regression equations control for all of the correlates of political ambition included in previous chapters, as well as the age of the respondent. Significance levels: * p < 0.05; ** p < 0.01.

and child care, it follows that eligible candidates with these responsibilities are less likely to consider running for office.

That household and familial responsibilities do not dramatically affect whether respondents have ever considered running for office may result from the fact that a supportive family unit can mitigate household and child care responsibilities. The survey asked the eligible candidates whether they ever received encouragement to run for office as an adult from a spouse or family member. More than one-third of the respondents reported spousal encouragement, and nearly half reported that another family member suggested that they run for office (see Table 5.7). For many respondents, this encouragement was not fleeting. Figure 5.1 breaks down family encouragement for a candidacy by the frequency with which respondents received the suggestion to run from their spouses and other family members. Nearly one of every four respondents received regular (at least three times) suggestions to run for office from a family member; the percentage receiving sustained encouragement from a spouse is somewhat lower (17 percent), but not rare. Levels of support also appear to be reciprocal. Roughly two-thirds of the members of the sample would be "very supportive" if their husband or wife wanted to enter the electoral area (see Table 5.7).

TABLE 5.7. *Encouragement from Family Members to Run for Office*

Support to Run for Office within the Family Unit	
Encouraged to run for office by a family member	47%
Encouraged to run for office by a spouse/partner	38
Discouragement to Run for Office within the Family Unit	
Discouraged from running for office by a family member	8
Discouraged from running for office by a spouse/partner	14
Attitudes Toward a Candidacy by Spouse/Partner	
Would be very supportive	65
Would be somewhat supportive	23
Would not be supportive	12
N	1,924

Notes: Results are based on the 2008 survey data. Number of cases varies slightly, as some respondents omitted answers to some questions. The percentages regarding spouses/partners are based on the subset of respondents who are married or living with a partner.

The effect of a supportive personal environment cannot be overstated. If we add to the model that predicts who considers running for office a measure of whether the respondent ever received encouragement or a suggestion to run from a family member or spouse, then the probability of considering a candidacy increases by approximately 38 percentage points. The predicted probabilities generated from the regression coefficients displayed in Table 5.8 reveal that the magnitude of the effect of an encouraging or supportive spouse is the same size as that of another family member. The data suggest, therefore, that interest in running for office increases not only if a spouse or partner triggers the notion of a candidacy, but also if someone else who is familiar with the family and professional obligations that would need to be reconciled with a campaign encourages the idea.

The notion of familial support as a prerequisite to considering entering politics emerged in many of the interviews. Mona Gregory, a college professor from Louisiana, attributed her ongoing interest in seeking elective office to support from her inner circle: "I wouldn't be able to do anything like run without the backing of my husband and friends." Paul Benson, an attorney from California, noted that the only reason he has ever considered running for office is because his spouse always pushes him to "get on a ballot . . . lately, she's been focused on the school board." Risa Gersten, who has always been interested in running for office, also identified the importance of familial sources of encouragement:

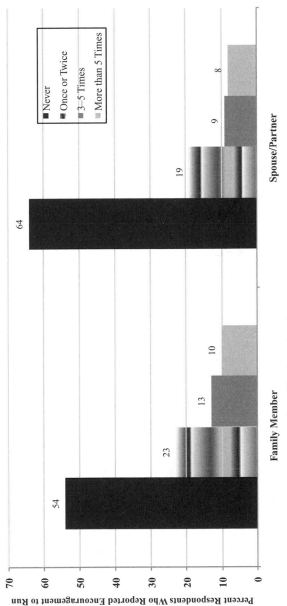

FIGURE 5.1. Encouragement to run for office by a family member or spouse.
Notes: Results are based on the 2008 data. N = 1,924.

TABLE 5.8. *Impact of Familial Encouragement on Considering a Candidacy (Logistic Regression Coefficients, Standard Errors, and Change in Probabilities)*

	Coefficient (and Standard Error)	Maximum Change in Probability (percentage points)
Support from Family Unit (in Adulthood)		
Encouraged to run for office by family member	1.08 (0.11)**	19.0
Encouraged to run for office by spouse/partner	1.09 (0.12)**	19.2
Politicized Upbringing Indicators		
"Political" household index	0.15 (0.04)**	18.6
Parent ran for office	0.37 (0.09)**	7.8
Ran for office as a student	0.45 (0.13)**	10.6
Minority Status		
Sex (female)	−0.74 (0.09)**	17.8
Black	−0.23 (0.16)	–
Latino/a	−0.30 (0.20)	–
Indicators of Political Engagement		
Political knowledge	0.15 (0.05)**	10.4
Political interest	0.12 (0.03)**	16.3
Political efficacy	0.03 (0.04)	–
Political participation	0.25 (0.02)**	49.3
Electoral Features and Opportunities		
Size of the congressional delegation	−0.01 (0.01)	–
Size of the state political opportunity structure	0.00 (0.00)	–
Size of the local political opportunity structure	0.00 (0.00)	–
Term limits	0.18 (0.11)	–
Part-time legislature	0.18 (0.13)	–
Legislative salary	0.00 (0.00)	–
Political Dynamics		
Democrat	0.17 (0.12)	–
Republican	−0.05 (0.13)	–
Percent Democratic presidential vote share	−0.01 (0.01)	–
Party congruence with the congressional delegation	0.06 (0.11)	–
Party congruence with the state legislature	−0.19 (0.12)	
Constant	−3.03 (0.54)**	
Percent correctly predicted	75.4	
Pseudo R-squared	0.40	
N	3,092	

Notes: Regression results are based on the 2001 data. Probabilities were calculated by setting all continuous independent variables to their means and dummy variables to their modes. The change in probability reflects the independent effect a statistically significant variable exerts as we vary its value from its minimum to maximum. Significance levels: * p < 0.05; ** p < 0.01.

> I know people in the State House and the White House. They've told me
> to run for office. They've pledged their support for a state legislative run,
> and even a congressional seat. But that's not the support I need. I need my
> husband to tell me to run and that he'll manage the household. I need my
> sister to tell me to run and that she'll take care of my carpool responsibilities.
> I need my parents to tell me to run and that they'll write a big check. That's
> the encouragement and support that really matters.

Eligible candidates are also well aware of the importance that their support for a candidacy confers to family members. Edward Copeland, for example, explained that his spouse does "everything in the house and with the kids." But when she was particularly concerned about a zoning ordinance and wanted to become active around that issue, Copeland supported her activism: "I told her, do what you need to do, I'll handle things around here. And she knew I meant it. I never said anything like that before. And I made good on my commitment, too. So, if I ever told her that she should run for office and that we'd figure things out at home, I think that would go a long way."

The lack of support from spouses, partners, and family members often corroborates the notion – particularly for women – that a political candidacy is just not possible, given their professional and personal obligations. But a supportive familial environment can mitigate concerns about how to balance household and child care responsibilities and, hence, propel eligible candidates' interest in running for office. When evaluating the relationship between family dynamics and political ambition, therefore, it is vital to look beyond the structures and roles, themselves; levels of encouragement and support for a future run for office are as important in adulthood as a politicized family can be during childhood.

Changes in Family Circumstances: Predicting Dynamic Ambition

When Barbara Cubin decided not to seek reelection to the U.S. House of Representatives in 2008, she told the Wyoming Republican State Central Committee that she "look[ed] forward to coming home to be a friend, a wife, a mother, and especially a grandmother."[32] With a husband suffering from an immune disorder, Ms. Cubin added, "None of us know how much time we have left, but what I do know is the time that he has left, I want to be with him." Parks Helms's decision not to seek reelection

---

[32] Bob Moen, "Cubin Announces She Will Not Seek Re-Election Next Year," *Associated Press State and Local Wire*, November 10, 2007.

as Mecklenburg County Commissioner in North Carolina could also be attributed to changes in his family circumstances. After sixteen years in office, Helms deferred to his spouse's plea to withdraw from politics so that they could finally take vacations and see their grandchildren: "It was so painfully obvious that for whatever reason, she thinks I should step aside. Sometimes if you love somebody like I love her, you do what's most important. And that's what I did."[33] Of course, terminating, as opposed to saving, a marriage can also affect political decisions. After losing a congressional race to Earl Pomeroy in 2006, Matt Mechtel planned a rematch in 2008. Ongoing divorce proceedings with his wife, however, led Mechtel to "sit back and get [his] life in order," which involved deciding not to enter the U.S. House race.[34]

The second-wave survey data allow me to delve more deeply into the manner in which family roles and responsibilities affect political ambition by assessing the relationship between changes in family structures and dynamics and interest in running for office. Over the course of the seven years between the two waves of the study, respondents underwent substantial changes in their family circumstances; from new marriages and children, to the dissolution of marriages and children moving out of the house, to dealing with a family illness or an aging relative, 77 percent of the eligible candidates experienced at least one such change (see Table 5.9). More specifically, nearly half the respondents grappled with a personal or family illness, and more than one-third experienced either a child moving out of the house or an aging parent joining the household.

TABLE 5.9. *Changes in Eligible Candidates' Family Structures and Responsibilities from 2001 to 2008*

Newly married	7%
Newly separated or divorced	6
Had or adopted a child	10
Had a child move out of the house	31
Dealt with a personal or family illness	46
Took care of an aging or sick parent	34
N	1,704

Notes: Number of cases varies slightly, as some respondents omitted answers to some questions.

[33] Jim Morrill, "This Time, No Race for Parks Helms: For 1st Time in 16 Years, Democrat Opts for Family Life, Not Politics," *The Charlotte Observer*, March 1, 2008.

[34] Jonathan Rivoli, "Mechtel Will Not Challenge Pomeroy," *Bismarck Tribune*, January 23, 2008, page 1A.

Overall, changes in family structures, and the concomitant shifts in family roles and responsibilities they bring, tend not to exert a systematic shift on respondents' political ambition. The regression equation presented in Table 5.10 includes gauges of changes in family structures, roles, and responsibilities, as well as the levels of support for a candidacy voiced by spouses, partners, and family members. The equation also controls for the correlates of dynamic ambition discussed in previous chapters. With the exception of a new family member joining the household – whether it be a new child or an aging parent – changes in family circumstances do not predict changes in ambition.[35]

TABLE 5.10. *Changing Interest in Running for Office: Effects of Family Dynamics on Predicting Dynamic Ambition (Ordered Logistic Regression Coefficients and Standard Errors)*

	Change in Ambition (5-point scale)
Changes in Family Roles and Responsibilities	
Newly married	− 0.07 (0.24)
No longer married	0.30 (0.29)
Had or adopted a child	0.69 (0.22)**
Had a child move out of the house	0.02 (0.14)
Dealt with a personal or family illness	0.25 (0.15)
Cared for an aging or sick parent	1.09 (0.12)**
Support from Family Unit (in Adulthood)	
Recently encouraged to run for office by family member	0.70 (0.20)**
Recently encouraged to run for office by spouse/partner	0.40 (0.23)
Politicized Upbringing Indicators	
"Political" household index	− 0.02 (0.06)
Parent ran for office	0.02 (0.18)
Ran for office as a student	− 0.05 (0.13)
Baseline level of political ambition (in Wave 1)	− 1.38 (0.11)**
(Threshold − 2)	− 9.15 (0.84)**
(Threshold − 1)	− 4.03 (0.45)**
(Threshold 0)	0.73 (0.43)
(Threshold + 1)	4.20 (0.62)**
Pseudo R-squared	0.21
N	1,409

Notes: Regression results are based on data from respondents who completed both the 2001 and 2008 surveys. The reduced number of cases results from listwise deletion. The equation also controls for the correlates of dynamic ambition presented in Table 4.3, as well as the respondent's age. Levels of significance: * $p < 0.05$; ** $p < 0.01$.

[35] At the bivariate level, new marriages depress levels of interest in running for office, especially among women. Of the 64 women and 74 men who entered marriages or civil

The fact that a new addition to the household spurs interest in running for office is consistent with the anecdotal evidence presented earlier in the chapter. When an individual takes on the additional responsibility of caring for someone else, the issues to which he or she is exposed and must navigate can trigger interest in running for office. George Terry, a history professor from New Mexico, serves as a case in point. Mr. Terry spent his adult life without "even a fleeting thought of running for office." When his 78-year-old father moved in with him in 2006, however, Mr. Terry grew increasingly frustrated with Medicare Part D and the difficulties of navigating the system:

> I spent more time online and on the phone with bureaucrats than I care to remember. And that was just so that my Dad could maintain the coverage he had. I began to think that someone needed to hold their feet to the fire. Senior citizens deserve better. For the first time in my life, I thought about running for office. I'm a smart guy. I could work on figuring out how to fix these problems.

Several respondents also noted that they became cognizant of and passionate about "failing schools," "neighborhood crime," "juvenile delinquency," "exorbitant costs of prescription drugs," and "Social Security" as they became responsible for new children and aging parents. The new issues that accompany new additions to the household, in other words, tend to propel interest in running for office, perhaps because it serves as a vehicle through which to address the issues and challenges that arrive with a new family member.

Conclusion

On July 3, 2009, Alaska Governor Sarah Palin announced her resignation. Although she acknowledged a litany of reasons for her decision – ranging from legal bills associated with charges of ethics violations, to nonstop media coverage of her every move – she told the group of supporters gathered outside her home in Wasilla, Alaska, that her decision ultimately came down to family concerns:

> This decision comes after much consideration, and finally polling the most important people in my life – my children, where the count was unanimous . . . well, in response to asking: "Want me to make a positive difference

unions between 2001 and 2008, 41 percent of women, compared with 32 percent of men, expressed less interest in running for office than they had in 2001. Sixteen percent of women, compared with 23 percent of men, reported heightened levels of interest in running for office (gender differences significant at $p < 0.01$). These findings, however, do not hold up in multiple regression analysis.

and fight for all our children's future from outside the Governor's office?"
It was four "yeses" and one "hell yeah!"[36]

Although many voters, pundits, and politicians viewed Governor Palin's justification for her resignation with skepticism, the central findings from this chapter suggest that most women and men who enter the political arena are heavily influenced by their family circumstances.

The manner and degree to which family roles and responsibilities affect the likelihood of considering running for office are complicated. Politicized upbringings positively influence political ambition, so eligible candidates who did not receive encouragement to run for office or engage in political discussions with their parents are disadvantaged from the outset. The lasting imprint of a politicized upbringing is truly remarkable, and cannot be fully compensated for regardless of how politically active an individual becomes later in life. Because politicized upbringings do not fall within the rubric of political opportunity structures, studies of expressive ambition tend to overlook their impact.

For as clear as the effects of a politicized upbringing are on political ambition, the effects of family in adulthood are as murky. The empirical measures of family structures and responsibilities do not, for the most part, predict political ambition. One important exception emerges from the analysis of the panel data, though; the addition of a new family member in the household spurs interest in running for office. Alternatively, strong qualitative evidence – both from actual candidates and elected officials and the eligible candidates themselves – suggests that serving as the primary caretaker of the children and the household complicates the likelihood of considering a run for public office. But when respondents receive encouragement to run from those who know them the best, such as their spouses, partners, and family members, this supportive home environment facilitates entry into the political sphere. Family roles and responsibilities, in other words, are often important considerations, but not, necessarily, impediments to or catalysts for running for office.

---

[36] Office of Alaska Governor Sarah Palin, "Palin Announces No Second Term, No Lame Duck Session Either," July 3, 2009. Accessed at http://www.gov.state.ak.us/exec-column.php (July 10, 2009).

6

On-the-Job Training

Professional Circumstances and the Decision to Run for Office

Heading into the 2010 midterm elections, journalists, pundits, and bloggers regularly commented on what appeared to be a proliferation of business executives running for high-level office, especially on the Republican side of the political aisle. "Business Backgrounds Are Working for First-Time GOP Candidates" graced the front page of the *Washington Post*. *The Hill* recognized the phenomenon when it ran a story titled "Republican Candidates Moving from the Boardroom to the Campaign Trail in '10." National Public Radio wondered, "Do CEOs Make Good Politicians?" And *Newsweek* featured a piece titled "America, Inc: A bumper crop of CEO politicians are campaigning to run the country like a bottom-line business."[1]

From California to Connecticut, former business executives threw their hats into the ring and competed in several of the highest-profile races across the country. Former CEOs Meg Whitman (eBay) and Carly Fiorina (Hewlett-Packard) secured the Republican nominations for governor and U.S. Senate in California, respectively. Republican Linda McMahon, the former CEO of World Wrestling Entertainment, vied to become the next U.S. senator from Connecticut. Plastics magnate Ron Johnson defeated

---

[1] Chris Cillizza, "Business Backgrounds Are Working for First-Time GOP Candidates," *Washington Post*, March 29, 2010, page A2; Sean J. Miller, "Republican Candidates Moving from the Boardroom to the Campaign Trail," *The Hill*, April 7, 2010. Accessed at http://thehill.com/blogs/ballot-box/gop-primaries/90885-republicans-move-from-boardroom-to-the-campaign-trail (December 17, 2010); Renee Montagne, "Do CEOs Make Good Politicians?" *National Public Radio*, November 4, 2010; Andrew Romano, "America, Inc.," *Newsweek*, February 12, 2010. Accessed at http://www.newsweek.com/2010/02/11/america-inc.html (December 17, 2010).

three-term incumbent U.S. Senator Russ Feingold in Wisconsin. Former Gateway CEO Rick Snyder was elected governor of Michigan.

Although candidates with business backgrounds garnered quite a bit of press attention in 2010, it has long been the case that candidates tend to come from the highest echelons of high-prestige occupations.[2] In the 111th Congress, for example, 203 members listed "business" as a previous profession. But public service and politics (215 members), law (202 members), and education (94 members) represented the other dominant backgrounds.[3] This is not surprising given that there is broad acceptance of the notion that anyone who ultimately decides to seek elective office is competitive and driven. Arthur Schlesinger (1966, 1) may have summarized it best when he began his pathbreaking work by stating flatly: "Ambition lies at the heart of politics." The women and men who emerge as candidates, especially for high-level office, are likely to have exercised that ambition to reach the top tier of professional accomplishment in their fields.

But why do some members of the candidate eligibility pool – all of whom occupy a space in the relatively high-prestige political pipeline – consider running for office, whereas others do not? To what extent do professional factors and success affect the candidate emergence process? This chapter offers an assessment of the manner in which eligible candidates' professional circumstances and experiences influence their interest in running for office. I find that, within the candidate eligibility pool, variations in income, political proximity, and the qualifications and professional credentials often relevant to a political career exert substantial effects on the likelihood of considering a candidacy. The empirical analyses, coupled with the qualitative evidence, indicate that, whereas higher incomes decrease the likelihood that an eligible candidate will consider running for office, greater access to the political arena and a heightened sense of one's qualifications to be a candidate bolster nascent ambition. Ultimately, the findings suggest that high levels of career ambition are

---

[2] Perhaps the poor economy and high unemployment rate drove more media attention to candidates' business credentials than would otherwise have been the case. After all, business leaders have always been well represented in the political arena. New York City mayor Michael Bloomberg; former governors Jon Corzine (New Jersey), Mitt Romney (Massachusetts), and Donald Carcieri (Rhode Island); and U.S. Senators Maria Cantwell (Washington) and Mark Warner (Virginia) serve as just a handful of examples of politicians who used their business experiences and credentials as foundations for high-level political careers.

[3] See Jennifer E. Manning, "Membership of the 111th Congress: A Profile," Congressional Research Service, November 19, 2010.

necessary to land in the candidate eligibility pool in the first place. But the politically relevant connections and skills acquired throughout the course of a career affect the likelihood of taking the next step in the candidate emergence process.

Professional Differences and Political Ambition in the Candidate Eligibility Pool: A Bivariate Analysis

We can begin an analysis of the manner in which eligible candidates' professions intersect with their levels of interest in running for office by examining the data at the bivariate level. Figure 6.1 presents respondents' political ambition, by profession. Several striking differences emerge across the professional subsamples. As we might expect, political activists report the greatest interest in entering the electoral arena. They are more than three times as likely as business leaders and educators to report "seriously" considering a candidacy, and they are only half as likely to report that they have never considered running for office. Because these women and men already work in the political arena, moving into an elective position would, in many cases, be a natural fit. Although lawyers exhibit lower levels of political ambition than activists, the members of the lawyer subsample are still more than twice as likely as the members of the business and educator subsamples to report that they "seriously" considered a run for office; they are about 30 percent less likely never to have thought about running for office.

When we delve more deeply into the specific offices in which eligible candidates express interest, further professional differences emerge. Turning first to the extent to which each professional subsample's interests are consistent with career ladder politics, the data reveal that lawyers and activists are significantly more likely than educators and business leaders to eschew the notion that local-level office is the first office an eligible candidate should pursue. More specifically, the data presented in the top half of Table 6.1 indicate that 29 percent of the lawyers and 30 percent of activists would enter the electoral arena by running for a state legislative, statewide, or federal office. Only 18 percent of the business leaders and 14 percent of the educators report such preferences (differences significant at p < 0.05).

The professional differences in office-specific preferences transcend the first elective office respondents would seek; lawyers and activists are also significantly more likely than business leaders and educators to report interest in ever pursuing a state legislative, statewide, or federal position

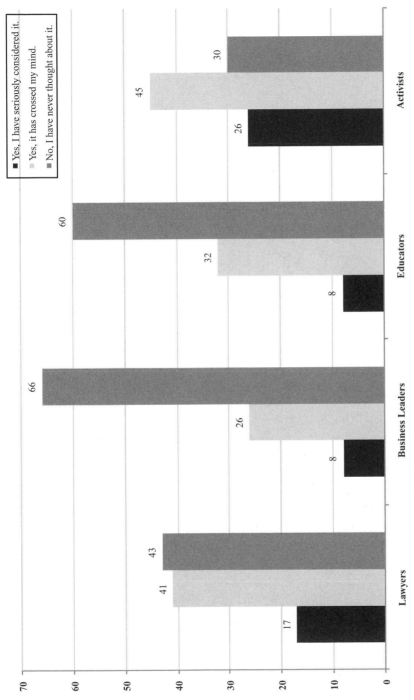

FIGURE 6.1. Interest in running for office, by profession.

Notes: Results are based on the 2001 survey data. Sample sizes: for lawyers, N = 1,128; for business leaders, N = 657; for educators, N = 925; and for activists, N = 814. Political activists are statistically more likely than members of the other three professional subsamples to have considered running for office (p < 0.01). Lawyers are statistically more likely than educators and business leaders to have considered running for office (p < 0.01).

TABLE 6.1. *Eligible Candidates' Elective Office Preferences, by Profession*

	Lawyers	Business Leaders	Educators	Activists
If you were going to run for office, then what level of office would you seek first?				
Local	44%	44%	60%	40%
State legislative	15	8	9	22
High (federal or statewide)	14	10	4	8
What level(s) of office would you ever be interested in seeking?				
Local	51	49	66	56
State legislative	33	19	23	46
High (federal or statewide)	40	24	17	30
N	1,138	667	936	831

Notes: Results are based on the 2001 survey data. In the top half of the table, entries indicate the percentage of respondents who said that, if they were to run for office, they would first seek the specified position. Percentages do not add up to 100 percent because respondents often expressed no interest in seeking elective office. In the bottom half of the table, entries indicate the percentage of respondents who indicated interest in running for each level of office. Percentages do not add up to 100 percent because respondents could select multiple offices. Chi-square tests comparing office-specific interests across profession reveal that educators are statistically more likely than members of the other three professional subgroups to choose local office and less likely to choose high-level office not only as the first position they would seek, but also as offices they would ever consider seeking ($p < 0.01$). Lawyers and activists are statistically more likely than educators and business leaders to express interest in entering electoral politics at the state legislative level, as well as ever seeking a state legislative position ($p < 0.01$). Lawyers are also the subgroup most likely to express interest in ever running for federal or statewide office ($p < 0.01$).

(see bottom of Table 6.1). Whereas approximately three-quarters of the lawyers and activists are interested in eventually running for an office beyond the local level, fewer than 45 percent of the business leaders and educators report such ambition (differences significant at $p < 0.05$).[4]

These findings are generally consistent with the policies that most directly exert an impact on members of each of the professions, as well as those that each of the professional subsamples might be best suited to influence. Consider the case of educators. Fifty-seven percent of the respondents in the educator subsample expressed interest in running for

---

[4] Levels of interest in local office for members of the business subsample might be somewhat understated. Many local officeholders are small business owners or self-employed entrepreneurs. This business subsample, however, is drawn from a national listing of corporate executives, many of whom may be less likely to have the time or professional support to seek local office. On the other hand, because the sample of business leaders is comprised of corporate executives, it is likely that their levels of interest in federal and statewide office are somewhat greater than that of the general population of business leaders.

the school board, compared with 30 percent of the lawyers, business leaders, and activists (differences significant at p < 0.01). A similar breakdown of office-specific interests came through in the interviews; forty of the seventy-five educators I interviewed said that if they were to seek an elective position, then they would run for school board. Concerns ranging from "fair teacher compensation" to "violence in the schools" to "making sure that kids are prepared when they start college" dominated these interviews.

Lawyers, business leaders, and political activists who are interested in running for a local position, on the other hand, are significantly more likely than educators to voice a preference for a mayoral or city council candidacy. Throughout the course of the interviews, they were more likely to discuss concerns regarding "zoning ordinances," "property taxes," and "judicial appointments by the city." Susan Marsh, a reproductive rights activist from New England, explained, for instance, that she is "more and more interested in running for the city council because of the protestors in front of the Planned Parenthood clinic who obstruct women's access to the facility." Although she acknowledged that she could run for the state legislature and "try to codify *Roe v. Wade* and pass buffer zone legislation," Marsh contended that "the most immediate way to solve the problem is to have control over the police department. And the mayor and city council have just that."

In some cases, office preferences are also consistent with the position respondents hold in their communities. Tom Barry, the executive director of a nonprofit organization in Wisconsin, for example, is well known and often quoted in local and statewide newspapers about education reform. He apologized for sounding "too egotistical," but said, "Having been a name in the Wisconsin press for the last 15 years, I can't imagine running for anything other than governor. My job has connected me to the top politicians in the state. People seek my views on statewide initiatives and policies. They'd be appalled if I announced a campaign for school board or town council."

Although respondents' professional interests shed light on their office-specific preferences, it is difficult to argue that the professions, in and of themselves, account for variation in nascent ambition. After all, the members of this candidate eligibility pool all work in one of the four professions from which most candidates emerge. Thus, the mere fact that an eligible candidate is a lawyer, business leader, educator, or activist can confer only limited explanatory power for why some respondents express interest in running for office, whereas others do not. An examination of the politically relevant experiences and credentials linked to respondents' professions, however, uncovers at least three elements of professional circumstances that contribute to eligible candidates' nascent ambition, or the lack thereof.

The Role of Income and Financial Success

Differences in eligible candidates' financial success serve as a starting point for exploring professional differences in political ambition. Not only is income often invoked as a key indicator of professional success, but it is also a significant predictor of mass-level political participation (Verba, Schlozman, and Brady 1995). Whether measured as personal income or household income, financial resources are substantially greater among the lawyers and business leaders in the sample than among the educators and activists. More specifically, the median personal income for lawyers and business leaders falls in the $100,000 to $200,000 range, compared with the $50,000 to $75,000 range for educators and political activists. Educators are approximately three times as likely as lawyers and business leaders to earn less than $50,000 per year; political activists are roughly six times as likely. Similar differences emerge in terms of household income: whereas more than 75 percent of lawyers and business leaders report household incomes of at least $100,000, only about half the educators and one-third of the political activists do so.

The manner in which these income differences account for variation in nascent ambition, however, is somewhat complicated. On one hand, financial success and freedom might affect whether an individual has the flexibility to consider running for office. Indeed, recent congressional elections have seen an increase in candidates who are political amateurs with substantial monetary resources (Canon 1990).[5] Nearly half the members of the 111th Congress were millionaires, fifty-five of whom reported wealth of $10 million or more.[6] Even nonwealthy candidates often must invest a substantial amount of their own money if they are to be considered serious congressional contenders. Personal wealth can also serve as a vital resource for candidates and elected officials at the state and local level, where most part-time positions offer little compensation. Nebraska State Senator Russ Karpisek, for instance, built a successful Czech

---

[5] See also Gail Russell Chaddock, "Can Campaign Finance Really be Reformed?" *Christian Science Monitor*, March 23, 2001, page 2.

[6] Dave Levinthal, "Congressional Members' Personal Wealth Expands Despite Sour National Economy," *Open Secrets*, November 17, 2010 (accessed November 23, 2010).

specialty meat market in Wilber, Nebraska, in large part because he used to work eighty hours per week. Since his election to the state house, though, he has incurred an extra $25,000 in labor costs because he must pay others to work the shifts he used to cover. Without the financial cushion he built, Senator Karpisek explained that he would likely have had to resign, noting, "I don't care about money, but I do like to keep the bills paid."[7]

This link between financial flexibility and candidate emergence is familiar to many respondents. Approximately one-third of the 300 eligible candidates I interviewed referred to financial freedom as a factor that propels political ambition. As John Garcia, a corporate executive from San Francisco, became increasingly successful professionally, he came to realize that "running for office was definitely in the cards." Reflecting on the state of his company, Garcia explained that he now has the financial resources and connections to pursue his political ambition:

> I took a one-man business and built a $150 million a year company. I have enough money to do whatever I want. But it's more than that. I also have a ton of business contacts. I give money to candidates all the time – usually Republicans, but I've been known to support some Democrats, too. The community knows me and respects me, so I wouldn't have a hard time raising money if I chose to do that rather than self-fund a campaign. And I pulled myself up by my bootstraps. It's a real American dream story, which voters would love.

Kevin Kendall, an attorney from Seattle, expressed a similar sentiment: "I worked like crazy to make partner in my firm so that I could have the kind of flexibility that's needed to pursue other endeavors and not check my work e-mail every ten minutes. I finally have the money and the time that a campaign, or any type of new project, would entail."

Several respondents who lacked the financial resources to pursue a political campaign mentioned the flexibility that a greater income would allow. Carrie Hodge, a political activist, believes that the costs of campaigns make running for office "too daunting to think about. And it's not only Congress. All campaigns have become so expensive.... I just don't have the money I need or the time it would take to raise it." Matthew Halloway, the executive director of a Montana branch of the Sierra Club, also noted that although he is very politically involved, he does not have the resources to think about electoral politics as "anything other than a hobby."

---

[7] Leslie Reed, "Some State Senators Must Decide: Serve the Voters or Pay Bills?" *Omaha World Herald*, December 9, 2007.

On the other hand, moving into the political arena from the private sector also often involves a substantial decrease in pay (see Ehrenhalt 1991; Rohde 1979; Prewitt 1970a). In other words, although financial resources might facilitate a candidate's emergence, the trade-offs involved in forgoing the income that makes a candidacy possible might depress interest in running for office. Former Alameda County, California, Supervisor Mary King, for instance, chose not to seek reelection because she could earn more money in the private sector:

> The job pays about $54,000 a year, you work seven days a week, you can't make any outside income without it being one kind of conflict or another, and the job can be very, very trying. I had to start thinking about retiring, as a single parent who had sent my kids through school.... I had to think, how am I going to take care of myself and take my skills and transfer them into something that is going to be more professionally lucrative?[8]

Pat Shea, a former gubernatorial candidate and deputy interior secretary in the Clinton administration, also decided that he is "finished for good" as far as running for office is concerned: "I really need to earn money to pay the mortgage and tuition bills."[9] Opting not to enter politics because of financial trade-offs can even occur at the local level. S. Gary Rosen planned to run for an at-large city council position, a seat that political operatives expected him to win, until he received an offer to teach chemistry at a local high school in Boylston, Massachusetts. Rosen had recently closed his business to run for a seat on the city council and realized that the lack of income was too much to bear. When given a more financially lucrative opportunity, he seized it.[10]

For the 27 percent of respondents with household incomes that exceed $200,000, a political career may represent a particularly costly endeavor. William Barnes, for example, is a businessman from the Midwest who has never given running for office any degree of serious thought. Although he is very interested in politics, Barnes explained that entering the electoral arena is "off the table." The sole provider for his wife and two children, he went on to note, "I am not aware of any political office that would provide comparable pay to my current job. I need to support my family at

---

[8] James Kellybrew, "An Exclusive Interview with Alameda County Supervisor Mary King," *Gibbs Magazine*, August 12, 2004.

[9] Dan Harrie, "Shea is Finished with Political Life; Shea is Done with Public Office," *Salt Lake Tribune*, April 8, 2001, page B1.

[10] Nick Kotsopoulos, "Rosen Abandons At-Large Council Race," *Telegram and Gazette*, August 8, 2001, page B1.

the level we're accustomed to enjoying. That's my job. That's my role."
Dina Ramirez, a college professor, arrived at a similar conclusion:

> I'm the primary breadwinner in a family of four. I work 60 hours a week, but I make a good living doing it. If I ran for office and lost, I'd have jeopardized my career. If I ran for office and won, I'd work at least as hard and at least as long for less pay. It just doesn't make financial sense. Isn't the whole point of earning money to buy flexibility down the road? As far as I can tell, politics involves little free time and with the paltry pay, it would make the future a lot harder for me and my family. Why do it?

Jennifer Williams, an attorney in New Mexico, also believes that she "work[s] too hard to get paid what elected officials – even members of Congress – earn." She came to this conclusion after witnessing another partner in her firm run for the U.S. House of Representatives. Williams recalled:

> He was well-known and well-liked, but it still took him an immense amount of time. And he had a really hard time balancing the campaign with his clients. I'd be in a similar situation. I wouldn't be able to afford to take a leave of absence, so I'd be working two full-time jobs. And the reward would be a huge income cut.

Summarized well by Daniel Ross, a high school principal in New York, "The single greatest impediment to my ever running for office comes down to money. Public officials get very little pay. I have too many degrees and too many financial obligations to forgo my current income, as inadequate as it often feels." Ellen Kaplan, an attorney from Pennsylvania, agreed: "On an abstract level, I would love to be more involved in politics. But practically, I'm a partner at a law firm that always seems to have huge trials. And if my two kids are going to go to college, then I need to be at the table for those huge trials. Until I no longer need the income from my firm, running for office isn't really an option." Attorneys Tom Corwin (Oklahoma), John Desmond (Colorado), and Barbara Judson (California) were among the twenty-six of seventy-five lawyers I interviewed who noted that the financial ramifications and opportunity costs that accompany a political candidacy would be too much to bear.

Perhaps because of the competing dynamics associated with higher levels of income – more financial freedom, but greater financial trade-offs – studies that address the impact of income on political ambition produce mixed results (Maisel and Stone 1997; Fowler 1996; Stone

1980).[11] Within the candidate eligibility pool, though, the financial trade-offs seem to carry more weight than the financial freedom associated with greater incomes. A majority (53 percent) of the respondents with household incomes in excess of $200,000 have never considered a candidacy; however, the majority (54 percent) of respondents who report household incomes that do not exceed $200,000 have considered running for office (difference significant at $p < 0.01$).[12]

The Role of Professionally Conferred Political Proximity

A second factor that likely contributes to the professional differences in ambition that emerge at the bivariate level is associated with political participation and proximity. Individuals who are already active in politics – for example, those who work and volunteer on campaigns, attend political and party meetings, interact professionally with elected officials, or have firsthand exposure to politics through personal and familial connections – may be more likely to envision themselves entering the political arena. This political proximity may both demystify the political process and foster relationships with politicians, community leaders, and donors who could be helpful throughout the candidate emergence process.

Political proximity, however, varies across profession in the candidate eligibility pool. Turning first to conventional types of political activism, lawyers and political activists are more likely than business leaders and educators to engage. Of nine different types of political participation – including voting, contributing money to campaigns, volunteering for candidates, attending political meetings, and serving on boards – the average political activist engaged in seven political activities over the course of the previous year.[13] Attorneys place second among the professions, with the average lawyer reporting that he or she participated in five political activities during the past year. Educators and business leaders trail

---

[11] These competing dynamics can even emerge at the local level, although the limited research finds that wealthier communities are often characterized by less city council electoral competition than are poorer communities (e.g., Eulau and Prewitt 1973).

[12] The findings are similar when I use personal income, as opposed to household income, to measure financial resources.

[13] See Chapter 4 for a description of the various types of political activities in which respondents engaged. This measure of political involvement taps into the diversity of respondents' political activity, not the sheer volume of their activism. This measure does not gauge, for example, how many campaign contributions an eligible candidate made, how many political meetings he or she attended, or the number of boards on which he or she serves.

the professional subsamples, averaging four political activities in the past year (difference of means across professions significant at $p < 0.05$).

A similar pattern emerges when we focus on more specific measures of political proximity. The data presented in Figure 6.2 illustrate that lawyers and activists are statistically more likely than business leaders and educators to report a connection to the political system. Some of these differences are relatively minor. In fact, more than 60 percent of the respondents in all four professional subsamples interact with elected officials not only as part of their job, but also socially. Yet the differences, overall, are consistent with the varying levels of political ambition expressed within each professional subsample.

When assessing these professional differences in political activism, it is important to recognize that individuals might be particularly likely to select into certain professions because of the political proximity they confer. Brad Cole, for instance, has been a real estate attorney in California for more than fifteen years. He entered the legal profession in general, and real estate law, in particular, because he "wanted to be at the center of things, politically." He elaborated, noting that "every political deal in this town has to do with space, property, and political interests." Brynn Mills, the executive director of an organization dedicated to ending gun violence, also chose her profession because she "wanted to be involved in politics every day." She speaks with candidates, lobbies elected officials, and engages donors "seven days a week, fifty-two weeks a year." In fact, Mills applied for her current job because she knew it would place her "at the hub of New Jersey politics, exactly where [she] wanted to be."

But there is no question that working in certain professions can generate politically relevant connections even if those connections were not a motivating factor for entering the field in the first place. Dora O'Keefe, for instance, assumed, when she started her own communications consulting firm four years ago, that her clients would be corporate entities with an interest in developing better relationships among their management teams and with their boards of directors. Much to O'Keefe's surprise, she was "repeatedly hired to help communicate a company's mission to key political players, both in the mayor's office and the state legislature." Cheryl Perry, a trial lawyer in Connecticut, also underestimated the political connections she would develop through the course of her career:

> I don't want to sound naïve. I always knew that trial lawyers were an easy base of support for politicians. We have disposable income. We have clients and connections in most industries. We're interested in politics because we

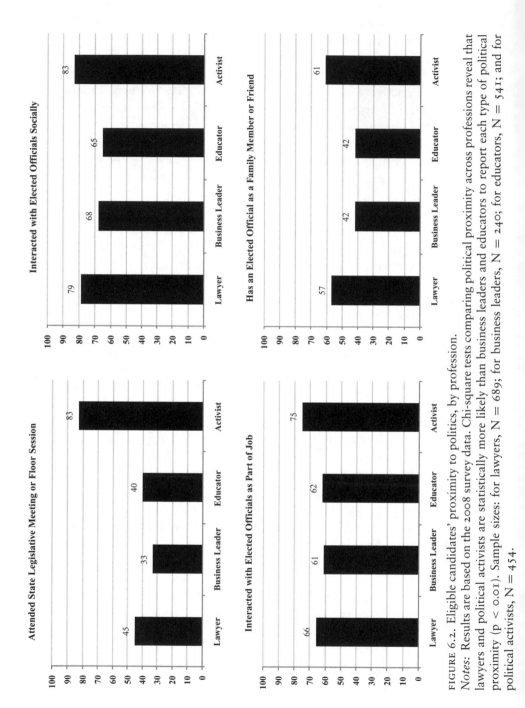

FIGURE 6.2. Eligible candidates' proximity to politics, by profession.

Notes: Results are based on the 2008 survey data. Chi-square tests comparing political proximity across professions reveal that lawyers and political activists are statistically more likely than business leaders and educators to report each type of political proximity (p < 0.01). Sample sizes: for lawyers, N = 689; for business leaders, N = 240; for educators, N = 541; and for political activists, N = 454.

have a lot to lose if tort reform goes in the wrong direction. But I never could have expected the number of candidates who parade in here one after another every campaign season.... I can't remember the last time I voted and hadn't actually met all of the candidates.

Mark Stanton, an environmentalist from Oregon, also remarked that he did not expect to make the political connections he developed when he first began his work: "I cared about clean air and clean water. I thought we'd be a grassroots kind of organization. We'd clean the beaches. But I'm never on the beach. I'm meeting with the members of the city council. Not what I ever would have anticipated."

Throughout the course of the interviews, many respondents linked the political proximity they acquired on the job to interest in running for office. Janet Upton, for instance, is a college administrator in South Carolina. She explained that she had "never once thought about running for office" before she assumed her current position. Although she cannot pursue any elective position now – "there would be far too many perceived conflicts of interest" – she realizes that her position has connected her to "the right people who would be helpful" should she decide to launch a candidacy at some point in the future. Mike McCulloch, a practicing attorney from the Midwest, averred that he had "absolutely no interest in running for office." But even he identified a connection between his career and the ease with which he could run:

> I'm fifty-six and probably the best commercial litigator in the state. I represent all the political players. Ironically, because I'm so well known and so respected by the politicians, I'd never want to enter politics. I have too much to lose, too solid a reputation to put on the line. If I'd been interested earlier in my career, then maybe it'd have been possible. There would sure as hell have been less to sacrifice.

Regardless of whether eligible candidates selected their professions because they already possessed high levels of political interest and sought to further their political connections, or were caught off guard by the political circles in which they often now find themselves operating, levels of political proximity vary considerably across professional domains. And this variation correlates with differences in respondents' nascent ambition across the four professional subsamples.

The Role of Professional Credentials and Qualifications
The third way that professional differences may be linked to eligible candidates' interest in running for office pertains to the politically relevant

credentials they acquire in their careers and their perceptions of these qualifications. Perceptions of electoral success have been shown to be the most important predictor of whether an individual decides to enter his or her first congressional race (see Maisel and Stone 1997). At the pre-candidacy stage of the candidate emergence process, however, relevant perceptions of success are likely longer-term and linked to an eligible candidate's internal psyche. Eligible candidates' estimates of their feelings of efficacy are based on a relatively broad set of criteria, including whether they think they have sufficient knowledge, credentials, and skills to enter the political sphere.[14] Importantly, these ingredients for self-efficacy are often acquired through professional experiences.

To gauge this general sense of self-efficacy, we can begin by measuring the degree to which an individual considers himself or herself "qualified" to run for office.[15] Respondents were asked to place themselves on a continuum from "not at all qualified" to "very qualified" to launch a candidacy. The survey results reveal that lawyers and activists are roughly twice as likely as business leaders and educators to consider themselves "very qualified" to seek an elective position (see Table 6.2). Members of the business and educator subsamples are twice as likely as members of the law and activist subsamples to assert that they are "not at all qualified" to run for office. Similar professional gaps appear when we consider respondents' assessments of whether they are qualified to perform the job of an elected official. Whereas approximately 80 percent of lawyers and activists contend that they are "qualified" or "very qualified" to do the job of an officeholder, fewer than two-thirds of business leaders and educators assess themselves this way. Members of the business and educator subsamples are more than twice as likely as lawyers and activists to rate themselves as "not at all qualified" to perform the job.[16]

---

[14] These credentials and experiences can translate into the political arena similar to the manner in which civic skills often acquired in nonpolitical settings can foster political participation at the mass level (see Verba, Schlozman, and Brady 1995).

[15] For some subset of eligible candidates, this assessment may be based on short-term electoral considerations and the structural forces at work in the political environment. For most eligible candidates, however, strategic considerations are probably more abstract. Because nascent ambition precedes the stage at which an eligible candidate faces a political opportunity structure, I expect individuals' estimates of their personal attributes and feelings of efficacy as political candidates, in general, to exert an impact on considering entering the electoral arena.

[16] The data pertaining to qualifications to perform the job of an elected official come from the 2008 survey; the 2001 survey instrument did not include this question.

TABLE 6.2. *Eligible Candidates' Perceptions of Their Qualifications to Seek and Hold Office, by Profession*

	Lawyers	Business Leaders	Educators	Activists
How qualified are you to run for public office?				
Very qualified	26%	11%	13%	31%
Qualified	35	23	29	29
Somewhat qualified	28	34	33	26
Not at all qualified	12	32	26	13
N	1,119	650	923	799

Notes: Results are based on the 2001 survey data. Chi-square tests comparing perceptions of qualifications across professions reveal that business leaders and educators are statistically less likely than lawyers and activists to contend that they are "very qualified" to run for office, and more likely to self-assess as "not at all qualified" to run for office ($p < 0.01$).

Eligible candidates' assessments of their qualifications cannot be separated from the skills they acquire and hone professionally. Like many respondents, attorney Hilda Morganthau cited her years of professional service as qualifications to enter politics: "I have eighteen years of experience working for two governors and serving on a statewide board. I am certainly qualified to seek a state-level position." Laura Thompson, an attorney from Arlington, Virginia, employed the same type of calculus in assessing her qualifications:

> I have worked with the local, state, and federal government for twenty-five years and I have been the government affairs liaison between organizations and legislative bodies during that time. I'm currently the chair of a partnership, which is a seven-county economic development corporation. I don't know what other experiences someone could have.

For a Washington attorney, more than thirty years of experience means that she "knows more about the details of the local law and the political system than most." In addition, her job requires that she be "well read and up to date on political issues at the local, state, federal, and international levels." Attorneys Michael Rudman (Minnesota), Jeffrey Townsend (California), and John Serlen (New York) were among other respondents who stated that their legal training qualified them to run for office.

Political experience was also a reference point for many educators, among them Millicent Tillman. The North Carolina college administrator served in three gubernatorial administrations and as a trustee for the public school system. She contended that her "immediate proximity to political life" qualified her to run for office. Carol Stewart has dealt with the public as a teacher and a principal for thirty years. She, too, invoked the experiences she acquired "on the job" as credentials for running for political office:

> I often call state representatives about budgetary and education issues. This has taught me to understand the difficult role of the states in times of budget cuts. My experiences in schools have also taught me how to deal with different types of people and understand their varying situations. So, I think that I would be qualified to run for office and serve the people.

Managing a four-year, 50,000-student operation with a "tremendous budget" conferred political qualifications to a college administrator from Florida. In another example, Philip Nichols, a middle school principal from the Midwest, was convinced that "compared to running a school with one thousand teenagers, politics would be a cakewalk."

Other respondents cited their professional responsibilities, such as the ability to "negotiate," "build coalitions," "articulate clear arguments to audiences large and small," "retain facts," "raise money," and "know who is connected to whom politically," as skills that would transfer well to the political sphere. According to Elizabeth Dixon, the executive director of a statewide organization devoted to children's issues and education, "Running an organization is probably not terribly different from sitting on a city council, or even in the state legislature." Sam Parker mentioned that his success in business and overseeing a staff of 6,000 employees positioned him to "manage a small town or county."

The majority of respondents I interviewed who self-assessed as "very qualified" to run for office drew similarities between the political arena and their current professional positions, and more than half stated the importance of concrete experiences in dealing with public officials or groups that influence the policy process. Eligible candidates' abilities to offer specific linkages between their professional responsibilities and the political arena, however, vary by profession. The data presented in Table 6.3 allow for comparisons across professions of self-assessments on skills that are generally considered important in electoral politics – skills that the respondents, themselves, often mentioned in the interviews. Regarding four of the five political skills about which the survey inquired, lawyers and activists are statistically more likely than business leaders and educators to perceive themselves as possessing the skill. Political activists, for instance, are twice as likely as educators and almost three times as likely

TABLE 6.3. *Eligible Candidates' Politically Relevant Skills, by Profession*

	Lawyers	Business Leaders	Educators	Activists
Perceptions of Skills				
Knowledgeable about public policy issues	56%	28%	39%	77%
Professional experience relevant to politics	82	60	60	70
Good public speaker	69	44	59	64
Good fundraiser	19	19	9	24
Well connected to the political system	24	15	11	45
N	687	236	537	454

Notes: Results are based on the 2008 survey data. Entries indicate the percentage of respondents who self-assess as possessing the skill. Sample sizes vary slightly because some respondents omitted answers to some questions. Chi-square tests comparing perceptions of each skill across professions reveal that, with the exception of fundraising, business leaders and educators are statistically less likely than lawyers and activists to contend that they possess each politically relevant skill ($p < 0.05$).

as business leaders to perceive themselves as knowledgeable about public policy issues. Lawyers are one-third more likely than business leaders and educators to contend that they have professional experience that is relevant to politics.

Overall, these perceptual differences across profession are largely consistent with the skills and experiences in which respondents report engaging in their professional capacities. That is, lawyers and activists are more likely than business leaders and educators to use regularly the public speaking skills, policy expertise, and political connections that are relevant when considering elective office. They are more likely to consider themselves qualified to run for office because they have already excelled at performing a series of tasks that are readily transferrable to the political arena.

A Side Note on the Gender Gap in Perceptions of Qualifications

Women in this sample of the candidate eligibility pool are, objectively speaking, just as qualified as men to hold elective positions. They have achieved comparable levels of professional success in the fields that precede political candidacies. They are equally credentialed and educated. And there are no notable gender differences either in levels of political knowledge and interest, or political participation and campaign experience. Yet women are more likely than men to dismiss their qualifications and doubt that they have what it takes to run for office.

Though not directly related to politics, investigators from a variety of disciplines provide evidence to suggest that women are less likely than men to contend that they possess the skills and traits necessary to enter electoral politics. Turning first to gender differences in skills-based measures, researchers find that women are more likely than men to diminish and undervalue their professional skills and achievements. Studies of gender differences in academic abilities provide a clear example. By the time of adolescence, male students rate their mathematical abilities higher than female students do, despite no sex differences in objective indicators of competence (Wigfield, Eccles, and Pintrich 1996). In the areas of language arts, male and female students offer comparable self-assessments, although objective indicators reveal that female students are actually higher achieving in these fields (Pajares 2002). Many of these misconceptions persist into adulthood, percolating up even to high-level professionals who have succeeded in traditionally male domains (Brownlow, Whitener, and Rupert 1998; Beyer and Bowden 1997). Controlling for a series of job-related functions and work experience, for instance, female MBAs accepted salary offers that were lower than the offers accepted by their male counterparts (Bowles, Babcock, and McGinn 2005). In the absence of clear compensation standards, women are also more likely than men to express lower career-entry and career-peak pay expectations (Bylsma and Major 1992).

Gender differences exist not only in the ways in which women and men perceive their objective skills, but also in the confidence they exhibit regarding their credentials, backgrounds, propensity to take risks, and willingness to compete. Studies reveal that, in general, men are more likely than women to express confidence in skills they do not possess and overconfidence in skills they do possess (Kling et al. 1999). Men tend to be more "self-congratulatory," whereas women tend to be more modest about their achievements (Wigfield, Eccles, and Pintrich 1996). Men tend to overestimate their intelligence, whereas women tend to underestimate theirs (Furnham and Rawles 1995; Beloff 1992). Men often fail to incorporate criticism into their self-evaluations, whereas women tend to be strongly influenced by negative appraisals of their capabilities (Roberts 1991). Further, a review of 150 studies in psychology concludes that in almost all personal and professional decisions, women exhibit significantly higher levels of risk aversion than do men (Byrnes, Miller, and

Schafer 1999). Perhaps because of this tendency, when comparing professional performance in competitive and noncompetitive environments, investigators find that men are more likely than women to seek out competitive environments and to exude confidence when competing (Niederle and Vesterlund 2010, 2007; Gneezy, Niederle, and Rustichini 2003).

The data on qualifications provide compelling evidence that women's inclination to undervalue their skills and experiences transcends into the electoral arena. After all, many of the patterns identified by researchers in other disciplines are only exacerbated by a culture that tends to reinforce traditional sex-role expectations and women's marginalization in politics. The data presented in Figure 6.3 reveal that, across professions, women are twice as likely as similarly situated men to consider themselves "not at all qualified" to run for office. In fact, almost half the women in the business subsample consider themselves completely unqualified to seek an elective position. Moreover, women are less likely than men to perceive themselves as possessing politically relevant skills. Men, for instance, are

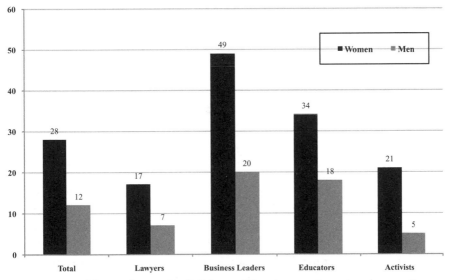

FIGURE 6.3. The gender gap in eligible candidates' perceptions that they are "not at all qualified" to run for office, by profession.
Notes: Results are based on the 2001 survey data. Sample sizes: for lawyers, N = 1,119; for business leaders, N = 650; for educators, N = 923; and for political activists, N = 799. Entries indicate the percentage of respondents who self-assess as "not at all qualified" to run for office. The gender gap in self-assessed qualifications is significant at p < 0.01 for the total sample and within each professional subgroup.

more than 60 percent more likely than women to think they could raise enough money to run for office; and they are almost 30 percent more likely than women to state that they are knowledgeable about public policy issues. These perceptual differences are striking in light of women and men's actual skills and experiences. Women and men in the sample are statistically indistinguishable from one another in terms of the key skills necessary to run for office. Thirty-three percent of women and 35 percent of men have conducted extensive policy research; 65 percent of women and 69 percent of men regularly engage in public speaking; and 69 percent of women and 64 percent of men report experience soliciting funds (in all comparisons, $p > 0.05$).

The exact source of women and men's different beliefs about their own qualifications to run for office is multifaceted. Relying on a mixed-method approach of quantitative analysis and interviews with eligible candidates, Richard L. Fox and I (2010) conclude that some women's self-doubts can be linked to their perceptions of a sexist political environment dominated by a masculinized ethos. Other women's self-assessed qualifications are the product of a stringent definition of "qualified" that encompasses both essential political background experiences and personal traits. Still other women hold themselves to an extremely high bar in assessing their readiness to pursue elective office.[17] For the purposes of this chapter, it is important to recognize that skills and credentials acquired "on the job" may vary by profession, but are undervalued by women, regardless of the professional sphere in which they operate.

The Impact of Professional Circumstances on Political Ambition: Multivariate Results

The bivariate analysis, coupled with evidence from the interviews, sheds light on the manner in which eligible candidates' nascent ambition varies across profession. The explanatory power of income, political proximity, and self-efficacy as a candidate – all of which are related to the professional environment in which a respondent works – is even more apparent in a multivariate context. Table 6.4 presents the logistic regression coefficients from the model of nascent ambition I have been building throughout this book (see Chapters 3, 4, and 5). The model also includes gauges

---

[17] For a nuanced, empirical examination of the gender gap in self-perceived qualifications, see Fox and Lawless 2011. For a mixed-method approach that includes both quantitative analysis and anecdotal evidence from interviews with eligible candidates as a way to shed light on the gender gap in self-perceived qualifications and political ambition, see Lawless and Fox 2010, chapter 6.

TABLE 6.4. *Impact of Professional Experiences and Qualifications on Considering a Candidacy (Logistic Regression Coefficients, Standard Errors, and Change in Probabilities)*

	Coefficient (and Standard Error)	Maximum Change in Probability (percentage points)
Professional Factors		
Income	−0.19 (0.04)**	22.8
Self-assessed qualifications to run for office	0.70 (0.05)**	45.4
Family Dynamics (in Childhood and Adulthood)		
Encouraged to run for office by family member	0.98 (0.12)**	24.0
Encouraged to run for office by spouse/partner	1.08 (0.13)**	26.3
"Political" household index	0.13 (0.04)**	18.6
Parent ran for office	0.36 (0.14)**	8.7
Ran for office as a student	0.32 (0.09)**	7.1
Minority Status		
Sex (female)	−0.53 (0.10)**	11.3
Black	−0.49 (0.17)**	10.5
Latino/a	−0.32 (0.21)	–
Indicators of Political Engagement		
Political knowledge	0.10 (0.05)	–
Political interest	0.05 (0.03)	–
Political efficacy	0.05 (0.05)	–
Political participation	0.20 (0.03)**	37.8
Electoral Features and Opportunities		
Size of the congressional delegation	−0.01 (0.01)	–
Size of the state political opportunity structure	0.00 (0.00)	–
Size of the local political opportunity structure	0.00 (0.00)	–
Term limits	0.21 (0.12)	–
Part-time legislature	0.24 (0.13)	–
Legislative salary	0.00 (0.00)	–
Political Dynamics		
Democrat	0.20 (0.13)	–
Republican	0.01 (0.14)	–
Percent Democratic presidential vote share	−0.01 (0.01)	–
Party congruence with the congressional delegation	0.01 (0.11)	–
Party congruence with the state legislature	−0.20 (0.12)	
Constant	−3.13 (0.58)**	
Percent correctly predicted	77.2	
Pseudo R-squared	0.46	
N	3,061	

Notes: Regression results are based on the 2001 data. Probabilities were calculated by setting all continuous independent variables to their means and dummy variables to their modes. The change in probability reflects the independent effect a statistically significant variable exerts as I vary its value from its minimum to maximum. Significance levels: * $p < 0.05$; ** $p < 0.01$.

of household income, political involvement, and self-assessed qualifications to run for office, all of which tap into the politically relevant skills and experiences eligible candidates acquire and build in a professional setting.[18]

A substantive interpretation of the regression coefficients reveals that professional factors exert a substantial, independent impact on nascent ambition. Respondents with higher incomes, for instance, are significantly less likely to consider running for office. Greater financial freedom, therefore, does not systematically increase the likelihood that an eligible candidate will think about a political career. Rather, the trade-offs associated with a loss of income that would likely accompany a candidacy depress the likelihood that an eligible candidate will even consider running for office. All else equal, respondents who report annual household incomes of at least $200,000 are more than 22 percentage points less likely than respondents who report annual incomes of less than $50,000 to consider throwing their hats into the electoral ring. Whereas greater incomes are associated with lower levels of nascent ambition, heightened levels of political proximity increase an eligible candidate's likelihood of running for office. The same is true when we consider perceptions of qualifications to run for office. Respondents who consider themselves "very qualified" to run for office have a 0.78 likelihood of having considered a candidacy. This predicted probability is 30 percent greater than that of an otherwise "average" respondent, and roughly two and one half times the likelihood of a respondent who considers himself "not at all unqualified."[19]

To demonstrate the extent to which income, political proximity, and qualifications contribute to professional differences in nascent ambition, I calculated the predicted probability that an eligible candidate has

---

[18] In this equation, I rely on the nine-point political participation scale to measure political activity. The specific indicators of political proximity were included only on the 2008 survey. When I restrict the analysis to respondents who completed the 2008 survey, and include a political proximity index, the results are comparable. To maintain a greater number of cases, as well as ensure that this regression equation builds on the models presented in earlier chapters, I present the equation that is based on the 2001 survey data. I also performed the regression analyses separately on each professional subsample. The results did not reveal any substantively or statistically meaningful differences; the same dynamics affect nascent political ambition across the professions.

[19] Moreover, the ability of an individual to imagine himself or herself as a qualified candidate for public office translates into a greater likelihood of envisioning oneself climbing the political career ladder in the future. Among respondents who express interest in seeking office, those who currently deem themselves very qualified to run are 42 percentage points more likely than those who do not self-assess this way to voice interest in eventually seeking a high-level position (regression results not shown).

considered running for office, by profession. For each predicted probability, I set all variables in the logistic regression equation presented in Table 6.4 to their overall sample means and modes, with the exception of the three variables that are linked to professional circumstances. I held the three professional variables – income, political proximity, and self-assessed qualifications – constant at their professional subsample means. This is important because the three gauges of professional circumstances do not all work in the same direction. The predicted probabilities, therefore, account for the fact that greater political proximity is often offset, at least in part, by greater annual incomes.

Figure 6.4 provides clear support for the claim that professional differences affect nascent ambition, and that those differences are driven by the variations in income, political proximity, and self-assessed

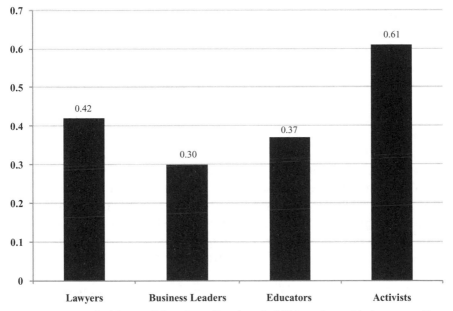

FIGURE 6.4. Eligible candidates' predicted probabilities of considering a candidacy, by profession.
Notes: Results are based on the 2001 survey data. Predicted probabilities are based on the regression equation presented in Table 6.4. The figure embeds within the calculations the statistically significant professional differences as measured by income, self-assessed qualifications, and political involvement. The predicted probabilities, therefore, are calculated based on the subsample means of these three variables for each profession. All remaining continuous variables included in Table 6.4 are held at their respective means. Dummy variables are held constant at their modes.

qualifications that characterize the professional subcultures in which respondents work. Holding constant political dynamics, electoral features, minority status, and family dynamics, the "average" political activist is twice as likely as the "average" business leader to consider running for office. The "average" lawyer is 40 percent more likely than the "average" business leader and nearly 20 percent more likely than the "average" educator to consider a candidacy. These differences in interest in running for office can be attributed entirely to variation in professional circumstances; all other predictors are held constant at their overall sample means and modes. Thus, merely working in a particular profession does not affect the likelihood that an eligible candidate will consider running for office; the income, political proximity, and skills and credentials associated with that profession influence nascent ambition. Lawyers and activists are most likely to possess a combination of the factors that work to propel thoughts of a candidacy.

Beyond the substantive effects of the professional variables, two additional findings emerge from the equation that merit further attention. Foremost, although sex remains statistically significant – and women, even accounting for income, political proximity, and self-assessed qualifications, are more than 11 percentage points less likely than their male counterparts to consider running for office – the professional variables reduce the gender gap in political ambition considerably. That women are more likely than men to doubt their qualifications to run for office goes a long way in shedding light on the reasons for the gender gap in ambition that was identified and explicated in Chapter 4.

Second, black respondents are significantly less likely to consider running for office. This result is driven by the self-assessed qualifications variable, although it operates the opposite way that it does with sex. Thirty-eight percent of black respondents, compared with 19 percent of white respondents, consider themselves "very qualified" to run for office. Black eligible candidates are also only half as likely as white respondents to self-assess as "not at all qualified" to run for office (10 percent of black respondents, compared with 20 percent of white respondents, self-assess this way; difference significant at $p < 0.01$).[20] A model that does not control for an eligible candidate's self-efficacy, therefore, suggests that race is not a statistically significant predictor of nascent ambition.

---

[20] No other racial differences emerge pertaining to qualifications. Latinos/as, as well as respondents who identify with another race, are not statistically indistinguishable from white respondents when asked to assess themselves on the qualifications continuum.

Once we take into account the fact that black respondents are actually more likely to consider themselves qualified, though, we see that, all else equal, they are less likely to report interest in running for office. Minority status – in terms of both gender and race – depresses the likelihood of considering a candidacy. The lack of a thorough investigation of professional differences that are linked to political ambition obscures these effects.

Changes in Professional Circumstances: Predicting Dynamic Ambition

Jan Henderson, a public school administrator in Kansas, mentioned during a phone interview her long-term plan to run for the state legislature. She explained, "I am a mom, so I have to wait until my girls are grown. They range in age from six to sixteen." But Henderson then elaborated on how she planned to pursue her political ambition:

> I can retire when I'm fifty-three, which is still young enough and energetic enough to launch a sort of second career, which could be politics.... And the timing coincides nicely with the ages of my children. I mean they'll be old enough where they won't need me at home as much and they could probably deal with me campaigning.

Lilly Bates, a lawyer from the Midwest, also detailed a plan to run for office that is contingent on her ability to retire early:

> [Running for office] is something I would seriously consider if I am able to retire in my late fifties and pursue politics as almost a second career. I am forty-one, a partner in my own law firm, and have three small children – ages four, five, and six. There is no way I could run now. School board or city council might seem like a good idea in fifteen or twenty years, though.[21]

---

[21] Several of the women with whom I spoke elaborated specifically on the different weight men and women place on children when considering entering the electoral arena and the manner in which their decision-making calculus involves professional considerations. Massachusetts attorney Denise Zauderer, for example, explained, "There's a season for everything. You establish your career, then your family, then you try to merge the two.... The mommy and career mix don't allow for much energy beyond that. So, you either wait until you retire, or until your children are grown." In many cases, balancing work and family does not preclude women from considering a candidacy. But these politically ambitious women mention the possibility of entering politics as an option only after their child care duties abate. Substantially delaying their entrance into the political arena makes it less likely that they will be able to climb very high on the political career ladder. For a more elaborate discussion of the intersection of gender, family roles, career responsibilities, and political ambition, see Lawless and Fox 2010, chapter 4.

Eligible candidates much closer to retirement age articulated similar plans. Ted Morrison, an investment banker from Florida, for example, has always been very active in the community. He serves on several boards and commissions, but has always perceived himself as "too busy" to run for office. Given his business success, though, he plans to retire within the next couple of years. According to Morrison, running for office would be a plausible way to fill his time. Amy Norton, an attorney from Seattle, will likely follow a similar path. After practicing law for 35 years, Norton is preparing to retire somewhat earlier than she expected:

> My husband is 10 years older than I am, so I'm leaving my profession a bit sooner than I otherwise might. But this means that I will have time for other pursuits, such as politics. A future run for office is not at all out of the question. It's a great way to continue to use my skills. What else do I have to do? Isn't that what retirement is for?

Of course, for every eligible candidate who mentioned politics as a way to fill his or her retirement, another respondent rejected the notion. Bill Hull, a former litigator who retired three years ago, captured the sentiment well when he voiced distaste about the prospects of pursuing a candidacy, now that he has the time: "I fish. I hunt. I spend time with my family. Running for office takes away from your life. It hardly pays anything. You hardly ever actually get to accomplish anything. No thanks. I would rather fish, hunt, and spend time with my family. That's what retirement is for."

Between the two waves of the study, one of every ten respondents retired from his or her career, so the extent to which a new career-free lifestyle can accommodate or foster political ambition is an important question. But retirement is not the only professional change eligible candidates underwent between 2001 and 2008. More than half the respondents – across each profession – took on more responsibilities at work, more than one-third experienced a change in household income, and nearly half arrived at new perceptions of their qualifications to enter the electoral arena (see Table 6.5). The panel data, therefore, allow for a systematic examination of the manner in which changes in professional circumstances affect interest in running for office.

The multiple regression analysis reveals that changes in professional circumstances do exert an impact on respondents' political ambition. Increases and decreases in interest in running for office, however, are driven not by actual changes in professional status, such as retirement, taking on more responsibilities at work, or variations in income. Rather,

TABLE 6.5. *Changes in Eligible Candidates' Professional Circumstances from 2001 to 2008*

Underwent a career change	18%
Took on more responsibilities at work	54
Retired	10
Experienced a decrease in household income	7
Experienced an increase in household income	27
Lower self-assessment of qualifications to run for office	15
Higher self-assessment of qualifications to run for office	33
N	1,924

Notes: Number of cases varies slightly, as some respondents omitted answers to some questions.

the regression equation presented in Table 6.6 – which controls for the baseline correlates of dynamic ambition, minority status, a politicized upbringing, and family dynamics – reveals that changes in respondents' perceptions of their qualifications to enter the electoral arena provide the most explanatory power when predicting the evolution of political ambition.

Consider, for example, respondents who considered themselves "very qualified" to run for office in 2008, but who self-assessed as "not at all qualified" in 2001. These women and men are nearly three times as likely as an otherwise "average" respondent who experienced no change in self-perceived qualifications to have become "definitely interested" in running for office. Alternatively, eligible candidates who considered themselves "not at all qualified" to run in 2008, but who self-assessed as "very qualified" seven years earlier, are 10 percentage points more likely than those whose perceptions did not change to have decided that they are "absolutely not" interested in running for office (0.28 predicted probability, compared with 0.18).

Granted, most respondents did not move from one end of the qualifications continuum to the other. But even a one-unit decrease in self-assessments – from "very qualified" to "qualified," for example – increases by 4 percentage points the likelihood that an eligible candidate will write off completely the possibility of running for office at some point in the future. This finding is far reaching, as nearly 50 percent of respondents reported some shift in their self-assessed qualifications; 33 percent considered themselves more qualified in 2008 than they were in 2001, and 16 percent assessed as less qualified (these shifts are consistent across the four professional subsamples). Clearly, perceptions of qualifications

TABLE 6.6. *Changing Interest in Running for Office: Effects of Professional Circumstances on Predicting Dynamic Ambition (Ordered Logistic Regression Coefficients and Standard Errors)*

	Change in Ambition (5-point scale)
Changes in Professional Circumstances	
Underwent a career change	−0.05 (0.19)
Took on more responsibilities at work	0.14 (0.14)
Retired	0.43 (0.24)
Change in household income (increasing)	0.07 (0.09)
Changes in Political Proximity and Perceptions of Politically Relevant Skills	
Change in political involvement (increasing)	0.07 (0.04)
Change in self-assessment of qualifications to run for office (increasing)	0.35 (0.08)**
Baseline level of political ambition (in Wave 1)	−1.38 (0.11)**
(Threshold − 2)	−8.92 (0.84)**
(Threshold − 1)	−3.81 (0.46)**
(Threshold 0)	1.05 (0.44)*
(Threshold + 1)	4.57 (0.63)**
Pseudo R-squared	0.23
N	1,388

Notes: Regression results are based on data from respondents who completed both the 2001 and 2008 surveys. The reduced number of cases results from listwise deletion. The equation also controls for the sex, race, and the baseline correlates of dynamic ambition presented in Table 4.3, as well as the politicized upbringing and family dynamics variables included in Table 5.10. Levels of significance: * $p < 0.05$; ** $p < 0.01$.

are not static gauges of concrete accomplishments or abilities that prepare eligible candidates to run for office.

Whereas recognizing individual-level shifts in qualifications is rather straightforward, identifying the underpinnings of eligible candidates' changing self-assessments is more complex. Respondents who were recruited to run for office between the two waves of the study, as well as those who engaged in more acts of political participation in 2008, as compared with 2001, were more likely to report stronger self-assessments of their qualifications. But changes in income, family dynamics, and interest in politics do not provide any leverage on explaining changes in respondents' perceptions of their qualifications to run. Even changes in attitudes toward politics and exposure to politicians, campaigns, and political institutions fail to shift self-perceived qualifications. Baseline demographics, such as race, age, sex, and party identification, are also not statistically significant. Quantitative measures may be limited in the extent to which they can capture the roots of what leads respondents to consider themselves qualified. These perceptions may be deeply rooted in personal psychology. Though it is possible to pinpoint only some of the sources of changes in these assessments, it is imperative to recognize the manner in which they fluctuate and the substantive impact they exert on explaining gains and losses in eligible candidates' political ambition over time.

Conclusion

When thinking about how best to "give back to the community," Kathy Taylor realized that her experience as a business executive and corporate lawyer positioned her well for politics. Serving first as state secretary of commerce and tourism and then as mayor of Tulsa, Oklahoma, Taylor explained that she first considered running for office when it occurred to her that she could "use all the skills [she] developed in business and [her] career to help the state."[22] Jay Christensen-Szalanski, a professor at the University of Iowa, concluded that the skills he developed teaching large lecture classes, as well as serving in the faculty senate, provided him with the credentials he needed to seek a position in the Iowa state house: "My main currency is my ideas and my experience at the university."[23] Darcy Burner spent years as a "software evangelist" who tried to convince small firms to write software for Microsoft products. She attributed her business success to Microsoft's excellent marketing. When Burner ran for the U.S. House of Representatives in Washington's 8th congressional district in 2006, she took the marketing lessons she learned in the corporate world onto the campaign trail: "You need a fairly simple idea that they can keep in their heads.... You've got to start simple: I'm a mother and businesswoman who wants to take the country in a different direction."[24]

Similar to the manner in which Kathy Taylor, Jay Christensen-Szalanski, and Darcy Burner attribute their entry into the political arena, at least in part, to their professional experiences, the quantitative and qualitative evidence presented in this chapter demonstrates that

[22] Cary Aspinwall, "Extreme Makeover: Forget Retirement. Baby Boom Women Dive into New Lives, Careers," *Tulsa World*, February 18, 2007.
[23] Bryce Bauer, "Senate Candidates Sport Different Styles," *Daily Iowan*, October 24, 2006.
[24] Jonathan Martin, "Political Novice Takes on GOP's Reichert," *Seattle Times*, May 15, 2006. Burner lost the race to Dave Reichert, whom she challenged unsuccessfully once again in 2008.

professional circumstances and credentials also affect eligible candidates' interest in running for office. The manner in which professional circumstances affect political ambition, however, transcends the specific fields in which eligible candidates work or the positions they hold. Political activists and lawyers are more likely than business leaders and educators to express interest in running for office not simply because they are political activists and lawyers, but rather, because they are more likely to have acquired politically relevant experiences and credentials throughout the course of their careers. More specifically, eligible candidates whose careers tend to confer a high level of political proximity, as well as those who perceive themselves to possess skills they use in their current careers that would transfer well to the political arena, are especially likely to consider running for office.

The findings in this chapter are instructive not only for identifying the professions and skills that are most likely to catapult ambition to run for office, but also for the study of candidate emergence more generally. The career path an individual selects at a relatively young age can shape his or her political ambitions well into the future. Without a certain degree of exposure to the political arena and the acquisition of politically relevant skills and traits, it is unlikely that an eligible candidate will consider running for office. Professional credentials and experiences that often seem only tenuously related to the decision to run for office, in other words, play a major role in fostering the nascent ambition that is a necessary condition for an eligible candidate to assess a political opportunity structure and consider entering a particular electoral contest at a given time.

7

You Think I Should Run for Office?

Political Parties, Political Recruitment, and Political Ambition

In a 2006 op-ed published in the *Philadelphia Inquirer*, Paul Hackett, who had recently dropped out of a U.S. Senate race in Ohio, reflected on the origins of his candidacy:

> When I got back from Iraq last year on March 18th after a seven-month combat tour with the First Marine Division in exotic cities like Ramadi and Fallujah, my wife arranged for a small group of friends and family to meet me at the Cincinnati airport. There, a good friend told me that U.S. Representative Rob Portman [(R–OH)] was about to resign and that I should run for the seat in southwest Ohio where I live and grew up. At first I thought he was kidding.

> But as I stood there in my desert utilities, tears running down my cheeks, my wife next to me, one kid on each leg and one in my arms for the first time in almost eight months, I thought of my service in Iraq, and the idea made sense. Service in Congress, as I saw it, would be a natural extension of service to my country in Iraq.[1]

Never before had Hackett considered running for office. But the strong beliefs about policies surrounding terrorism and national security that he acquired while serving in Iraq, coupled with the encouragement he received, propelled Hackett to run as the Democrat in a special election for Ohio's second congressional district. Although he lost the race to Republican Jean Schmidt, Hackett recounted that "the phone kept ringing." Impressed by his congressional campaign – Hackett had become a "political rock star" – U.S. Senators Harry Reid (D–NV) and Chuck Schumer (D–NY) implored Hackett to challenge Mike DeWine, Ohio's

---

[1] Paul Hackett, "Culture of Careerism Scuttled a Political Bid," *Philadelphia Inquirer*, February 28, 2006, page A11.

two-term Republican incumbent senator. Told that his country needed him, Hackett viewed the U.S. Senate race as "another opportunity to serve [his] country and [his] party."[2]

Recruitment by the Democratic Party also paved the way for Tammy Duckworth's decision to run for Congress in 2006. The previous year, U.S. Senator Dick Durbin (D–IL) invited wounded Illinois veterans to the State of the Union address. Duckworth, who had recently lost both legs in combat in Iraq, attended as one of the guests. A few months later, when she earned a promotion to major, she once again found herself face to face with Senator Durbin; Duckworth's new responsibilities involved advocating on behalf of military families and testifying before Congress about military health care. Amid the increasingly unpopular Iraq war, and in an attempt to refute the notion that Democrats were "soft" on national security, the party sought to convince veterans to enter U.S. House races in traditionally Republican districts.[3] So, Senator Durbin targeted Duckworth, who had never before considered a career in elective office. Within two months, Duckworth found herself on the campaign trail, often accompanied by Democratic heavy hitters such as Rahm Emanuel and Barack Obama.[4]

As the candidacies of Paul Hackett and Tammy Duckworth demonstrate, political parties can play a critical role in the candidate emergence process. Not only do eligible candidates' party affiliations often affect their issue priorities and policy preferences, but their exposure to and interaction with party officials and political elites can also generate the support and encouragement that bolster interest in running for office. This chapter focuses on the various ways that political party and political ambition intersect in the candidate eligibility pool. I begin with an examination of respondents' political views, ideology, and partisanship. Although the eligible candidates I surveyed and interviewed tend to hold strong views, the majority of which fall on the liberal side of the

[2] Shortly after Hackett entered the race, Senators Schumer and Reid threw their support behind Sherrod Brown. Facing fundraising difficulties and a lack of support from the political establishment, both locally and nationally, Hackett withdrew from the Democratic primary. Sherrod Brown went on to defeat Mike DeWine in the November 2006 general election.

[3] Naftali Bendavid, *The Thumpin': How Rahm Emanuel and the Democrats Learned to Be Ruthless and Ended the Republican Revolution.* New York: Doubleday, 2007.

[4] Peter Slevin, "After War Injury, an Iraq Vet Takes on Politics," *Washington Post*, February 19, 2006, page A01. Duckworth won a competitive Democratic primary against Christine Cegelis by a 4 percent margin, but lost the general election to Peter Roskam by 2 percentage points.

ideological spectrum, party affiliation does not predict political ambition. This null finding, however, should not be interpreted to mean that the parties exert little influence on interest in running for office. Rather, recruitment from party leaders, elected officials, and political activists is one of the most important predictors of whether a respondent considers a candidacy. Attitudes toward party leaders and political institutions also account for much of the variation in eligible candidates' political ambition over time. Overall, the evidence presented in this chapter demonstrates that political ambition is deeply intertwined with and related to the political parties, even if partisanship, itself, does not affect interest in running for office.

Eligible Candidates' Political Attitudes and Partisanship

As we have seen throughout this book, citizens with relatively high levels of political activism, interest, and proximity to the political arena are more likely to consider a candidacy. Specific issue motivations, however, often bolster an individual's propensity to participate politically. Indeed, Sidney Verba, Kay Lehman Schlozman, and Henry Brady (1995) recognize that having a direct stake in a policy may increase an individual's likelihood to engage the political system around that issue (see also Craig and O'Brien 1993; Verba and Nie 1972). Even citizens who tend to lack the time, money, and civic skills that foster political activism are more likely to participate when they are concerned about or directly affected by a particular policy. Among public assistance recipients, for example, severe economic hardship, as well as formative contact with government agents whom citizens living in urban poverty routinely face, bolsters the willingness to participate in the political system (Lawless and Fox 2001).

Issue passion spurs activism not only at the mass level, but also among political elites. Consider Erskine Bowles, who had served as President Bill Clinton's chief of staff and was living in New York at the time of the September 11, 2001 attacks. Although he had always been politically involved and connected, Bowles had never considered running for office, himself. September 11, however, sparked his political ambition: "I gave blood, I wrote some checks to charities, but it just wasn't enough. I decided I wanted to spend the rest of my life in public service."[5] Bowles moved back to his home state of North Carolina and entered the 2002

---

[5] Dawn Ziegenbalg, "Senate Candidate Bowles Visits Class at North Forsyth," *Winston-Salem Journal*, May 10, 2002, page B1.

U.S. Senate race, in which he defeated seven candidates to win the Democratic primary (although he lost the general election to Elizabeth Dole).

Many previously politically unconnected women and men responded to the events of September 11 with candidacies as well. Joe Finley, for example, was a New York firefighter who served as one of the first responders on September 11. He challenged Congressman Steve Israel in 2002, largely because of experiences at Ground Zero: "I feel compelled to try to help, to make sure that we don't get complacent about what happened. We need someone in Congress who's worked down there, not just people who passed through there for a photo."[6] Adam Taff, a pilot who had flown from Washington, DC, to Los Angeles on September 10, entered a 2002 congressional race in Kansas because he considered himself lucky enough not to be flying the day of the attacks; he wanted to give back by entering a career of public service.[7] Texas attorney and former marine Mike Ortega initially planned to respond to the attacks by reenlisting. At age 33, though, he was told that he was too old. He decided, instead, to challenge Martin Frost for his seat in the U.S. House of Representatives.[8]

More generally, David Canon (1990) finds that strong policy goals serve as motivating factors for congressional candidates who have no previous political experience (see also Wilson 1962). Other studies reveal that, once individuals actually seek and hold state legislative positions, ideological preferences and passion often motivate their agendas (e.g., Swers 2002; Thomas 1994). Similar results apply at the congressional level. In fact, members of the U.S. House of Representatives with relatively long congressional careers, but who do not hold powerful positions, are much more likely to retire than are their less experienced and more powerful colleagues (Lawless and Theriault 2005; see also Fisher and Herrick 2002; Theriault 1998). These voluntary retirements occur because members do not have the power (through their committee assignments) to exert sufficient influence over the policy areas for which they are passionate and responsible.[9] It follows, therefore, that individuals

---

[6] Malia Rulon, "September 11 Inspires Novice Candidates," *Associated Press*, October 21, 2002.

[7] Dave Ranney and Eric Weslander, "Ex-Candidate Taff Indicted Over Home Loan," *Lawrence Journal World and News*, August 18, 2005. Accessed at http://www2.ljworld.com/news/2005/aug/18/excandidate_taff_indicted_over_home_loan/?state_regional (January 16, 2011).

[8] Dawn Ziegenbalg (note 5).

[9] The effect of reaching a career ceiling is more dramatic for women than men, perhaps because of gender differences motivating the decision to run for Congress. Whereas men seem to be satisfied – at least in part – by mere service in the House, women might need

might be more likely to contemplate a candidacy when an ideological drive accompanies their resource base.

To assess the extent to which political views affect interest in running for office, it is important first to examine eligible candidates' issue positions and priorities. The top half of Table 7.1 lists five broad policy statements with which respondents were asked to express their levels of agreement. Two important trends emerge from the data. First, regarding four of the five issues, the majority of respondents fall on the left side of the ideological spectrum. More specifically, from gun control and reproductive freedom to hate crime legislation and universal health care, at least 56 percent of respondents favor a relatively progressive position. Only on the issue of taxes does more than half the sample voice more moderate policy preferences.[10] Overall, these issue preferences are somewhat more liberal than the respondents' self-designated political ideology (see Chapter 2, Table 2.1). Of course, roughly half the sample identifies as "moderate," a likely result of citizens' tendency to eschew "extreme" labels.[11] The second central finding to emerge from the top half of the table is that, across issues, eligible candidates are very willing to express their opinions. At least 75 percent of respondents either agree or disagree with each policy statement, even though "neither agree nor disagree" was an available option to select.

Not only do respondents hold strong positions regarding a series of public policy issues, but they also consider many of these issues important motivators for political activism. Overall, the average respondent deems 3.4 of the eight fiscal and social policy issues with which he or she was presented "very important." In all but one case (gay rights), more respondents consider the issue "very important" than "not very" or "not at all

policy influence to satisfy their career goals, since policy influence, and not status, often leads them to seek office initially (Fox 1997; Bledsoe and Herring 1990; Costantini 1990).

[10] On a broad host of these fiscal and social policy issues – taxes, abortion, health care, and crime – women are significantly more likely than men to express progressive attitudes. The same general pattern is true in the general population. For recent analyses of the intersection of gender, voting behavior, political ideology, and attitudes about contemporary policy issues, see Norrander and Wilcox 2008; Simon and Hoyt 2008; Whitaker 2008; Jennings 2006.

[11] It is also important to recognize that belief systems of the mass public are multidimensional, so many individuals hold liberal preferences on one dimension and conservative preferences on another. These cross-pressured individuals tend to self-identify as moderate when asked to place themselves on the liberal–conservative scale (Treier and Hillygus 2009).

TABLE 7.1. *Eligible Candidates' Policy Preferences and Issue Priorities*

	"Agree" or "Strongly Agree"	"Disagree" or "Strongly Disagree"
Policy Preferences		
More gun control laws should be passed.	65%	25%
Abortion should always be legal in the first trimester.	64	23
Congress should enact hate crime legislation.	57	25
The U.S. should move toward universal health care.	56	29
Taxes are too high.	52	23
	Issue is "Very Important"	Issue is "Not Very Important"
Issue Priorities		
Education	60	3
Economy	44	7
Health care	42	11
Foreign policy	38	10
Environment	35	15
Abortion	33	27
Crime	25	21
Gay rights	14	56
N	3,544	

Notes: Results are based on the 2001 survey data. For policy preferences, cell entries in each row do not total 100 percent because respondents could also choose "neither agree nor disagree" for each policy. For issue priorities, the "not very important" column also includes respondents who considered each issue "not at all important" (no more than 5 percent of respondents assessed any issue this way). Cell entries in each row do not total 100 percent because respondents could also choose "important" as a response.

important" (see bottom of Table 7.1).[12] The policies around which there is the most consensus, however, are not, necessarily, the policies that promote activism. Consider the case of reproductive freedom. Nearly two-thirds of respondents believe that abortion should always be legal in the first trimester, yet only one-third of respondents consider the issue "very important" to them. In another example, whereas a majority of

[12] Notably, men are less inclined than women to rate almost all issues as "very important" determinants of their political activity. This finding suggests that women may be more likely than men to view politics as an avenue through which to implement policy goals (see also Lawless and Fox 2010, chapter 5).

the eligible candidates surveyed contend that Congress should enact hate crime legislation, only about one of every eight respondents places gay rights on his or her issue priority list. Rather, education, the economy, and health care round out the sample's issue priorities.[13]

Despite some variation in the sample as far as ideology, policy preferences, and issue priorities are concerned, these differences confer virtually no explanatory power when we turn to interest in running for office. The data presented in Table 7.2 make clear that neither self-designated political ideology, nor issue passion for any particular policy or policy domain, accounts for political ambition. Approximately 50 percent of liberals, moderates, and conservatives have considered running for office. And roughly half the eligible candidates who feel strongly about each issue have considered running for office, whereas the other half have not.

The same null finding holds in a multivariate context. Table 7.3 presents the percentage of Democrats, independents, and Republicans who have considered running for office, as well as the predicted probabilities, by political party, that result from the logistic regression equation that models whether a respondent ever considered running for office (see Table 6.4). No statistically significant differences emerge at either the bivariate level or from the multiple regression analysis; party identification does not predict interest in running for office.[14]

It is important to recognize, however, that even though party affiliation and ideology do not, in and of themselves, affect eligible candidates' political ambition to seek office, party can still play an important role

---

[13] The data regarding issue priorities and positions come from the 2001 survey, which was conducted prior to the war in Iraq and the economic downturn that began in 2007. The purpose in presenting these data is not to identify the most important issues of the day, but rather, to demonstrate the broad policy preferences and magnitude of political priorities. I expect that eligible candidates would confer greater importance to the economy as a pressing issue if asked the question today.

[14] Men in the eligibility pool, regardless of party affiliation, are approximately one-third more likely than women to have thought about seeking public office. The gender gap is remarkably consistent across the three party identifications. Democratic women are no more likely than Republican or independent women to consider running for office. These findings suggest, therefore, that substantially more women officeholders identify as Democrats than as Republicans not because Democratic women are particularly likely to be politically ambitious, but rather, because women in the candidate eligibility pool are much more likely to be Democrats than Republicans (see Lawless and Fox 2010, chapter 5). When I add interaction terms between sex and party identification, the results remain the same. The coefficients are in the expected directions (Female * Democrat is positive; Female * Republican is negative), but neither coefficient approaches statistical significance (p > 0.60 in both cases).

TABLE 7.2. *Bivariate Relationship Between Political Ideology, Issue Priorities, and Considering a Candidacy*

	Considered Running for Office
Political Ideology	
Liberal	54%
Moderate	50
Conservative	51
Issue Priorities (respondent considers the issue "very important" when participating politically)	
Foreign policy	54
Gay rights	54
Environment	53
Economy	52
Abortion	52
Education	50
Health care	50
Crime	45
N	3,496

Notes: Results are based on the 2001 survey data. Number of cases varies slightly, as some respondents omitted answers to some questions.

in the candidate emergence process. After all, political parties are often critical in candidate recruitment and nomination, especially at the state legislative and congressional levels (Jewell and Morehouse 2001; Aldrich 2000). Party organizations' leaders, elected officials, and activists serve as formal electoral gatekeepers who groom eligible candidates to run for office. Any thorough assessment of the manner in which partisanship and political parties shape interest in running for office, therefore, must also include an examination of the candidate recruitment process.

Who Gets Asked to Run for Office?

In October 1991, the U.S. Senate readied for a vote to confirm Clarence Thomas to the Supreme Court. The nomination had already moved from the Judiciary Committee to the floor of the Senate when Anita Hill, a law professor at the University of Oklahoma, reluctantly accused Thomas of making unwanted sexual advances toward her when she worked under his supervision at the Equal Employment Opportunity Commission. Forced

TABLE 7.3. *Considering a Candidacy, by Party: Bivariate and Multivariate Comparisons*

	Democrat	Republican	Independent
Have you ever considered running for office?			
Yes, I have seriously considered it.	14%	16%	14%
Yes, it has crossed my mind.	39	34	36
No, I have never thought about it.	47	50	50
Predicted Probability of Considering a Candidacy *(based on regression equation presented in Table 6.4)*	0.61	0.57	0.57

Notes: Results are based on the 2001 survey data. For the bivariate comparisons of interest in running for office by party, N = 3,461. The predicted probabilities are based on setting the variables included in Table 6.4 to their respective means. Dummy variables are held constant at their modes. None of the comparisons achieves conventional levels of statistical significance.

to conduct additional hearings, several members of the all-male Senate Judiciary Committee criticized Hill for coming forward so many years after the alleged incidents occurred. Many questioned the validity of her claims, even suggesting that Hill committed perjury in her FBI affidavit when recounting her interactions with Thomas (Miller 1994). Following four days of televised hearings and debates, the 98 percent male Senate ultimately voted 52–48 to confirm Clarence Thomas.

Angered by the manner in which the Senate handled Thomas's confirmation, a number of Democratic women candidates sought and won seats in the 103rd Congress. As Senator Barbara Boxer (D–CA) (1994, 39–40) summarized:

> The American public realized that Anita Hill struck an honest chord; Clarence Thomas struck a disturbing chord; and the Senate Judiciary Committee, looking like a relic from another time and place, struck a chord of irrelevancy. And all of these chords played together had a very dissonant sound.... The Anita Hill incident became a catalyst for change.

Of course, the Clarence Thomas confirmation hearings did not serve as the only catalyst for 1992's "Year of the Woman" elections. The record number of women candidates represented the culmination of several factors: an increase in the number of open seats as a result of the decennial census, an electoral context dominated by "women-friendly issues," and higher than usual levels of voter discontent with government and incumbents (see Dolan 1998; Wilcox 1994). This environment, however, translated into women's candidacies and victories in large part only because the Democratic Party recognized a favorable set of circumstances that paved the way for the party to recruit women to run in targeted districts.

Indeed, scholars have long known that contemporary dynamics often drive patterns of political recruitment and that electoral gatekeepers are strategic in their recruitment efforts (Maestas, Maisel, and Stone 2005). Even the earliest research identified socially stratified patterns of candidate recruitment, not only for the highest elective offices (Matthews 1984; Aberbach, Putnam, and Rockman 1981), but also for the state legislature (Seligman et al. 1974) and the city council (Prewitt 1970b). Although encouragement from political parties can be instrumental in propelling a candidacy for anyone, political parties tend not to tap "just anyone" to run for office.

Who gets asked to run for office, and do Democrats and Republicans recruit the same types of people? To begin to answer these questions, the survey asked respondents whether they ever received the suggestion to run for any political office from a party leader, elected official, or political activist (this includes nonelected individuals working for interest groups and community organizations). Certainly, not all political offices are alike, and patterns of recruitment might vary across level of office. But overall, as illustrated in Figure 7.1, half the Democrats in the sample, and nearly half the Republicans and independents, report receiving the suggestion to run for office from at least one of these electoral gatekeepers. A few party differences do emerge, though. Democrats are roughly one-third more likely than Republicans to receive encouragement to run for office from nonelected activists; Republicans, by contrast, are approximately 15 percent more likely than Democrats to report recruitment efforts from party leaders and elected officials (differences significant at $p < 0.05$). Not surprisingly, independents are less likely than their partisan counterparts to receive encouragement to run for office from party leaders and elected officials.

Because encouragement to run for elective office is perceived more seriously as the number of recruitment contacts increases, the 2008 survey included a battery of questions about the breadth and frequency with which the eligible candidates have been recruited. Figure 7.2 presents data pertaining to two types of recruitment intensity: whether the respondent received encouragement to run by all three types of gatekeepers and whether the respondent was recruited to run at least three times by any one gatekeeper. On both measures of recruitment intensity, no substantive

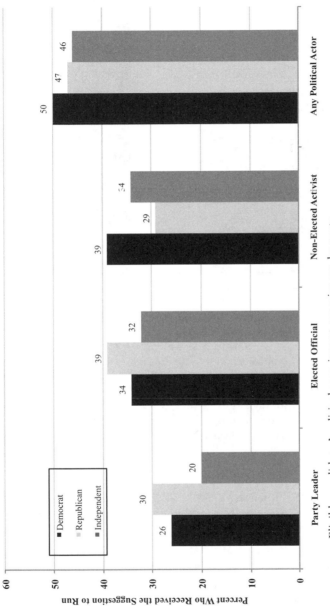

FIGURE 7.1. Eligible candidates' political recruitment experiences, by party.

Notes: Results are based on the 2008 survey data. Chi-square tests comparing differences across party affiliation are significant at p < 0.05 for recruitment from party leaders and nonelected activists. Sample sizes: for Democrats, N = 925; for Republicans, N = 527; and for independents, N = 390.

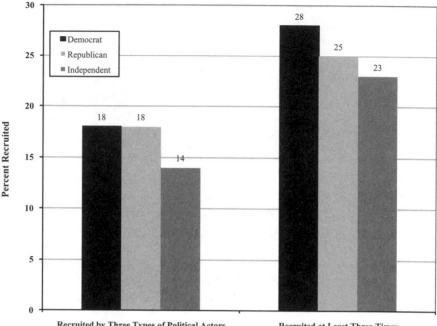

FIGURE 7.2. Frequency and breadth of eligible candidates' political recruitment experiences, by party.

Notes: Results are based on the 2008 survey data. Chi-square tests comparing differences between Democrats and Republicans fail to achieve statistical significance. Independents are statistically less likely than both Democrats and Republicans to have received the suggestion to run for office by three political actors; independents are statistically less likely than Democrats to have been recruited to run at least three times by any one political actor ($p < 0.05$). Sample sizes: for Democrats, $N = 925$; for Republicans, $N = 527$; and for independents, $N = 390$.

or statistically significant differences separate Democrats from Republicans. Independents, however, are less likely to receive broad, sustained recruitment efforts, more evidence that they operate in fewer partisan circles from which party leaders and elected officials recruit candidates.

The aggregate data tell a story that suggests comparable levels of political recruitment by the two major political parties. These data, however, obscure significant professional and gender differences in Democratic and Republican patterns of recruitment. Turning first to professional differences, Democratic and Republican lawyers are significantly more likely to report having been recruited to run for office than are business leaders or educators. More specifically, among lawyers, 40 percent of Democrats and 41 percent of Republicans report receiving encouragement to run for office from a party leader, elected official, or political activist. By contrast, only one-quarter of Democratic and 20 percent of Republican business leaders and educators report such recruitment efforts (party differences for educators and business leaders not significant at $p < 0.05$). As we might expect, political activists represent the professional subsample most likely to receive encouragement to run for office from political gatekeepers. Republican activists, however, are at a particular advantage: 61 percent of Democratic and 72 percent of Republican activists were recruited to run for office. This statistically significant difference is driven in large part by the fact that Republican activists are approximately 60 percent more likely than their Democratic counterparts to report recruitment by an elected official (36 percent of Democrats, compared with 58 percent of Republicans). Consistent with the findings in Chapter 6, the bivariate data suggest, therefore, that professional subcultures play a role in positioning eligible candidates for political recruitment, and that the Republican Party is more likely than the Democratic Party to tap fellow activists to join the ranks.

The party differences by gender are more striking. The results from the 2001 survey indicate that, among Republicans, men are two-thirds more likely than women ever to have received the suggestion to run for office from a gatekeeper (25 percent of women, compared with 42 percent of men; difference significant at $p < 0.05$). Among Democrats, the gender gap is still substantively important and statistically significant, but much smaller (36 percent of women and 47 percent of men report recruitment by an electoral gatekeeper).[15] These party differences are consistent with the party gap among elected officials.[16] By 2008, however, the gender gap in political recruitment among Democrats decreased from 11 percentage points to 6 percentage points. The gender gap in political

---

[15] These gender differences are generally comparable across professions. Women attorneys and educators are significantly less likely than men to be tapped to run for office by party leaders, elected officials, and political activists. Among businesspeople, the ratio of men to women who have been recruited is comparable, although not statistically significant.

[16] In the 112th Congress, approximately 70 percent of the women serving in the House of Representatives and Senate are Democrats. Seventy percent of all women serving in state senates are Democrats, as are 71 percent of women serving in the states' lower chambers. The numbers of women occupying most statewide offices, such as governor and attorney general, reveal a similar partisan divide: of the 73 women who hold statewide elective positions, 50 affiliate with the Democratic Party. Democratic women outnumber Republican women in roughly 90 percent of state legislatures. By contrast, at both the federal and state levels, the majority of male legislators are Republicans.

recruitment among Republican respondents decreased slightly, to 13 percentage points.

The party gap in women's political recruitment does not appear to result from divergent strategies by the parties, or more concerted, systematic recruitment activities by Democratic leaders and elected officials. Democratic and Republican women are equally unlikely to have received encouragement to run for office from elected officials (32 percent). And Democratic women (23 percent) are about as unlikely as Republican women (25 percent) to report recruitment from party leaders. The smaller recruitment gap among Democrats, therefore, can be attributed to the party gap in recruitment from political activists. Thirty-six percent of Democratic women, compared with 24 percent of Republican women, have been recruited to run for office by a political activist in the community (gender difference significant at $p < 0.05$).[17]

Multiple regressiom analysis lends support to the central findings uncovered at the bivariate level. Table 7.4 presents a logistic regression equation predicting whether a respondent received the suggestion to run from an electoral gatekeeper. The model, which relies on the 2008 survey data, controls for basic demographics, party identification, and the types of political participation and proximity that facilitate direct contact with political actors who might suggest a candidacy. As is the case at the aggregate level, party identification does not predict whether a respondent receives the suggestion to run from an electoral gatekeeper. And as we would expect, eligible candidates who are politically active and well connected to the political arena are particularly likely to receive encouragement to run for office.

Even after accounting for political participation and proximity, though, the gender gap in recruitment is dramatic. Women are 18 percentage points less likely than men to have a political actor suggest that they run for office. The typical woman has a 0.44 predicted probability of being recruited to run for office, compared with the 0.62 likelihood of her typical male counterpart. Politically active women who occupy the same professional spheres as politically active men are not equally

---

[17] For a nuanced discussion of gender differences in political recruitment, see Fox and Lawless 2010 and Lawless and Fox 2010. We argue that gender differences in political recruitment across parties are likely the result of the work of women's organizations, both nonpartisan and those affiliated with a particular political party or its positions and priorities. Because the objective of many of these organizations is to promote progressive women's candidacies, they likely disproportionately propel Democratic women into the circles and networks from which candidates tend to emerge.

TABLE 7.4. *Who Gets Recruited to Run for Office by Electoral Gatekeepers? (Logistic Regression Coefficients, Standard Errors, and Change in Probabilities)*

	Coefficient (and Standard Error)	Maximum Change in Probability (percentage points)
Sociodemographic Factors		
Sex (female)	-0.73 $(0.14)^{**}$	18.0
Black	0.68 $(0.25)^{**}$	14.3
Latino/a	-0.15 (0.29)	–
Income	0.03 (0.06)	–
Education	-0.16 $(0.07)^{*}$	16.4
Political Factors		
Democrat	0.24 (0.23)	–
Republican	0.34 (0.24)	–
Political participation	0.31 $(0.04)^{**}$	59.3
Proximity to the Political Environment		
Worked or volunteered on a campaign	0.81 $(0.15)^{**}$	19.9
Attended a political meeting	0.54 $(0.18)^{**}$	13.2
Served on a nonprofit board	0.42 $(0.15)^{**}$	10.2
Attended political party meeting or event	0.37 $(0.15)^{*}$	9.1
Interacted with elected officials at work	0.93 $(0.14)^{**}$	22.8
Contact with women's organization(s)	2.42 $(0.24)^{**}$	32.9
Constant	-3.52 $(0.57)^{**}$	–
Percent correctly predicted	77.9	
Pseudo R-squared	0.47	
N	1,660	

Notes: Results are based on the 2008 survey data. Maximum changes in probabilities are based on the logistic regression results. Probabilities were calculated by setting all continuous independent variables not under consideration to their means and dummy variables not under consideration to their modes. The change in probability reflects the independent effect a statistically significant variable exerts as I vary its value from its minimum to maximum (i.e., the change in probability for Sex (female) reflects the fact that a woman is 18.0 percentage points less likely than a man, all else equal, to receive the suggestion to run for office from an electoral gatekeeper). Significance levels: * $p < 0.05$; ** $p < 0.01$.

sought by electoral gatekeepers, regardless of the side of the political aisle on which they find themselves. These findings are consistent with studies that argue that political parties have historically been enclaves of male dominance that contribute to women's underrepresentation.[18] More specifically, both because of overt bias on the part of party leaders

[18] See, for example, Freeman 2000; Carroll 1994; Bernstein 1986; Rule 1981; Fowlkes, Perkins, and Tolleson-Rinehart 1979; Welch 1978; Diamond 1977.

(Niven 2006, 1998), as well as a tendency to recruit from their own male-dominated networks (Sanbonmatsu 2006), parties' recruitment practices continue to embody a masculinized ethos that favors the selection of male candidates.

Minority status, however, does not appear to depress racial minorities' likelihood of being encouraged to run for office in the same way it does women's. All else equal, and across political parties and professions, black eligible candidates are more than 14 percentage points more likely than their white and Latino counterparts to report having been recruited to run for office by an electoral gatekeeper. Neither the survey data nor the interview evidence sheds much light on why this might be the case. A few respondents did mention that they have witnessed party operatives and elected officials reach out to racial minorities to broaden the party's appeal. A political activist from New Jersey, for example, noted that he and his colleagues "do everything possible to identify racially diverse candidates." Bob Lerner and Phyllis Nathan, both of whom practice law, also commented on the appeal that black lawyers in their firms appear to have for both political parties. Nathan, a Democrat, recounted "numerous conversations" with the vice chair of the state party in which she was asked to introduce him to partners in the firm who might be open to running for a county-level position. She recalls that the party leader's enthusiasm "went through the roof" when she arranged a meeting with a colleague who happened to be African American. Lerner relayed a similar story about the Republican Party chair:

> He [the party chair] has a lunch at the firm every year or so, just to see whether there might be some attorneys who would be willing to write fat checks or maybe even one day run for office. He never says it, but it's clear that he's especially interested in [people of color.] They can probably fund their own races, and they'd send the signal that the Republicans are working hard to broaden their base.

Although we should be careful generalizing from these eligible candidates' experiences to the broader political pipeline, it may be the case that the parties place more of a premium on racial, as opposed to gender, diversity when recruiting candidates to run for office.

Political Recruitment and Considering a Candidacy

The extent to which political parties cast their nets when recruiting candidates is critical not only because it highlights the sociodemographic and social stratification within the candidate recruitment process, but also because it highlights the important role parties play in the candidate emergence process. Stacey DeBoise Luster, for example, had always been involved in her Worcester, Massachusetts, community. Indeed, it was her connection to several nonprofit organizations in the area that helped her "develop as leader." But she did not consider running for the city council in 1997 until politically connected colleagues in these organizations encouraged her to take the plunge: "They planted the seed, and then the community and the ministers came and said they would help."[19] Party recruitment was also vital for Patty Wetterling's eventual candidacy. The mother of an abducted child, Ms. Wetterling successfully advocated for the national AMBER Alert system and was instrumental in passing federal legislation that required states to implement registries of individuals who commit crimes against children.[20] But until the Democrats heavily recruited her to run for Congress when their presumed candidate withdrew from the 2004 race in Minnesota's 6th district, Ms. Wetterling had never "really seriously considered [running]" at all.[21] Even U.S. House Minority Leader Nancy Pelosi (D–CA) – who was a Democratic activist from an early age – did not consider entering the political arena as a candidate, herself, until Congresswoman Sala Burton, who was dying of cancer, urged Pelosi to run. She ran for Burton's House seat in 1988 and has represented the San Francisco Bay Area ever since.[22]

The power of political recruitment came through in the interviews with eligible candidates. In fact, for many individuals, recruitment from political leaders served as the key ingredient in fomenting their consideration of a candidacy. Attorney Mark Powers, for example, considered running for the state legislature because Republican Party leaders suggested that he do it: "That was really influential for me. You need to have the party's support in order to have a viable run for any office. That's so ingrained in me that running wouldn't have occurred to me without the suggestion from the party." Tim Barry, an attorney from Michigan, offered a similar reflection:

> I had never really thought about running for office. Well, not in any serious way. But about 5 years ago, I was at a town meeting; I try to go every month.

19 Clive McFarlane, "Perennial Candidate Urged to Run," *Telegram and Gazette*, July 20, 2007, page B1.
20 Tom Schenck, "Wetterling Foundation Ponders Its Future in a Political World," *Minnesota Public Radio*, March 10, 2006.
21 Greg Gordon, "Wetterling Sets Her Sights on House Seat; Experts Say She is a Long Shot Against Incumbent Kennedy," *Star Tribune*, April 27, 2004, page 1A.
22 Dana Wilkie, "From Political Roots to Political Leader, Pelosi is the Real Thing," *Copley News Service*, November 13, 2002.

We were talking about the next elections and that we needed candidates. The minute the Republican Committee chair mentioned that he thought I'd be great in office, he had me. I never realized it until he said the words, but I guess I was waiting for someone to suggest that I think about running.

Marsha Pollack, a high school principal from New England, also first thought about running for office after party officials raised the idea of a candidacy. She explained:

I was on the board of a women's fund and we were discussing the open seat for county commissioner. Someone on the board said that I should run, and the rest of the board members jumped on the bandwagon. I laughed it off. But a couple of days later, a woman who had run for governor a few years back and is now an influential party operative called me. She told me that I would make a great candidate and should think seriously about the commissioner position. For the first time in my life, I actually started thinking about running for office.

In some cases, encouragement from party organizations and electoral gatekeepers even spurred actual candidacies, as was the case for Dan Warton, who currently operates a business in West Virginia:

I once ran for Democratic Alderman back when I lived in Buffalo. It was a pretty low-key thing. Someone from the Democratic Council asked me to run, I did, and then I got the most votes. Since then, I have thought about running for the state legislature. Colleagues and party officials have all asked me to run. I know a lot of politicians. I know all the state legislators, too. I have the right connections with the party, so it's something that might be possible.

Even respondents who never received encouragement to run for office from a party leader or elected official are cognizant of the legitimacy and viability that recruitment efforts confer. Men and women – across parties – intimated that such support would bolster their willingness to run for office. A Nashville, Tennessee, businesswoman epitomized this sentiment when she explained that she cannot really think about running for office because she does not have support from a political party: "I have never really thought about running in a serious way because I'm not a card carrying member of a party. I'm an issues person, not a party person. Colleagues and friends would be supportive, but without the party leaders, it's hard to imagine running a viable campaign, let alone winning." A college dean from a small liberal arts college in Maine drew the same conclusion: "I'm not politically naïve enough to think that the kind of support I've had [from colleagues and friends] to run for mayor means anything. I'm not politically connected. I have very little name recognition. Without party support, there's nothing to consider." Jason Madden, an attorney in Arizona, consistently receives suggestions from colleagues and clients to run for the city council. He dismisses this encouragement as "nice enough, but not sufficient. Until the party approaches [him], it just seems silly to think about it." A lack of recruitment has also kept an Illinois high school principal from running, despite her political interest:

> Sadly, the only person who has ever told me I should run is my husband. He always tells me that I'd be a good candidate because I listen well and I'm smart and I consider different sides of an issue before making any decisions.... If I had more support, particularly the support of those from the party.... I [would] be more likely to run.

Several respondents even indicated that recruitment would serve as the only catalyst for a serious consideration of a candidacy:

> People have suggested that I run for office, but nothing that serious. It's not like I've had members of political parties lined up with volunteers to pass out fliers and get my name out there. That's what it'd take to get me to really consider running for any position. (Carrie Hodge, political activist, Maryland)

> Last year, a group of people started talking to me about running for the State Supreme Court. There was a vacancy and they thought I knew the right people and had the right personality to run. I told them, "Tell the governor and the party chair to call me and tell me and then I'll think about it." They never called. And I never thought much more about it. (Patrick Sewell, attorney, Oregon)

> If I had serious people, like party officials, urging me to run, I wouldn't be able to not think about doing it. (Jason Roberts, educator, Pennsylvania)

> I'd run if someone from one of the political parties said they wanted me to run. I'm very easily influenced. It's just that right now, there's not enough support. (Roberta Simmons, political activist, Ohio)

In total, 73 of the 300 women and men with whom I spoke raised at some point during the interview the notion that party support would enhance their likelihood of considering a candidacy.

To demonstrate more broadly the substantive effects of political recruitment, Table 7.5 presents the coefficients and predicted probabilities from a logistic regression equation that models whether a respondent ever considered running for office. In addition to the main explanatory variable – whether the respondent ever received the suggestion to run from an electoral gatekeeper – I control for all of the correlates of political ambition that have been introduced and analyzed in previous chapters.

TABLE 7.5. *Impact of Political Recruitment on Considering a Candidacy (Logistic Regression Coefficients, Standard Errors, and Change in Probabilities)*

	Coefficient (and Standard Error)	Maximum Change in Probability (percentage points)
Political Recruitment		
Recruited by an electoral gatekeeper	1.02 (0.11)**	9.0
Professional Factors		
Income	−0.18 (0.04)**	13.4
Self-assessed qualifications to run for office	0.61 (0.06)**	21.4
Family Dynamics (in Childhood and Adulthood)		
Encouraged to run for office by family member	0.88 (0.12)**	15.0
Encouraged to run for office by spouse/partner	0.97 (0.13)**	17.0
"Political" household index	0.12 (0.05)**	9.8
Parent ran for office	0.34 (0.14)*	5.0
Ran for office as a student	0.30 (0.10)**	3.4
Minority Status		
Sex (female)	−0.52 (0.10)**	5.5
Black	−0.62 (0.17)**	6.3
Latino/a	−0.35 (0.21)	−
Indicators of Political Engagement		
Political knowledge	0.09 (0.06)	−
Political interest	0.03 (0.04)	−
Political efficacy	0.08 (0.05)	−
Political participation	0.13 (0.03)**	14.0
Electoral Features and Opportunities		
Size of the congressional delegation	−0.00 (0.01)	−
Size of the state political opportunity structure	0.00 (0.00)	−
Size of the local political opportunity structure	0.00 (0.00)	−
Term limits	0.22 (0.12)	−
Part-time legislature	0.24 (0.13)	−
Legislative salary	0.00 (0.00)	−
Political Dynamics		
Democrat	0.21 (0.13)	−
Republican	0.02 (0.14)	−
Percent Democratic presidential vote share	−0.01 (0.01)	−
Party congruence with the congressional delegation	0.01 (0.12)	−
Party congruence with the state legislature	−0.20 (0.12)	
Constant	−2.83 (0.59)**	−
Percent correctly predicted	77.9	
Pseudo R-squared	0.48	
N	3,055	

Notes: Regression results are based on the 2001 data. Probabilities were calculated by setting all continuous independent variables to their means and dummy variables to their modes. The change in probability reflects the independent effect a statistically significant variable exerts as I vary it from its minimum to maximum. Significance levels: * $p < 0.05$; ** $p < 0.01$.

Support from electoral gatekeepers provides a large boost in eligible candidates' political ambition.[23] Both men and women who receive encouragement to run are significantly more likely than those who receive no such support to think about running for office. Consider an otherwise average male respondent who receives support to run for office from a spouse and family member. Political recruitment from an electoral gatekeeper increases his likelihood of considering a candidacy from 0.29 to 0.53. A similarly situated woman who has not been recruited by a gatekeeper has only a 0.20 likelihood of considering a run for office. Women who receive support from a party leader, elected official, or political activist have a 0.41 probability of considering a candidacy. Thus, not only does recruitment increase the likelihood of considering a run for office, but it can also partially close the gender gap and race gap in political ambition. Moreover, political recruitment can offset any disadvantage a respondent suffers from not growing up in a politicized home.

The quantitative and qualitative evidence supports the claim that recruitment by electoral gatekeepers spurs eligible candidates' interest in and willingness to run for office. Comments from women and men who have been recruited reflect the political viability conveyed by gatekeepers' suggestions to run; party support brings the promise of an organization that will work on behalf of a candidate. Statements from individuals who have yet to receive political support for a candidacy demonstrate that, without encouragement, a political candidacy feels far less feasible. External support is important to eligible candidates from all political parties and professional backgrounds, so even if party affiliation does not predict political ambition, the parties with which eligible candidates are affiliated can certainly promote their interest in running for office.

Changes in Relationships With and About the Political Parties: Predicting Dynamic Ambition

Public opinion scholars have documented declining levels of political trust and increasing cynicism toward government for the past forty years (see Clawson and Oxley 2008). Much of this research links distrust of government to monumental events, such as the Vietnam War and the riots and demonstrations accompanying the civil rights movement (Hetherington

---

[23] When I substitute measures of recruitment intensity for the overall measure of ever having been recruited to run for office by a gatekeeper, the same variables achieve statistical significance, although the magnitude of recruitment's impact is somewhat greater.

2005). Shorter-term political and economic circumstances, however, can also fuel fluctuations in political trust, as can presidential behavior and approval ratings (Keele 2007). Timothy Cook and Paul Gronke (2005), for example, find that Americans' trust in government increased following September 11, 2001, and then gradually declined.

Consistent with the extant literature, the evidence from the interviews reveals that vagaries in the political climate between the two waves of the study moved many eligible candidates to acquire more negative views of government and the political system. Don Jackson, the executive director of a nonprofit organization in Mississippi, highlighted this phenomenon by explaining that he had not changed between 2001 and 2008, but that politics had: "I am a Democrat, always have been, and always will be. But national politics is now a disaster. The fighting, the positioning. Makes me doubt that anything meaningful will ever get done." Hank Wright, who has worked as an environmentalist in Alaska for more than two decades, agreed:

> I never had a *Mr. Smith Goes to Washington* outlook, but twenty years ago when I'd testify at congressional hearings, actually even ten years ago, the committee chair and the members were real statesmen. No more. They receive factually wrong information from interest groups that don't believe in science. Some of them have probably never heard of the Congressional Research Service. They're often rude and make very clear that they have no interest in acquiring new information or hearing opposing viewpoints. It's all about positioning themselves and winning a fight.

Charlotte Kramer, a high school principal in Missouri, also referenced the extent to which the last five years have been a "political turnoff": "Swift Boat Veterans for Truth. People standing on roof tops in New Orleans. George Bush. Karl Rove. Do I need to say more? I am a Republican and I am conservative. But this is not how politics should be." Respondents also raised former New York Governor Eliot Spitzer's sex scandal, allegations of sexual harassment in the Illinois attorney general's office, former Connecticut Governor John Rowland's resignation and subsequent imprisonment, Vice President Dick Cheney's ties to Enron, and the financial indiscretions and illegalities committed by former members of Congress, including Tom DeLay (R–TX), Bob Ney (R–OH), Randy "Duke" Cunningham (R–CA), and William Jefferson (D–LA), as evidence that "the system is broken." According to Kate Bender, an attorney from Olympia, Washington, "Politics has become a dangerous sport that, ironically, always ends in a tie. Both parties are to blame. I'm still a Republican. But not a proud one. My husband is still a Democrat. But he's disgusted, too."

Indeed, changes in ideological or partisan identification were very rare. Only 1 percent of eligible candidates who considered themselves liberal in 2001 identified as conservative in 2008; the same is true when we consider movement from the conservative side to the liberal side of the ideological spectrum. The numbers for changes in party identification, though somewhat higher (4 percent of Republicans came to consider themselves Democrats and 1 percent of Democrats became Republicans), are still extremely low. But even though respondents did not change their party affiliation or ideology, they did alter their attitudes toward the parties and the political system. Nearly two-thirds of both Democrats and Republicans became more cynical toward government between 2001 and 2008. Moreover, nine of ten Democrats, as well as nearly one-third of Republicans, developed animosity toward the Bush administration. Three-quarters of Republicans, along with half the Democrats in the sample, grew frustrated with the Democratic Congress (see Figure 7.3). The data also reveal that during this seven-year interval, respondents began following foreign affairs more closely, thereby suggesting that their attitudes toward the political system may have been influenced not only by the divisive rhetoric and gridlock that came to characterize Washington, DC, during this time, but also the wars in Iraq and Afghanistan and the United States' position globally.

For Democrats, Republicans, and independents alike, the shifting sands of the political context exerted a direct impact on political cynicism. Table 7.6 presents the results of a logistic regression equation predicting whether a respondent grew more cynical between the two waves of the panel study. Controlling for the conventional predictors of political trust and efficacy, the model indicates that animosity toward the Bush administration, frustration with the gridlocked Democratic majority in Congress, and increased attention to foreign affairs all increase the likelihood that a respondent grew more cynical about politics and the political process. A respondent with no more interest in following foreign affairs in 2008 than in 2001, and who had not grown increasingly frustrated with the Bush administration or the Democratic Congress, for instance, had a 0.39 likelihood of having become more cynical. A heightened awareness of foreign affairs, coupled with frustration with both the executive and legislative branches of the federal government, increased the predicted probability of increased cynicism to 0.92.[24]

---

[24] The substantive effects of animosity toward the Bush administration and frustration with the Democratic Congress are comparable in size; each increases the likelihood of growing more cynical by 13 to 14 percentage points. Increased attention to foreign

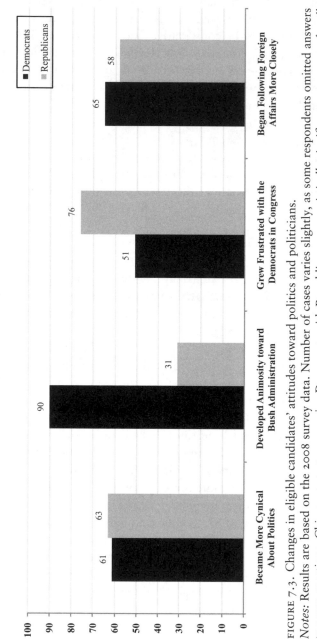

FIGURE 7.3. Changes in eligible candidates' attitudes toward politics and politicians.

Notes: Results are based on the 2008 survey data. Number of cases varies slightly, as some respondents omitted answers to some questions. Chi-square tests comparing Democrats with Republicans are statistically significant at p < 0.05 for all comparisons except "Became more cynical about politics." Sample sizes: for Democrats, N = 1,127; for Republicans, N = 604.

TABLE 7.6. *Increasing Levels of Cynicism, Since 2001 (Logistic Regression Coefficients, Standard Errors, and Change in Probabilities)*

	Became More Cynical Coefficient (and Standard Error)	Maximum Change in Probability (percentage points)
Current Political Context		
Began following foreign affairs more closely	0.69 (0.11)**	11.1
Animosity toward Bush administration	0.40 (0.18)*	6.5
Frustration with Democrats in Congress	1.13 (0.13)**	22.3
Number of political leaders considered inspiring	−0.06 (0.03)	−
Animosity toward Bush administration * Democrat	0.94 (0.30)**	27.8
Frustration with Democrats in Congress * Republican	−0.30 (0.24)	−
Baseline Predictors of Political Cynicism		
Sex (female)	−0.09 (0.11)	−
Black	0.04 (0.20)	−
Latino/a	0.03 (0.24)	−
Age	−0.01 (0.01)	−
Democrat	−0.97 (0.30)**	21.7
Republican	0.08 (0.26)	−
Change in household income (increasing)	0.06 (0.06)	−
Change in political interest (increasing)	0.03 (0.04)	−
Baseline level of cynicism (in Wave 1)	−0.34 (0.05)**	13.9
Constant	0.84 (0.41)	−
Percent correctly predicted	69.5	
Pseudo R-squared	.19	
N	1,857	

Notes: Results are based on the 2008 survey data. Maximum changes in probabilities are based on the logistic regression results. Probabilities were calculated by setting all continuous independent variables not under consideration to their means and dummy variables not under consideration to their modes. The change in probability reflects the independent effect a statistically significant variable exerts as I vary its value from its minimum to maximum. Because of the inclusion of the interaction terms, the coefficient (and predicted probability) associated with the Democrat variable – in and of itself – does not accurately capture the partisan gap in increased cynicism. We must assess the joint effect of the principal components and the interaction term. Democrats who did not develop animosity toward the Bush administration, for example, have a 0.539 predicted probability of having become more cynical. The predicted probability of experiencing an increase in cynicism for Democrats who did develop animosity toward the Bush administration increases to 0.817. Significance levels: * $p < 0.05$; ** $p < 0.01$.

Heightened political cynicism is important not only because it pervades the candidate eligibility pool, but also because it plays a critical role in accounting for eligible candidates' net decrease in interest in running for office. Regardless of the causes of fluctuating cynicism and trust, most political scientists agree that the degree to which one perceives that political institutions and public officials are responsive to citizens' preferences carries consequences for political behavior. Citizens are more likely to engage the political system when they trust government and view it as responsive (King 1997; Piven and Cloward 1997; Conway 1991). Cynicism, on the other hand, leads to lower levels of political and community engagement (Cohen and Dawson 1993; Hirlinger 1992; Wilson 1991).

The multiple regression analysis reveals that changes in cynicism affect eligible candidates' interest in running for office statistically and substantively. Table 7.7 presents a regression equation that includes a measure of the change in respondents' cynicism between the two waves of the study. I control for the correlates of dynamic ambition discussed in previous chapters, as well as a measure of whether the respondent was recently recruited to run for office, as we know that political recruitment spurs interest in running for office and that changes in the political environment affect the parties' recruitment patterns.

As we would expect, eligible candidates who received the suggestion to run for office from a party leader, elected official, or political activist between the two waves of the study are more likely to have gained interest in running for office. But regardless of recruitment efforts and their interaction with electoral gatekeepers on either side of the political aisle, eligible candidates who grew more cynical about politics and the political system between the two waves of the study were 46 percent more likely than their counterparts whose levels of political cynicism did not change to lose all ambition to run for office. More specifically, an "average" respondent with no change in cynicism has a 0.19 predicted probability of having lost all interest in running for office. The likelihood of writing off entirely the notion of a future candidacy grows to 0.28 in cases in which the "average" respondent grew more cynical. Heightened levels of cynicism predict decreases in political ambition even when I restrict the sample to people with interest only in state and local office. Relatively

affairs exerts a smaller effect (5 percentage points). As we would expect, Democrats' increasing cynicism is driven particularly by their attitudes toward George W. Bush (as indicated by the statistically significant interaction term).

TABLE 7.7. *Changing Interest in Running for Office: Effects of Changes in Attitudes Toward and Support from the Political Environment (Ordered Logistic Regression Coefficients and Standard Errors)*

	Change in Ambition (5-point scale)
Changes in Attitudes Toward and Support from the Political Environment	
Became more cynical about politics and the political system	-0.54 (0.14)**
Recruited recently to run for office by a political actor	0.53 (0.18)**
Baseline level of political ambition (in Wave 1)	-1.43 (0.11)**
(Threshold -2)	-9.46 (0.86)**
(Threshold -1)	-4.35 (0.48)**
(Threshold 0)	0.60 (0.45)
(Threshold $+1$)	4.13 (0.64)**
Pseudo R-squared	0.25
N	$1,386$

Notes: Regression results are based on data from respondents who completed both the 2001 and 2008 surveys. The reduced number of cases results from listwise deletion. The equation also controls for the baseline correlates of dynamic ambition and minority status presented in Table 4.3, the politicized upbringing and family dynamics variables included in Table 5.10, and the professional circumstances variables presented in Table 6.6. Levels of significance: * $p < 0.05$; ** $p < 0.01$.

short-term changes in the political environment at the national level – such as assessments of a presidential administration or a change in congressional leadership – can, therefore, leave a significant imprint on an individual's attitudes toward entering all levels of the political system as a candidate. And even if the seven years between the two waves of the study represent a "worst case scenario" in that presidential and congressional approval ratings sank to historic lows, the fact remains that these somewhat unique times carried long-term consequences for political ambition and engagement with the democratic process.

Conclusion

The findings presented in this chapter demonstrate the manner in which eligible candidates' affiliation and interaction with, as well as attitudes toward, the political parties affect their interest in running for office. In terms of specific party positions, policy preferences, and issue priorities, neither the Democrats nor the Republicans carry an advantage as far as political ambition is concerned. Roughly half the eligible candidates who identify with each party report at least some interest in running for office. Neither party's agenda or platform, in other words, is any more likely than the other's to motivate its eligible partisans to consider throwing their own hats into the ring.

The fact that Democrats and Republicans are similar with respect to aggregate levels of interest in running for office, however, does not mean that the parties do not play an important role in triggering and/or suppressing political ambition. On both sides of the political aisle, party leaders, elected officials, and activists recruit candidates to run for office. And the survey data and interview evidence paint a compelling picture that encouragement and support for a candidacy – even in the most general terms – markedly increase respondents' likelihood to consider entering the electoral arena. The parties, therefore, play a pivotal role influencing candidate emergence. Accordingly, given the heavy weight eligible candidates place on recruitment and the degree to which support for a candidacy bolsters political ambition, both major political parties will continue to field an overwhelming majority of male candidates unless they make conscious efforts to recruit more women.

Political parties also exert an influence on dynamic ambition. The political tumult of the seven years between the two waves of the panel study appears to have pushed many qualified, well-situated potential candidates away from considering a run for elective office. This is not to say that there have been no moments of unity. Following the events of September 11, 2001, the divisive partisanship that plagued the first eight months of the Bush administration disappeared as Democrats and Republicans joined together on the steps of the Capitol for a congressional rendition of "God Bless America." Then-Speaker of the House Dennis Hastert (R–IL) remarked, "Senators and House members, Democrats and Republicans will stand shoulder-to-shoulder to fight this evil that has perpetrated on this nation. We will stand together to make sure that those who have brought forth this evil deed will pay the price."[25] In the aftermath of the January 8, 2011, shooting of Congresswoman Gabrielle Giffords (D–AZ) – an act of violence that many suggested was an indirect, unintended product of partisan rhetoric taken a step too far – members of Congress attempted to curb partisan rancor by sitting with colleagues

---

[25] "Congress Vows Unity, Reprisals for Attacks," CNN.com, September 11, 2001, accessed at http://articles.cnn.com/2001–09–11/us/congress.terrorism_1_attacks-world-trade-center-cowardly-acts?_s=PM:US (January 29, 2011).

from the opposite party at the 2011 State of the Union address. U.S. Senator Lisa Murkowski (R–AK), who crossed the aisle and sat on the Democratic side of the House chamber, asked, "Why not start off this new 112th Congress with a gesture, an effort to try to come together if even for just a couple of hours?" She added that "there are no cooties to be had" when colleagues sit next to their political rivals.[26]

But symbolic gestures of cooperation and collegiality in Washington have been fleeting and short-lived. Hotly and bitterly contested presidential elections, such as the 2004 general election for president and the 2008 Democratic presidential primary, may increase mass-level political participation. But the hyperpartisan bickering that dominated Washington for the seven years between the two waves of the study has taken a toll as far as candidate emergence is concerned. Increased levels of political cynicism – which the evidence suggests relate directly to attitudes toward the presidency of George W. Bush and the Democrat-controlled Congress – have made serving in office less appealing for eligible candidates across the ideological and partisan spectrum. And despite calls for increased civility in Washington, polarized vitriol continues to characterize the manner in which the Obama administration and the U.S. House of Representatives under Speaker of the House John Boehner (R–OH) interact with one another. The effects of this discourse and the nature of electoral politics do not affect Democrats and Republicans differently; they culminate to detract eligible candidates from all walks from exhibiting a healthy interest in entering the political fray and engaging fully in democratic governance, regardless of the level of office.

---

[26] Annie Groer, "State of the Union Bi-Partisan Date Night Update," PoliticsDaily.com, January 25, 2011. Accessed at http://www.politicsdaily.com/2011/01/25/state-of-the-union-bipartisan-date-night-update/ (January 29, 2011).

8

Biting the Bullet

Deciding to Run for Office

Deciding whether to run for office can be very difficult, even for high-profile potential candidates or experienced politicians. Consider the case of Illinois Attorney General Lisa Madigan, who was wooed by Barack Obama to seek a U.S. Senate seat in 2010.[1] Madigan was thought to be the clear favorite in the race for the open seat. Not only did Rahm Emanuel (then-chief of staff to President Obama) deem Madigan the "most popular political figure in Illinois," but Madigan's father is also Illinois House Speaker Michael J. Madigan, whose connections and influence played a major role in his daughter's previous campaigns.[2] In fact, Congressman Mark Kirk, the strongest potential candidate on the Republican side of the aisle, made clear that he would not enter a race against Madigan.[3] Yet after months of "agonizing" over the decision, Madigan informed supporters and the media that she would not run for the seat: "I have a job that I love right now and I also have a family that I love and I plan on continuing to serve as your attorney general."[4]

---

[1] Seyward Darby, "A Few Good Dems," *The New Republic*, February 15, 2010. Accessed at http://www.tnr.com/article/politics/few-good-dems (February 26, 2011).

[2] Lynn Sweet, "Lisa Madigan Nixes Senate or Governor Bid," *Chicago Sun Times*, July 8, 2009. Accessed at http://blogs.suntimes.com/sweet/2009/07/lisa_madigan_is_not_running_fo.html (February 26, 2011).

[3] Josh Kraushaar, "Kirk Running for the Senate," *Politico*, July 8, 2009. Accessed at http://www.politico.com/blogs/scorecard/0709/Kirk_running_for_the_Senate.html (February 26, 2011).

[4] John Chase, Mike Dorning and Rick Pearson, "Madigan: Decision to Pass on Senate, Governor 'Agonizing' but Best for Family," *Chicago Tribune*, July 8, 2009. Accessed at http://newsblogs.chicagotribune.com/clout_st/2009/07/madigan-to-seek-reelection-as-attorney-general.html (February 26, 2011).

In another example, Congressman Sam Graves (R–MO) announced in January 2011 that he would not challenge Democratic U.S. Senator Claire McCaskill for her seat in 2012. The Republicans' prospects of winning the seat in a race expected to be one of the most competitive of the cycle, regardless of their nominee, would have been brightest if Graves had thrown his hat into the ring. First elected to the House of Representatives in 2000, Congressman Graves was thought to have a unique ability to tap into McCaskill's base in Kansas City. Moreover, his rural background, opposition to the Democrats' stimulus package, and recent ascension to chair of the House Small Business Committee were expected to carry broad appeal with Missouri voters.[5] Following drawn-out speculation about his political ambition, however, Graves finally issued a public statement: "It was an agonizing decision for me, determining the best way for me to serve and my ability to get there. I believe it is a winnable race for me. However, I also believe that I can have a greater impact on federal policy in the next six years as a chairman in the House."[6]

Individuals deliberating an initial run for office might face an even more difficult decision process than did Lisa Madigan and Sam Graves, both of whom enjoyed high levels of name recognition, support for their candidacies, and what appeared to be favorable political opportunity structures. Most first-time candidates are moving into unfamiliar territory and cannot fully envision what a candidacy would entail and whether they could endure it. A former president of an ACLU chapter in the South who was interviewed for this study, for example, said that he gets "anxious when articulating interest in running for office." When asked to elaborate, he explained:

> I have thought about running for office for the last 25 years, ever since I ran for president of the student council in high school. But anytime I try to talk to anyone else about it, I get frazzled and worried. What if people don't like me? What if they won't vote for me? What if I can't raise the money? What if I'm not good at the job? I just don't know.

Reproductive rights activist Susan Marsh voiced a similar sentiment. Although she is interested in running for the city council, "being interested

---

[5] David Lieb, "Decision Nearing for GOP Senate Hopefuls," *Associated Press*, January 30, 2011. Accessed at http://www.kmov.com/news/local/Analysis-Decision-nearing-for-GOP-Sen-hopefuls-114901584.html (February 26, 2011).

[6] Ken Newton, "Graves Won't Run for Senate," *St. Joseph News-Press*, February 3, 2011. Accessed at http://www.newspressnow.com/localnews/26734587/detail.html (February 26, 2011).

and actually running are two different things." On two occasions, she "chickened out of running" because "the uncertainty of what it would be like was insomnia-inducing." Harriet Goodwin, a political activist from South Carolina, also referred to the angst involved in the decision process, concluding: "I am too old now – but I thought about running at many different times across my life. I always made excuses, but I guess looking back now, I just never had the nerve." Regardless of whether the candidacy is situated at the local, state, or federal level, deciding whether to enter electoral politics is a complex endeavor.

In this chapter, I turn to the second stage of the candidate emergence process and examine the factors that distinguish those who choose to run for office from those who think about running, but do not. Although the overwhelming majority of respondents view many typical campaign activities – and the toll that a candidacy might take on themselves and their families – with disdain, more than 350 of the eligible candidates surveyed did run for office at some point. An analysis of their decisions to run reveals that many of the same personal, professional, and political factors that affect whether an eligible candidate considers running for office also influence the likelihood of launching an actual campaign. More specifically, minority status, financial concerns, perceptions of qualifications to run for office, and patterns of political recruitment play a role in transforming nascent interest in running for office into expressive ambition. The data also indicate that, barring fundamental changes to the manner in which respondents view themselves and the political environment, pursuing elective office will remain an unlikely path for most eligible candidates.

So Many Reasons Not to Run for Office: Negative Perceptions of the Electoral Environment and the Campaign Process

Americans hold a high degree of cynicism toward elected officials and disdain for the political process. According to a 2010 Gallup poll, only 11 percent of Americans have "a great deal" or "quite a lot" of confidence in Congress, the lowest evaluation the political institution has ever received.[7] That same year, only 26 percent of citizens reported that they trust the federal government "always" or "most of the time." Levels of

---

[7] Lydia Saad, "Congress Ranks Last in Confidence in Institutions," Gallup Poll, July 22, 2010. Accessed at http://www.gallup.com/poll/141512/congress-ranks-last-confidence-institutions.aspx (March 12, 2011).

trust in state government (33 percent) and local government (52 percent) are considerably higher, but still not widespread.[8] These attitudes are consistent with survey research that finds that a majority of Americans do not believe that elected officials are qualified for the positions they hold (Knowledge Networks 2002). Moreover, when Americans are asked how they would rate the "honesty and ethical standards" of people working in a variety of professions, politicians fare poorly. Only 20 percent of Americans believe that local officeholders have "high" or "very high" ethical standards; the percentages for state officeholders (12 percent) and members of Congress (9 percent) are even lower.[9]

Relatively negative attitudes about the political environment and the electoral arena are not restricted to mass population samples; many eligible candidates in the sample drew similar conclusions. Forty percent contend that most current officeholders are not "well intentioned" in their desire to enter public service. Thirty-five percent do not think that the majority of elected officials are qualified to hold elective office. And, as the data presented in Chapter 7 make clear, negative and cynical impressions of the political system became more widespread over the seven years between the two waves of the survey.

These opinions certainly stem from a series of factors. The federal government with which so many Americans have grown frustrated likely contributes to the record low presidential and congressional approval ratings documented by national pollsters. Moreover, these events shape attitudes toward state and local governments (Gartner and Segura 2008; Maestas et al. 2008). In short, polarizing political leaders on both sides of the aisle and controversial government actions at home and abroad have taken their toll as far as the status of politics is concerned.

In addition, the negative political advertising that saturates high-level competitive elections has turned politics into a blood sport that focuses on destroying the opponent (Swint 2006; Mark 2006; Kamber 2003). Further, the mainstream television networks and newspapers, in response to increasing competition from the Internet and cable news, incorporate scandal and partisan conflict into the central aspects of political reporting (Graber 2010; Fox, Van Sickel, and Steiger 2007; Sabato 2000). The

[8] "Poll Finds Trust of Federal Government Runs Low," *CNN.com*, February 23, 2010. Accessed at http://articles.cnn.com/2010-02-23/politics/poll.government.trust_1_new-national-poll-government-cnn?_s=PM:POLITICS (March 12, 2011).

[9] "Honesty/Ethics in Professions," Gallup Poll, November 19–21, 2010. Accessed at http://www.gallup.com/poll/1654/honesty-ethics-professions.aspx (March 12, 2011).

emergence of openly partisan reporting adds to the contentious atmosphere in the presentation of politics (Jamieson and Capella 2008; Cohen 2006). It is no surprise, therefore, that broad national sentiment tends not to identify politics as a noble calling.

Given their negative attitudes toward the political system, it is somewhat surprising that so many respondents consider engaging with the system as a means to influence the public policy process. The data presented in Figure 8.1 indicate that more than two-thirds of the eligible candidates are "likely" or "very likely" to give money to a candidate who favors their positions, or lobby already elected government officials. Nearly 60 percent of respondents are likely to volunteer for a candidate or group. And more than two of every five respondents report that they would be likely to organize people in their communities to affect policy. On the other hand, only one of every ten respondents is likely to run for office as a way to influence public policies about which they hold strong convictions. Moreover, when asked to identify the most effective way for a citizen to ensure that the government addresses an important problem, running for office garners the least support.[10] The rankings for the best means through which to implement change in the community are consistent across race, sex, and profession; as the political activity becomes more complex and demanding, the less likely respondents are to embrace it. Overall, though, respondents' willingness to influence the policy process suggests that negative attitudes toward the political system in general serve less as a deterrent for political activism than we might expect.

Negative attitudes about specific features of the campaign process, however, do cloud individuals' willingness to engage in the activities associated with running for office. The 2008 survey included a battery of questions pertaining to eight aspects of electoral politics and campaigning. Five of the activities refer to the mechanics of a campaign; three focus on the personal toll a campaign might take. Respondents were asked the extent to which they would feel comfortable undertaking each activity, as well as whether negative feelings about any specific aspect of electoral politics would ultimately deter them from running for office. The

---

[10] Forty-eight percent of respondents believe that supporting a candidate with similar views is the best way to ensure that the government addresses an important problem. Twenty-five percent contend that forming an organization is the most effective route. Making financial contributions to candidates and elected officials (15 percent) and running for office (13 percent) place a distant third and fourth.

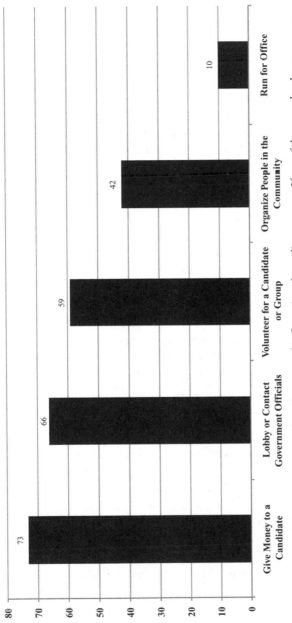

FIGURE 8.1. Eligible candidates' preferred means of influencing the policy process. If you felt strongly about a government action or policy, how likely would you be to. . . .

Notes: Results are based on the 2001 survey data. Bars represent the percentage of respondents who answered "likely" or "very likely." Number of cases varies slightly, as some respondents omitted answers to some questions.

data presented in Table 8.1 reveal that respondents view most campaign activities in a negative light.

Turning first to the mechanics of a campaign, even the activities about which respondents express the highest levels of comfort are quite unpopular. No more than one-quarter of the eligible candidates report that they would be "comfortable" engaging in any of the tasks typically involved in running for office. Respondents are more likely to feel so negatively about engaging in a negative campaign and soliciting campaign contributions that they consider these activities deterrents to running for office. The findings are similar in terms of the personal toll a campaign often takes. The bottom half of Table 8.1 reveals that the loss of privacy and the lack of family time deter far more respondents from running for office than strike them as something they would be willing to endure.[11] Notably, the overwhelming majority of respondents would be more likely to express interest in a political position if they did not have to campaign at all. In fact, 73 percent of women and 69 percent of men report that they would be more likely to seek a position of political power if they could do so without engaging in campaign activities.

Throughout the course of the interviews, disdain for the political process and what entering an actual political contest might entail was also readily apparent. More than three-quarters of the eligible candidates expressed some degree of negativity about several aspects of running for office. In particular, fundraising, the potential loss of privacy, and engaging in a negative campaign emerged as the most common deterrents.

Fundraising as a Deterrent to Running for Office

Eligible candidates are well aware that the amount of money needed to run a competitive federal race is exorbitant. Indeed, the 2010 federal elections cost approximately $4 billion, or, according to a press release issued by the Center for Responsive Politics, "enough to run the city of Pittsburgh for two years. Buy every resident of Topeka a nice used car. Or treat each and every American to a Big Mac and fries."[12] More specifically, in the

---

[11] Women are statistically more likely than men to view all eight aspects of running for office so negatively that they serve as deterrents to running for office. Overall, 67 percent of women, compared with 54 percent of men, were deterred by at least one typical campaign activity (difference significant at $p < 0.05$).

[12] Center for Responsive Politics, "Center for Responsive Politics Predicts Midterms Could Cost Nearly $4 Billion," opensecrets.org, October 27, 2010. Accessed at http://www.opensecrets.org/news/2010/10/election-2010-to-shatter-spending-r.html (February 19, 2011).

TABLE 8.1. *Eligible Candidates' Willingness to Engage in Campaign Activities*

	"Comfortable"	"So negative it would deter me from running"
Mechanics of the Campaign		
Engaging in a negative campaign	5%	37%
Soliciting campaign contributions	12	25
Dealing with party officials	19	13
Going door-to-door to meet constituents	25	16
Dealing with members of the press	26	12
Personal Aspects of the Campaign		
Loss of privacy	5	41
Spending less time with family	8	29
Potentially hindering professional goals	14	17
N	1,908	

Notes: Results are based on the 2008 survey data. Number of cases varies slightly, as some respondents omitted answers to some questions.

ninety-two congressional races characterized as the most competitive in the 2010 election cycle, the average Democrat raised $1.9 million and the average Republican raised $1.3 million.[13] The average spending in the 2010 U.S. Senate races reached an all-time high; the average incumbent's fundraising receipts totaled roughly $11.4 million; the typical challenger managed to raise $4.1 million.[14]

These levels of campaign spending undoubtedly affect eligible candidates' interest in running for office. Daniel Rodman, the vice president for finance at a large accounting firm in Chicago, articulated many respondents' concerns about the vast amounts of money required to run for office:

> I always thought the idea of raising money was unappealing. But after seeing the millions of dollars that second- and third-tier candidates raised in 2008 – guys like Mike Huckabee, Bill Richardson, and even Ron

[13] Michael Beckel, "In Tightest House Races, Democrats Maintain Financial Advantage Heading into Campaign's Final Weeks," opensecrets.org, October 18, 2010. Accessed at http://www.opensecrets.org/news/2010/10/in-tightest-house-races-democrats-m.html (February 19, 2011).

[14] Dave Levinthal, "Election 2010 to Shatter Spending Records as Republicans Benefit from Late Cash Surge," opensecrets.org, October 27, 2010. Accessed at http://www.opensecrets.org/news/2010/10/election-2010-to-shatter-spending-r.html (February 19, 2011).

Paul – and the fact that they still were not taken seriously, no way. I'd never be able to raise even a fraction of what they managed to take in. And I'd never want to.

Concern over the amount of money needed to run for office trickles down to the local level as well. Carrie Hodge, a political activist, believes that the costs of campaigns make running for office "too daunting to think about. And it's not only Congress. All campaigns have become so expensive." Patrick Barnett, a politically active attorney from Connecticut, explained that he "always thought that someday" he would run for office. When a close friend had to raise $25,000 for a seat on the school board, though, Barnett changed his mind: "About 500 people vote in those elections. That is not a good use of anyone's time, even if the activity of fundraising, itself, was more appealing than it actually is." Other respondents described the prospects of raising money for a campaign as "daunting," "petrifying," "disgusting," "off-putting," and "more painful than a root canal without anesthesia."

Invasion of Privacy as a Deterrent to Running for Office
Also necessary for a viable candidacy is a willingness to endure a loss of privacy (Sutter 2006). Consider 2010 Democratic congressional candidate Krystal Ball, who competed for the U.S. House seat in Virginia's 1st district. Three weeks prior to the general election, a conservative blogger posted on Facebook and leaked to the media nine photos of Ball and her ex-husband at a 2002 holiday party. The candidate, who was 22 years old at the time, donned a "sexy Santa suit" and posed suggestively with sex toys.[15] Although Ms. Ball lost the race for reasons other than the racy photos (she ran as a progressive Democrat in a Republican district), she contends that the release of the photos was intended to force her to "collapse in a ball of embarrassment and to hang [her] head in shame."[16] Individuals who seek local-level offices also often reference the unwelcome intrusion into one's personal life that can accompany a political campaign and public service. Sandy Freedman, the former mayor of Tampa, Florida, for example, reflected on the "demeaning, almost ridiculous" campaign process: "There is a loss of privacy, a feeling that

---

[15] Nate Jones, "Candidate's Sexy Santa Photos Leaked: Sexism in Action?" *Time*, October 7, 2010. Accessed at http://newsfeed.time.com/2010/10/07/candidates-sexy-santa-photos-leaked-sexism-in-action/ (February 19, 2011).
[16] Krystal Ball, "The Next Glass Ceiling," *Huffington Post*, October 11, 2010. Accessed at http://www.huffingtonpost.com/krystal-ball/the-next-glass-ceiling_b_757819.html (February 26, 2011).

nothing is off limits. . . . I think [we] are already seeing candidates of a lesser quality in many cases because people don't want to put themselves through this."[17] It is no surprise, therefore, that when the *Mobile (AL) Register* surveyed roughly 400 city residents in 2008 about their interest in running for office, only 12 percent of those surveyed expressed any interest in a future run. And among the 88 percent with no ambition to enter the electoral arena, loss of personal privacy was a leading reason.[18]

The eligible candidates with whom I spoke also identified the potential loss of privacy as a primary reason not to run for office. Janie Lopes, a professor at a large university in New England, follows politics very closely, but would never run for office because of "the intrusive nature of campaigns." She elaborated, explaining that "watching the politics of personal destruction is bad enough. I can't imagine what it would be like to be the target. It'd be humiliating, embarrassing, and I'd be grief stricken." Michigan attorney Bill Lee often thinks about running for municipal office. But shortly after the thought arises, he dismisses it: "The process is so personal and nasty. I would love to serve. But in order to do that, you need to run. And given the invasion of privacy you have to endure, you practically have to be a sociopath and not care at all about what anyone thinks or what they'll find out." Ben Finkelstein, an attorney from Washington, arrived at a similar conclusion: "If you run, you're treated horribly, your life ravaged like a piece of meat fed to hungry vultures. Who could deal with that? Who'd want to deal with that?"

Respondents frequently associated the loss of privacy with the contemporary news media's willingness to delve into almost all aspects of a candidate's life. A businesswoman from Columbia, Missouri, bemoaned the "news media's obsession with interfering in everything that has nothing to do with the issues that are pertinent to the election. I get that they have bottom-line concerns, but it's gotten ridiculous." Florida business owner George Ortega explained that he would never run because "the press launches personal attacks and places your life under a microscope." High school principal Elizabeth Logan does not believe that she has "any skeletons in the closet." She would never step forward as candidate, though, "just in case [she's] wrong about that."

---

[17] George Coryell, "Election Losers Find Life Goes On," *Tampa Tribune*, September 10, 2000, page 1.
[18] "Ethics Training Could Ease Voters' Distrust," *Mobile Register*, April 21, 2008, page A06.

Not all respondents view the invasion of privacy as a deterrent, but even those who expressed a willingness to endure "background checks" and "unfounded allegations" quickly noted that they would be unlikely to throw their hats into the ring because they would never subject their families to such a heightened level of personal scrutiny. Tom Clawson, who practices law outside Seattle, for example, wondered, "If you love your family, then why open them up to the irrelevant and inane discussions about whether you smoked a joint in your twenties and how that affects your ability to be a responsible husband, father, and public servant?" Marjorie Lieberman, the executive director of an environmental nonprofit organization, commented, "I have the stomach for the way the press treats candidates. But I don't know if my husband and children do. And I don't plan to find out." The words of a California attorney represent, almost verbatim, many respondents' conclusions: "The intrusion into one's privacy that comes with a campaign is such that one would have to be insane to run for office."

Negative Campaigning as a Deterrent to Running for Office

Linked to the loss of privacy are concerns about enduring a negative campaign. Although campaigns for high-level office have always included personal and political attacks, recent election cycles have seen an increase in such rhetoric. The 2010 congressional and gubernatorial elections, for example, set a record for negative campaign advertising (Fowler and Ridout 2010). Governor Pat Quinn (D–IL) accused Republican opponent Bill Brady of sponsoring a bill that would "mass-euthanize sheltered dogs and cats in gas chambers."[19] Sharron Angle, the Republican U.S. Senate candidate from Nevada, accused Senate Majority Leader Harry Reid of voting "to use taxpayer dollars to pay for Viagra for convicted child molesters and sex offenders."[20] Angle, herself, was the target of what became a high-profile ad when she competed for the Republican nomination against Sue Lowden. Lowden accused "career politician and Senate candidate Sharron Angle of sponsoring a bill that would have used tax dollars to give massages to prisoners" based on a plan "developed by the

---

[19] Molly Ball, "This Year's Attack Ads Cut Deeper," *Politico*, October 17, 2010. Accessed at http://www.politico.com/news/stories/1010/43698.html (February 20, 2011).

[20] Andy Barr, "Sharron Angle Ad: Harry Reid Gives Viagra to Predators," *Politico*, October 7, 2010. Accessed at http://www.politico.com/news/stories/1010/43282.html (February 20, 2011).

Church of Scientology."[21] Overall, more than 50 percent of candidates' television ads between Labor Day and Election Day 2010 attacked their opponents; more than 90 percent of the ads run by political parties fell into this category (Fowler and Ridout 2010).

Negative campaigns, however, transcend statewide and federal elections. In the 2010 school board race in Manatee, Florida, for example, Jane Pfeilsticker accused her opponent, Julie Aranibar, of tax fraud, failure to manage her finances, and suffering a foreclosure and failed business. A flier sent to thousands of voters not only contained these accusations, but also included copies of IRS paperwork and tax liens.[22]

Eligible candidates are cognizant of the possibility of being dragged through the mud, regardless of the level of office they might seek. Michael Mason, for instance, is a tax lawyer from Florida. A self-designated conservative Republican, he fondly remembers the attacks launched against Democrat John Kerry in the 2004 presidential election: "The Swift Boat Veterans were great. They provided a lot of information that people needed to know. I always appreciate when things like that happen in a campaign." Mason, however, has "no interest in being a target of the mudslinging, even if serves a purpose." Small business owner Peter Hernandez observed that the "cutthroat nature of campaigns means that nothing is off-limits these days. To be a formidable candidate means to be willing to take cheap shots and receive cheap shots." Elaine Minor agrees and, because she is "missing the backbone to take all the personal attacks, to see [her] views distorted, and to have [her] integrity impugned," she would "never in a million years" run for office.

Despite the widespread negative views of campaigning and the electoral process, 320 members of the sample of the candidate eligibility pool had – by the time of the 2001 survey – stepped forward as candidates and run for office at some point in their lives (182 of these candidates won their races). By the second wave of the study in 2008, 54 additional respondents had emerged as candidates (41 of whom won their races). Thus, we have a unique opportunity to assess the factors that transform politically engaged

---

[21] Reid Wilson, "Can Sue Lowden Still Win?" *Hotline on Call*, June 1, 2010. Accessed at http://hotlineoncall.nationaljournal.com/archives/2010/06/can_sue_lowden.php (February 20, 2011).

[22] Natalie Neysa Alund, "School Board Hopeful Alleges Smear Campaign," Bradenton.com, October 14, 2010. Accessed at http://www.bradenton.com/2010/10/14/2653393/school-board-hopeful-alleges-smear.html (February 20, 2011).

citizens into actual candidates, as well as the manner in which personal, professional, and political factors influence the calculus.

Expressing That Ambition: The Decision to Enter an Actual Race

In beginning an empirical analysis of who launches an actual candidacy, it is important first to paint a portrait of the eligible candidates who reach this second stage of the candidate emergence process. The regression coefficients and predicted probabilities presented in Table 7.5 yield from a fully specified model of who considered a candidacy (see Chapter 7). Because the models presented throughout the book are additive – and each chapter controls for the main explanatory factors presented in previous chapters – we can assess the relative extent to which minority status, family dynamics, professional factors, political recruitment, and electoral features and political engagement affect nascent ambition. Overall, the model performs well; not only does each explanation offered in Chapters 4, 5, 6, and 7 independently exert an effect on the likelihood of considering a run for office, but taken together, these factors account for much of the variation in considering a candidacy. Indeed, if we compare the fully specified model to the "null model" presented in Chapter 3 (see Table 3.6), which controlled only for electoral features and political dynamics, then we can see the leverage we gain by moving beyond traditional gauges of the political opportunity structure when predicting the initial decision to run for office. More specifically, the fully specified model correctly predicts 42 percent more of the cases than does the null model.[23]

The data reveal a substantial winnowing process that occurs in the candidate emergence process long before eligible candidates decide to run for particular offices at particular times. Minority status, family dynamics, professional factors, and broad recruitment efforts play critical roles, independently and in concert with one another, in predicting whether eligible candidates will ever reach the political opportunity structures central to expressive ambition. All else equal, for example, women are approximately 6 percentage points less likely than men to consider running for office; the same is true of blacks in the candidate eligibility pool. Minority status – in terms of both sex and race – systematically

---

[23] The pseudo-R^2 measure also increases from 0.01 in the null model to 0.48 in the fully specified model. This gain in explanatory power – despite the measure's imperfection – is consistent with the change in the cases correctly predicted.

depresses the likelihood of considering a run for office, regardless of concrete credentials, perceptions of qualifications, patterns of recruitment, and family dynamics. By contrast, growing up in a political household and interacting with family members who encourage entering the political arena propel nascent ambition, as does political recruitment by an electoral gatekeeper. Professional factors play an important role, too, in that a heightened sense of qualifications more than offsets concerns regarding the financial risk and loss often associated with a candidacy.

Another way to highlight the manner in which the eligibility pool narrows throughout the candidate emergence process is to compare the respondents who have considered running for office with the entire sample of the candidate eligibility pool. The first column of data in Table 8.2 presents the frequencies of each of the central predictors of nascent ambition in the overall sample of eligible candidates. Women, for example, comprise 47 percent of the sample. Slightly more than 20 percent of the respondents consider themselves "very qualified" to run for office. And 38 percent report having been encouraged to run for office by a party leader, elected official, or political activist. The second column presents the same frequencies, but restricts the analysis only to respondents who have considered running for office. Simple comparisons between the first and second columns demonstrate the effects of several key variables on considering a candidacy. Among eligible candidates with nascent ambition, women comprise only 39 percent of the subsample. One-third of these respondents consider themselves "very qualified" to run for office. Nearly 60 percent report having been recruited to run by an electoral gatekeeper.

The third column in the table reports the frequencies for these key variables only among people who actually ran for office. Despite being almost 50 percent of this sample of the candidate eligibility pool, women represent only one-third of the actual candidates. Among these candidates, more than 50 percent self-assess as "very qualified" to run for office; and more than four of five were recruited by an electoral gatekeeper. At the aggregate level, therefore, we see that many of the same variables that affect nascent ambition also affect expressive ambition.

The same is true in a multivariate context. Table 8.3 reports the logistic regression coefficients predicting who launches a candidacy, controlling for the baseline correlates of political ambition, as well as the personal, professional, and political factors introduced in Chapters 4 through 7. Prior to explicating the findings, it is important to acknowledge that the model does not include a measure of eligible candidates' perceived

TABLE 8.2. *Comparison of Considering a Candidacy and Actually Running for Office, by Minority Status, Family Dynamics, Professional Circumstances, and Political Recruitment*

	Total Candidate Eligibility Pool	Considered Running (Nascent Ambition)	Actually Ran (Expressive Ambition)
Minority Status			
Woman	47%	39%	34%
Black	10	11	13
Family Dynamics/Early Upbringing			
Ran for office as a student	55	63	65
Received suggestion to run from a family member	35	53	54
Received suggestion to run from a spouse/partner	27	43	48
Professional Factors			
Considers self "very qualified" to run for office	21	32	56
Household annual income of at least $200,000	27	25	19
Political Recruitment			
Encouraged to run by at least one electoral gatekeeper	38	59	84
N	3,568	1,812	331

Notes: Entries indicate the percentage of respondents who fall into each category throughout the candidate emergence process. In the total pool of eligible candidates, for example, 47 percent of respondents were women. Among the subsample of eligible candidates who considered running for office, 39 percent were women. And among the respondents who actually ran for office, 34 percent were women.

likelihood of winning. Many studies find that officeholders' motivations to seek higher office are guided by how they assess their likelihood of winning, as they are unwilling to sacrifice their current levels of power if they are not confident they will acquire more of it.[24] A study geared to uncover the decision to run, however, cannot easily tap into the perceived likelihood of winning, as it requires a retrospective assessment

[24] As discussed in Chapter 2, a wide body of literature employs objective indicators of the likelihood of winning a race as chief predictors of static, progressive, and discrete ambition. See, for example, Maestas et al. 2006; Stone, Maisel, and Maestas 2004; Stone and Maisel 2003; Kazee 1994, 1980; Rohde 1979; Black 1972; Schlesinger 1966.

that is likely shaped by the outcome of the election in which the respondent competed. Of the respondents who sought elective positions and won their races, 64 percent contend that they thought they were "likely" or "very likely" to win their race. Among respondents who lost their races, only 37 percent report believing that were "likely" or "very likely" to win (difference statistically significant at $p < 0.01$). For similar reasons, the model does not include as an explanatory variable respondents' attitudes about engaging in campaigns. Individuals who ran for office expressed more negative attitudes than did women and men who never launched a candidacy, probably a result of actual candidates' firsthand experiences.

The results that emerge from the regression analysis highlight a distinction between personal and family factors versus professional and political factors. Political recruitment, income, and self-assessed qualifications continue to exert substantive and statistically significant effects at this stage of the candidate emergence process. On the other hand, the effects of minority status and family dynamics – which play an important role in fomenting nascent ambition – are muted when we turn to the decision to enter an actual race. Although sex remains a statistically significant predictor of ambition, race exerts no effect on expressive ambition.[25] Further, family dynamics in both childhood and adulthood fail to achieve statistical significance.

We can gain an even better handle on the manner in which the factors that affect nascent ambition also influence expressive ambition by focusing on the eligible candidates who decided to run for office between the two waves of the survey. Certainly, we should be cautious when analyzing these data, as only 54 respondents emerged as new candidates between 2001 and 2008. But consistent with the multiple regression results presented in Table 8.3, the distinction between sociodemographic and family

---

[25] Several studies suggest that the political environment has a gendered effect on citizens' attitudes about entering the political system. David Hill (1981) finds, for example, that women are more likely to emerge as candidates in states that established an early pattern of electing women to the state legislature, support women's political participation, and do not have a tradition of gender disparities in income or educational achievement. Women are less likely to run for office in states with a traditional culture (Fox 2010; Rule 1990; Nechemias 1987). Thus, it is important to note that the role sex plays in the second stage of the candidate emergence process withstands controls for political culture. Eligible candidates are more likely to emerge in more Democratic states and in states with a higher percentage of women in the state legislature. But the interaction between political culture and sex is not statistically significant.

TABLE 8.3. *Who Runs for Office? Expressive Ambition in the Candidate Eligibility Pool (Logistic Regression Coefficients, Standard Errors, and Change in Probabilities)*

	Ran for Office Coefficient (and Standard Error)	Maximum Change in Probability (percentage points)
Minority Status		
Sex (female)	−0.40 (0.20)*	4.9
Black	0.17 (0.26)	–
Latino/a	−0.51 (0.48)	–
Family Dynamics		
Age	0.06 (0.01)**	18.4
"Political" household index	−0.12 (0.08)	–
Parent ran for office	−0.19 (0.22)	–
Ran for office as a student	−0.03 (0.17)	–
Marital status (married/living with partner)	0.32 (0.29)	–
Responsible for majority of household tasks	0.25 (0.21)	–
Responsible for majority of child care	0.33 (0.30)	–
Encouraged to run for office by family member	−0.27 (0.29)	–
Professional Factors		
Income	−0.22 (0.08)**	18.4
Self-assessed qualifications to run for office	0.61 (0.11)**	22.1
Political Recruitment		
Recruited by an electoral gatekeeper	0.97 (0.24)**	9.8
Indicators of Political Engagement		
Political knowledge	0.10 (0.15)	–
Political interest	0.10 (0.07)	–
Political efficacy	0.00 (0.08)	–
Political participation	0.17 (0.05)**	17.4
Electoral Features and Opportunities		
Interested in high-level office	−0.10 (0.17)	–
Size of the congressional delegation	0.00 (0.01)	–
Size of the state political opportunity structure	0.00 (0.00)	–
Size of the local political opportunity structure	0.00 (0.00)	–
Term limits	0.07 (0.20)	–

	Ran for Office Coefficient (and Standard Error)	Maximum Change in Probability (percentage points)
Part-time legislature	0.10 (0.24)	–
Legislative salary	0.00 (0.00)	–
Political Dynamics		
Democrat	0.29 (0.23)	–
Republican	0.36 (0.24)	–
Percent Democratic presidential vote share	0.03 (0.02)	–
Party congruence with the congressional delegation	0.22 (0.20)	–
Party congruence with the state legislature	0.29 (0.22)	–
Constant	– 10.17 (1.20)**	–
Percent correctly predicted	85.3	
Pseudo R-squared	0.30	
N	1,506	

Notes: Sample is restricted to respondents who have considered running for office. Regression results are based on the 2001 data. Probabilities were calculated by setting all continuous independent variables to their means and dummy variables to their modes. The change in probability reflects the independent effect a statistically significant variable exerts as I vary it from its minimum to maximum. Significance levels: * $p < 0.05$; ** $p < 0.01$.

dynamics, as opposed to professional and political factors, emerges when we focus on just the new candidates.

Turning first to minority status, 20 percent of the men, compared with 15 percent of the women, who considered running for office actually chose to seek an elective position. Put somewhat differently, 12 percent of the men from the initial pool of eligible candidates actually threw their hats into the ring and sought elective positions, whereas only 7 percent of the women did so (difference significant at $p < 0.01$). The results are similar when we include the new candidates who emerged between the two waves of the study. Taking into account the total number of women and men who ran for office, 22 percent of the men who considered running, compared with 17 percent of the women, actually emerged as candidates. Race, however, exerts no direct effect on the decision to enter an actual race. Three percent of white respondents, 3 percent of black respondents, and 5 percent of Latino respondents emerged as new candidates between the two waves of the survey (differences not statistically significant).

Family dynamics also fail to exert any systematic role in triggering an actual candidacy. Of respondents who had or adopted a child between 2001 and 2008, 3 percent emerged as candidates; the same proportion holds for women and men who did not expand their families between the two waves of the study. Candidate emergence across changes in marital status, as well as changes in household and child care responsibilities, was also consistent.

With the exception of sex, therefore, the explanatory power of minority status and family dynamics when accounting for candidate emergence tends to be restricted to the nascent phase of political ambition. The same is not true of professional and political factors. Thirty-five percent of the new candidates, for example, increased their self-assessments of their qualifications to run for office between the two waves of the study; 52 percent maintained their level of self-assessed qualifications. In other words, self-efficacy as a candidate – which, as established in Chapter 6, is closely linked to professional roles and responsibilities – held steady or increased for all but seven of respondents who decided to run for office between 2001 and 2008. The data reveal a similar pattern as far as political recruitment is concerned. Twenty-one percent of the new candidates reported having been recruited to run for office for the first time between 2001 and 2008. Sixty percent received recent and sustained encouragement from at least one party leader, elected official, or nonelected activist over time. The professional and political circumstances that are relatively more proximate to the actual decision to run for office, therefore, affect the likelihood not only that an eligible candidate will consider running for office, but also that he or she will enter a race.

Because the overwhelming majority of respondents who have considered running for office have not yet chosen to launch a candidacy, we can also assess how nascent ambition might develop into expressive ambition by asking eligible candidates directly about what factors, if any, might propel them to run for office. The survey presented respondents with a list of eleven items that might encourage them to run for office in the future. The data presented in Table 8.4 reveal that many of the factors that affected whether respondents ever ran for office also emerge when we ask eligible candidates what might lead them to run for office in the future.

Foremost, factors associated with an encouraging political environment are the most influential for all eligible candidates who are considering running for office. More than half the respondents would be

TABLE 8.4. *Factors That Might Encourage Eligible Candidates to Run for Office in the Future*

Percent of Eligible Candidates Who Would Be More Likely to Run for Office if...	
Encouraging Political Environment	
There was a lot of support for the candidacy	57%
Campaigns were publicly financed	43
Received the suggestion from party or community leader	40
Encouraging Personal and Professional Environment	
Had more financial security	47
Had more free time	42
Received the suggestion from spouse/partner	29
Received the suggestion from a friend	23
Credentials, Experience, and Self-Motivation	
Had more passions for political issues	37
Had previous experience working on a campaign	32
Had more public speaking experience	23
Had more impressive professional credentials	20
N	3,143

Notes: Results are based on the 2001 survey data. Cell entries represent the percentage of respondents who said that they would be more likely to run for office under the specified condition. N includes only respondents who have never run for public office.

more inclined to run for office if they knew there was strong support for the candidacy. Attorney Jose Espinoza highlighted the importance of external support when asked about the circumstances under which he could foresee running for office: "The only thing that would accelerate my running for office would be if an opportunity came about and there was substantial encouragement. If this were the case, I might take a chance and run even if it was not the best time for me." Similarly, Tom Johnson, a Virginia executive, noted that if many people came to him and demonstrated that he had grassroots support, he would be more likely to run. Lisa Cantwell, the owner of a small business located outside San Diego, will not run for office until "the party and the community's leaders put their money where their mouths are." Although she is interested in running for the state legislature and has received encouragement from elected officials and party operatives, Cantwell will not agree to run for office until her supporters help her raise the money or "pass a law that takes the money chase out of campaigning."

The data presented in Table 8.4 also indicate that a more encouraging professional environment would facilitate a candidacy, much more so than would a more encouraging personal environment. Men and women emphasize that free time is one of the most important factors that would encourage them to run for office in the future; the importance of more free time is second only to external support for a candidacy. As Colorado attorney Nina Henderson stated, "My current job is extremely time consuming. If that were somehow to change, I would consider running for office." Despite her high level of interest in politics, Maureen Martin, a high school principal from New Jersey, cannot run because of her job. She commented that the only thing that would let her pursue a candidacy, even for a local office, would be "retirement." Oregon lawyer Rick Peters agrees: "I work 18 hours a day and I do that because it brings my family financial security. If there was another way I could do that, or if my firm valued public service and pursuing it wouldn't involve a pay cut, then, sure, I'd love to run for the legislature."

Finally, the bottom category presented in Table 8.4 focuses on eligible candidates' credentials, political experience, and self-motivation. The lack of self-efficacy as a candidate serves as a deeply embedded obstacle to running for office now and in the future. Respondents react positively to the notion of running for office once they acquire more public speaking experience, campaign experience, and impressive professional credentials. Notably, the data pertaining to credentials and qualifications are particularly damning for women's expressive ambition. Women are 33 percent more likely than men to state that having more impressive credentials would heighten their likelihood of pursuing public office. They are 50 percent more likely than men to assert that more public speaking experience would increase their likelihood of running. And women are nearly 20 percent more likely than men to say that they need additional campaign experience before running for office.

Overall, regardless of whether we examine the data in a multivariate context, restrict the analysis to the women and men who emerged as candidates between the two waves of the survey, or consider respondents' attitudes toward the extent to which a series of factors might affect their likelihood of running for office, the findings are generally the same. Minority status (at least in terms of sex), professional credentials and qualifications, and patterns of encouragement to run for office are key predictors of turning the consideration of a candidacy into a reality.

For developing a broader theory of political ambition, these findings are important, as they are separate and distinct from the political opportunity structure an eligible candidate confronts.

The Role of the Political Opportunity Structure

As discussed in Chapter 2, structural variables that tap into the political contexts in which respondents live also might affect the initial decision to run for office. The regression results presented in Table 8.3, however, reveal that measures of legislative professionalization, the size and openness of the state's political opportunity structure, whether the state imposed term limits, and whether the respondent's party identification is congruent with the majority of the residents in the state all fail to achieve conventional levels of statistical significance.[26] This is not altogether surprising, as fewer than 4 percent of the men and women who considered running for office actually sought a statewide or congressional office. When I restrict the sample only to individuals who expressed interest in seeking a state or federal office and predict whether the respondent actually ran, the coefficients on the structural variables are all in the expected directions, but they still fall short of reaching statistical significance.

Of course, these null results must be viewed with at least some degree of skepticism. It is not possible to capture fully the extent to which structural variables play a role in the initial decision to run for office because of a lack of indicators of the local political context. The total number of local governmental units by state – which serves as the one available local structural variable – is statistically insignificant. But I do not have gauges of the partisan composition of local constituencies, or information pertaining to the size and levels of incumbency associated with local offices, such as school board and city council.

Despite the limited quantitative evidence that taps into the extent to which structural variables affect the initial decision to run for office at the local level, the comments relayed by the eligible candidates in the interviews suggest their effect. Eligible candidates frequently mentioned that they would not run for office if they had to face a strong incumbent or if they were not politically in sync with their communities. Attorney Ellen Chapman noted, for instance, that Denver is becoming increasingly conservative. She explained that she could not run for the city council or

---

[26] For a more detailed discussion of the influence structural variables exert on this sample of the eligibility pool's candidate emergence process, see Fox and Lawless 2005.

any other municipal position: "I am definitely not in sync with this new majority. I would be unelectable." Mitchell Reston, a businessman who lives outside Tulsa, has "very strong political aspirations." But "as the only gay man living amid neoconservative religious types," he does not think that running for office would be "feasible." Phil Bensen, a history professor at a large university in the South, feels the same way: "I don't fit in here politically. I'd like to run, but I'd never get elected locally, so it would be a waste of my time." On the other hand, Danielle Keaver, who runs a nonprofit organization in New Hampshire, decided to run for local office in 2008 because it was a "good year for Democrats for all levels of office." She explained, "The timing wasn't perfect for me personally, but I had to seize the opportunity. My views were as close to the people in my town as they ever would be."

Structural variables and strategic considerations, in essence, likely affect the decision to run for office at all levels, even if the empirical data are limited in the extent to which they can measure the effects. There is, however, no reason to believe that gauges of the local political opportunity structure would render insignificant the personal, professional, and political factors that also affect expressive ambition.

Conclusion

The data presented in this chapter provide evidence that most eligible candidates express distaste for the nuts and bolts associated with a political campaign. Yet several hundred respondents still chose to enter the electoral arena as candidates. At this second stage of the candidate emergence process – the decision to enter the first actual race – factors not related to the political opportunity structure operate somewhat differently than they do in predicting nascent ambition. More specifically, sex, professional factors – such as income and self-perceived qualifications – and political recruitment exert an impact on both nascent and expressive ambition. On the other hand, whereas an eligible candidate's race and family dynamics affect whether he or she will consider a candidacy, these explanations shed little light on who decides to enter an actual race. Of course, race, a politicized upbringing, and a supportive family environment play a vital role in the initial decision to run for office because these factors affect whether eligible candidates ever reach the second stage of the process and confront the decision to run for office.

The conclusions I draw from the data presented in this chapter do not mean that the political opportunity structure is not an important predictor of whether an eligible candidate will enter a race at a given time. Indeed, the data are limited in the extent to which they can shed light on the relative importance of the opportunity structure, so I err on the side of caution and argue that previous research paints a sufficiently compelling picture of the influence of structural variables for me to stipulate their effects. But data from this sample of the candidate eligibility pool demonstrate that, beyond the opportunity structure, a series of personal, familial, professional, and political dynamics also affect the initial decision to run for office. Overlooking the power of these variables – all of which are key predictors of considering a candidacy, and many of which also exert an additional influence on the decision to enter a race – leaves scholars with an incomplete conception of political ambition.

Future Patterns of Candidate Emergence and Studies of Political Ambition

Peter Hernandez opened a small business in New England more than a decade ago. He devotes the overwhelming majority of his time to his profession, but politics is always in the back of his mind. Even though he works "upwards of 70 hours a week," Hernandez thinks about running for office "all the time. It's percolating seven days a week." This is not surprising given that he was raised in a highly political home; his parents never ran for office, but according to Hernandez, "They might as well have. They were always hosting candidate events and attending political meetings." Indeed, he credits his parents with encouraging him to seek elective positions in both high school and college. He is not sure when he will run for office, but it is likely only a matter of time. Convinced that his political connections, business experiences, and lifelong passion for politics would make him a "solid candidate" and an "excellent politician," Hernandez is never surprised when clients and business associates urge him to run for the city council or the state legislature. He also knows he would have support should he enter a race; the state legislators who do business with his firm have already pledged their help, as have his family, friends, and colleagues.

Texas attorney David Robinson reports that he, too, has considered running for office, although he no longer thinks about it very often. Raised in a fairly political home – his parents spoke about politics regularly and he remembers accompanying his parents to the polls on Election Day – Robinson recalls being encouraged to develop strong beliefs about a host of national and foreign policy issues. By the time he completed college and law school, he had contributed financially to "more candidates and issue campaigns than [he] can remember." Now a partner in a law firm that handles the business of many elected officials, Robinson acknowledges that he is "closer to politics than ever before." But he explains that he has also become "frustrated, disgusted, and increasingly turned off" by politicians and government: "I used to think – very naively – that if you got the right guys in there, then we'd see positive change. But that never happens. It doesn't matter who we elect. The system changes them for the worse. I know people who started out with the right intentions and are now unrecognizable." Because of his increasing cynicism toward politics, as well as the fact that "the job doesn't pay enough to make the trade-offs worthwhile," Robinson no longer has any interest in running for office.

Unlike Peter Hernandez and David Robinson, Jill Gruber has not given running for office much thought. She rarely discussed politics with her parents when growing up, although she is quite politically involved as an adult. Not only does she try to attend school board and city council meetings, but she is also an active member of several political organizations that focus on the environment and education. Gruber's political activism is somewhat limited by her lack of free time; she has three school-aged children and performs more of the household tasks and child care than does her spouse, who is an elementary school principal. No friend or family member ever suggested that Gruber run for office. No colleague ever encouraged a candidacy. And no party official, officeholder, or fellow political activist ever mentioned that she should consider entering electoral politics. Although she has not considered running for office, Gruber is open to the idea "at some point down the road when the children are grown." But she doubts she could win. She does not view herself as qualified to seek most offices and she does not think she "know[s] the right people."

The sentiments of these three individuals exemplify the manner in which the early stages of the candidate emergence process are set into motion long before an opportunity to enter a specific race occurs. They all possess excellent qualifications and credentials to run for office. They are well educated, have risen to the top of their professions, serve as active members in their communities, and express high levels of political interest. Yet because of different sociodemographic backgrounds, family dynamics, professional circumstances, and attitudes toward the political system, they are not equally likely to exhibit nascent ambition, let alone actually run for office. The factors that lead an individual first to consider running for office and then to decide to seek an actual position are complex and multifaceted. But the evidence presented throughout this book indicates that the early stages of the candidate emergence process are driven by far more than a strategic assessment or cost–benefit analysis of the political opportunity structure. Overlooking nascent ambition and its dynamic nature, therefore, likely means misgauging not only who will ultimately emerge as candidates, but also prospects for electoral competition, democratic legitimacy, and political representation.

Summary of the Findings: Contemporary Patterns of Candidate Emergence

For decades, political scientists have bemoaned the dearth of research pertaining to the initial decision to run for office.[1] Because of the many methodological and sampling design challenges involved in identifying and compiling a sample of women and men in the candidate eligibility pool, the overwhelming majority of the research on political ambition focuses on the end stage of the candidate emergence process. That is, scholars tend to develop theories and generate predictions regarding the decision to enter a particular race at a given time. Typically based on data from actual candidates or elected officials, study after study provides evidence that the political opportunity structure plays an important role in the decision to run for office. In short, when individuals face favorable opportunity structures – for example, open seats, term-limited incumbents, or politically congruent constituencies – they will be more likely to throw their hats into the electoral ring than when doing so would involve a less appealing set of structural circumstances. Political ambition, itself, is taken almost as a given. Eligible candidates all tend to have it; the question is under what conditions they will exercise it.

There is no question that studying political ambition this way has allowed political scientists to gain a solid grasp on static, progressive, and discrete ambition. Relatively short-term strategic calculations linked to the external political environment serve as important predictors of the manner in which individuals navigate their political careers. We know from a wide body of literature, for instance, that politicians tend to behave in ways that maximize their likelihood of attaining higher office, or at least maintaining the position they currently hold (Schlesinger 1966). Perceptions of electoral success have been shown to be a key consideration in an individual's decision to enter his or her first congressional race (Maisel and Stone 1997). Studies of congressional retirement conclude that as an

---

[1] Among others, Donald Matthews (1984), Thomas Kazee (1994), and Walter Stone and L. Sandy Maisel (2003) call attention to the little research that focuses on eligible candidates, despite its importance in helping political scientists develop a fuller understanding of the electoral process, candidate quality, and issues of representation.

electoral margin decreases, so, too, does a member's likelihood of seeking reelection (e.g., Lawless and Theriault 2005; Theriault 1998; Moore and Hibbing 1992). For many members of Congress, it is preferable to exit the chamber voluntarily, as opposed to engaging in an arduous reelection bid that might end in defeat.

But because the study of political ambition has largely been limited to the decision making of political actors who are already fully immersed in electoral politics, we have been limited in the extent to which we can assess empirically the fundamental assumption that all eligible candidates are, in fact, interested in running for office and ready to exercise that political ambition given the right political opportunity structure. We have been unable to shed much light on the factors that promote a general, abstract interest in running for office. And we have barely scratched the surface in terms of the extent to which broad interest in running for office changes over time. The Citizen Political Ambition Panel Study and the eligibility pool approach on which it relies overcome the methodological challenges involved in identifying and sampling a broad cross-section of eligible candidates and allows for a systematic analysis of the critically important initial decision to run for office.

The survey results and interview evidence presented throughout this book substantiate the theoretical distinction between nascent and expressive political ambition. Levels of interest in running for office among the eligible candidates in the study are quite high; roughly half considered a candidacy, and more than 10 percent actually sought elective office at some point. But even among a sample of women and men who occupy the professions that are most likely to lead to political careers, 50 percent of respondents never had the notion of a candidacy even cross their minds. These individuals do not assess the costs and benefits of entering a particular electoral contest; running for office does not appear on their radar screens. Among eligible candidates who have considered running for office – individuals with nascent ambition – focusing on the political opportunity structure to predict specific political career decisions can provide leverage for understanding the late stages of the candidate emergence process. But it is imperative to examine the factors that lead women and men in the candidate eligibility pool to consider a candidacy in the first place, as well as the extent to which those circumstances change over time.

My findings and analysis demonstrate that the initial decision to run for office is linked to four sets of factors that fall outside the traditional political opportunity structure, but that systematically exert an influence on interest in running for office. *Minority status, family dynamics, professional experiences*, and *political attitudes and recruitment* overlap, interact, and simultaneously affect eligible candidates' inclinations to pursue public office. Table 9.1, which summarizes and categorizes the empirical and qualitative evidence, illustrates the broad range of findings and underscores the value of homing in on the earlier phase of the candidate emergence process.

TABLE 9.1. *Summary of Findings*

Evidence of the Effects of Minority Status in the Candidate Emergence Process:

- Men are nearly twice as likely as women to report having "seriously considered" a candidacy; women are more likely than men never to have thought about running for office.
- The gender gap in nascent ambition exists among white, black, and Latino eligible candidates.
- Not only are women less likely than men to consider running for office in general, but they are also particularly less likely to express interest in high-level (i.e., federal or statewide) offices.
- Across profession and party, women are less likely than men to be recruited to run for office by party leaders and elected officials and less likely to consider themselves qualified to run for office.
- African Americans are more likely than their white counterparts to be recruited to run for office and to consider themselves qualified to run for office.
- Women are less likely than men to emerge as actual candidates.

Evidence of the Effects of Family Dynamics in the Candidate Emergence Process:

- Eligible candidates who report growing up in a household in which their parents frequently suggested that they run for office are more likely to consider running for office as adults.
- Encouragement or a suggestion to run for office from a family member or spouse increases the likelihood that an eligible candidate will consider a candidacy.
- The addition of a new family member in the household spurs interest in running for office.

Evidence of the Effects of Professional Circumstances in the Candidate Emergence Process:

- Lawyers and activists are significantly more likely than business leaders and educators to consider running for office and to report interest in ever pursuing high-level office.
- As an eligible candidate's income rises, his or her likelihood of considering a candidacy decreases.

- Eligible candidates whose careers confer a high level of political proximity are especially likely to consider running for office.
- Lawyers and activists are roughly twice as likely as business leaders and educators to consider themselves "very qualified" to seek and hold an elective position. These assessments of qualifications cannot be separated from the skills acquired and honed on the job.
- Changes in respondents' perceptions of their qualifications to enter the electoral arena predict changes in interest in running for office.

Evidence of the Effects of the Role of Political Parties in the Candidate Emergence Process:

- Party identification predicts neither whether a respondent considers running for office nor whether a respondent receives the suggestion to run from an electoral gatekeeper. But recruitment from party leaders, elected officials, and political activists is one of the most important predictors of whether a respondent considers a candidacy, regardless of party.
- For Democrats, Republicans, and independents alike, the shifting sands of the political context exert a direct impact on political cynicism.
- Eligible candidates who grew more cynical about politics and the political system between the two waves of the study are significantly more likely than their counterparts whose levels of political cynicism did not change to lose all ambition to run for office.

Consistent with the three anecdotes that opened this chapter, the list of findings highlights the fact that personal and professional considerations and experiences – many of which might seem quite removed from the decision to run for office – play a major role in positioning eligible candidates along the candidate emergence continuum. Family circumstances that promote political activism and engagement often trigger eligible candidates' interest in running for office from an early age. Encouragement for a candidacy from politically engaged family members can sustain that interest over time and make the notion of a candidacy seem feasible and desirable. Professional circumstances also exert a substantial effect on nascent ambition. More specifically, politically relevant connections and skills acquired throughout the course of a career not only provide eligible candidates with greater proximity to the political arena, but also enhance women and men's self-perceptions of their qualifications to run for office. Finally, attitudes toward, and experiences with, party leaders and political institutions exert an effect on eligible candidates' interest in running for office. Broad recruitment efforts from electoral gatekeepers, for instance, often plant the seed for a future candidacy, even when those recruitment efforts are not attached to any particular elective office. Eligible candidates' attitudes about the political arena and its players shape their interest in running for office, too. Increased levels of cynicism toward the political process – often directed at the federal government, the president, and Congress – can depress the likelihood that an eligible candidate expresses interest in a future candidacy, even at the local or state level.

Importantly, minority status plays a role in the candidate emergence process as well, often underlying the family, professional, and political factors that affect nascent ambition. More specifically, political organizations and institutions that have always been controlled by men continue to operate with a gendered lens that promotes men's participation in the political arena and does not sufficiently encourage women to break down barriers in traditionally masculine spheres and environments. Moreover, a gendered psyche imbues many women with a sense of doubt as to their ability to thrive in the political sphere. These same deeply internalized attitudes about gender roles and women and men's receptivity in the political arena lead men to envision and, in some cases, embrace the notion of running for public office. Race operates somewhat differently, but also affects interest in running for office. Although black and Latino eligible candidates are as likely as their white counterparts, at least at the aggregate level, to report having considered running for office, the gender gap in political ambition persists across racial and ethnic lines. In addition, once we account for professional circumstances and recruitment experiences, black eligible candidates are statistically less likely than whites to consider running for office.

The empirical findings also indicate that, over the course of seven years, interest in pursuing a candidacy fluctuated for nearly 40 percent of the panel respondents. Between the two waves of the study, a significant number of respondents gained strong interest in running for office, whereas an even larger group became adamantly opposed to running. Importantly, measurable changes in the political opportunity structure do not account for these shifts. Rather, changes in internal and external political efficacy, as well as patterns of political recruitment and family circumstances, explain the individual-level changes in interest in running for office. These results suggest that ebbs and flows in political ambition also often precede the decision to enter an actual race at a given time.

Taken together, the findings presented throughout this book reveal that nascent ambition is a necessary condition for expressive ambition, and that it is far more fluid than current theories suggest.

Implications for Candidate Emergence and the Study of Political Ambition

When we consider the broader implications of the two-stage candidate emergence process, it becomes clear that the results speak to fundamental questions of electoral competition, political representation, and democratic legitimacy. Overall, this examination of the initial decision to run for office should quell some anxiety regarding perceptions of limited electoral competition, but it should also raise a series of grave concerns over the quality of democratic governance and political representation in the United States.

Turning first to electoral competition and political accountability, the U.S. political system – which is composed of more than half a million elected positions – can function and sustain itself only if a large, engaged group of citizens exhibit interest in running for elective office. Indeed, competitive elections tend to increase voter turnout, enhance citizens' political activism, and elevate the extent to which candidates and elected officials respond to their constituents (Barreto and Streb 2007; see also Jacobson 2001). In this vein, the results of the Citizen Political Ambition Panel Study provide mixed prospects. The majority of eligible candidates convey a willingness to run for office if the opportunity presents itself and the circumstances are right; only three in ten rule out the possibility completely. That said, the political tumult of the seven years between the two waves of the study appears to have pushed many qualified, well-situated eligible candidates away from considering a run for elective office. The net decrease in political ambition in the candidate eligibility pool indicates that serving in office has become less appealing. If interest in running for office is a powerful barometer of civic engagement, then theories of candidate emergence and the metrics by which we measure the health of democracy in the United States must begin to account for the manner in which political trends, events, and conditions affect eligible candidates' levels of nascent ambition and attitudes toward entering the political fray.

The results of the study also reveal that prospects for political representation and democratic legitimacy are likely far less rosy than the increasing gender and racial diversity in the pipeline professions to a political career might suggest. As I argued at the outset of this analysis, the willingness of a large and diverse group of citizens to seek elective office is necessary for a healthy democracy. More specifically, and as detailed in Chapter 1, a compelling body of evidence suggests that particular sociodemographic groups are best able to represent the policy preferences of that group. In addition, political theorists ascribe symbolic or role model benefits to a more diverse body of elected officials (Amundsen 1971; Bachrach 1967; Pitkin 1967). If interest in seeking office is in any way restricted to citizens with certain demographic profiles, then serious questions emerge regarding the quality of descriptive, symbolic, and substantive representation.

The results of the investigation indicate that, despite policy-related and symbolic benefits, the prospects for increasing women and racial minorities' numeric representation in our political institutions are not promising. Only a combination of profound changes – not only in terms of how women in the eligibility pool perceive themselves, but also in terms of how their professional, political, and personal networks perceive them – can begin to lessen the gender gap in considering a candidacy. Women's increasing presence in the candidate pipeline, as well as voters' willingness to elect female candidates, are certainly necessary for moving toward gender parity in elected bodies. But the empirical evidence, coupled with the words of the eligible candidates themselves, suggests that even if women were much better represented in the candidate eligibility pool, they would still be less likely than men to run for office. Women's full inclusion in our political institutions requires more than open seats and a steady increase in the number of women occupying the professions that most often precede political careers. It depends on closing the gender gap in political ambition. Barring such change, women will continue to be less likely than men to consider running for office, so they will remain less likely than men ever to reach the second stage of the candidate emergence process.

The prospects for black eligible candidates are more positive because perceptions of qualifications and patterns of political recruitment work to their advantage and offset the negative effect of race, in and of itself. Of course, this sample of eligible candidates approximates the race and gender breakdowns in society. In terms of the pipeline professions that lead to a career in politics, though, white men continue to dominate disproportionately, especially in the fields of law and business. Without substantial changes to the types of candidates electoral gatekeepers recruit, fundamental shifts in family dynamics both in childhood and adulthood, or widespread improvement in the manner in which citizens assess politicians and political institutions, politically connected white men will continue to dominate not only the individuals who decide to run for office, but also the pool of eligible candidates who think seriously about a candidacy.

The results of the Citizen Political Ambition Panel Study make clear that the two-stage conception of the candidate emergence process poses many critical obstacles that affect eligible candidates long before they face the decision to enter an actual race. Considering the fundamental ways in which minority status, family dynamics, professional circumstances, and interactions with and attitudes toward the political system influence the pre-candidacy stage of the electoral process, I propose three avenues of future research to pick up where this study leaves off.

We might begin by studying early family, education, and career experiences that can affect the candidate emergence process, paying special attention to the manner in which these experiences interact with sex and race. For most people, choosing to run for office is not a spontaneous decision; rather, it is the culmination of a long, personal evolution that often stretches back into early family life. From an early age, do women and men develop different conceptions of what political careers embody and entail? In school, does American political history's focus on white men's accomplishments leave enduring effects on the psyches of young women and men? Does eligible candidates' access to strong role models and mentors encourage their professional achievement and facilitate their political ambition? And does the power conferred by these role models and mentors vary along gender and racial lines? In conducting these analyses, researchers may want to focus on high school and college students. Many attitudes about running for office and the electoral environment are in place long before women and men find themselves in the candidate eligibility pool. Investigating gender or race differences in ambition at their source, as opposed to relying on retrospective assessments of events that occurred decades earlier, may prove fruitful.

Second, the findings in this book point to the importance of determining the specific factors that might spur ambition among eligible candidates. What types of recruitment messages are particularly effective in encouraging candidacies? To what extent can positive messages about the importance of government service combat increasing levels of political cynicism and negative attitudes toward U.S. politicians and institutions? Does the general anti-government message disseminated by Tea Party activists – a message that appears to have triggered some candidacies in the 2010 election cycle – ultimately depress interest in running for office in the long run? What specific steps can political parties, electoral gatekeepers, and political activists take to improve eligible candidates' assessments of themselves as candidates? Can the dissemination of information that shows that women, as well as African Americans, actually perform as well as white men at the polls combat negative attitudes and pessimistic expectations about the electoral process? This type of research carries clear normative implications for organizations and individuals working to increase racial and gender diversity in electoral politics, but it will also shed light on the circumstances by which we can foster and sustain civic engagement at the utmost levels.

Finally, a full assessment of the candidate emergence process must incorporate the manner in which perceptions of the political opportunity structure, as well as the actual political opportunity structure, play a role in the initial decision to run for office. Because perceptions tend to dictate behavior, they are just as important as reality. Indeed, Richard L. Fox and I (2011) demonstrate the extent to which perceptions of skills and traits account for eligible candidates' assessments of their qualifications to run for office (see also Chapter 6). But research that examines the manner in which perceptions of the political opportunity structure affect the decision to run for office is scant (see Githens 2003). We have only very limited gauges of how eligible candidates perceive the specific political climates and seats for which they could potentially run. And we continue to lack data that allow for an examination of the actual structural factors surrounding most localities and municipalities, even though local-level positions are the most common to pursue. How do eligible candidates view the opportunity structures associated with different levels of office? To what extent do attitudes about competitive federal races trickle down to the local level? Are women and men even aware of all of the local offices in their communities? Do eligible candidates' perceptions of gender or racial bias in electoral competition affect their interest in running for particular offices? Only by answering these questions can we fully understand the extent to which the political opportunity structure affects both the nascent and expressive stages of the initial decision to run for office.

I began this book by asking why anyone makes the move from politically minded citizen to candidate for public office. What factors contribute to the initial decision to run for office? What circumstances serve to encourage and suppress political ambition over time? Nine chapters, 300 interviews, and thousands of surveys later, I can conclude that eligible candidates move along the candidate emergence continuum only if they first consider running for office. And importantly, the key ingredients for considering a candidacy are far less proximate to entering a political contest than most studies of political ambition suggest. Minority status, family dynamics, professional circumstances, and attitudes toward and interactions with the political system – all of which are removed from the traditional political opportunity structure – determine the likelihood that an eligible candidate will emerge from the eligibility pool. With this broader conception of political ambition, we can continue to investigate who would ever run for office, and we can ensure that these investigations are more nuanced and grounded not only in a cost-benefit analysis of political reality, but also in individual-level circumstances, many of which are deeply embedded and the product of long-standing patterns of socialization.

APPENDIX A

The Citizen Political Ambition Panel Study

Richard L. Fox and I drew the "candidate eligibility pool" from a national sample of women and men employed in the four professions that most often precede state legislative and congressional candidacies: law, business, education, and politics. In assembling the sample, we created two equal-sized pools of candidates – one female and one male – that held the same professional credentials. Because we wanted to make nuanced statistical comparisons within and between the subgroups of men and women in each profession, we attempted to compile a sample of 900 men and 900 women from each.

We drew the names of lawyers and business leaders from national directories. We obtained a random sample of 1,800 lawyers from the 2001 edition of the *Martindale-Hubble Law Directory*, which provides the addresses and names of practicing attorneys in all law firms across the country. We stratified the total number of lawyers by sex and in proportion to the total number of law firms listed for each state. We randomly selected 1,800 business leaders from *Dun and Bradstreet's Million Dollar Directory, 2000–2001*, which lists the top executive officers of more than 160,000 public and private companies in the United States. Again, we stratified by geography and sex and ensured that men and women held comparable positions.

No national directories exist for our final two categories. To compile a sample of educators, we focused on college professors and administrative officials, and public school teachers and administrators. Turning first to the higher education subsample, we compiled a random sample of 600 public and private colleges and universities from the roughly 4,000 schools listed in *U.S. News and World Report's* "America's Best Colleges" guide (2001), from which we selected 300 male and 300 female professors and administrative officials. Because we did not stratify by school size, the college and university portion of the sample yielded a higher number of educators from smaller schools; however, we found that the size of the institution was not a significant predictor of political ambition. We then compiled a national sample of 1,200 public school teachers and principals (600 men and 600 women). We obtained the sample through an Internet search of public school districts, from which we located the websites of individual schools and the names of their employees. This technique might result in a bias toward schools that had the resources to provide computers in 2001. A 2001 study by the U.S. Department of Education, however, found that 98 percent of public schools had Internet access and 84 percent had a web page.

Our final eligibility pool profession – "political activists" – represents citizens who work in politics and public policy. We created a list of political interest groups and national organizations with state and/or local affiliates and sought to strike a partisan and ideological balance. We randomly selected state branch and local chapter executive directors and officers of organizations that focus on the environment, abortion, consumer issues, race relations, civil liberties, taxes, guns, crime, Social Security, school choice, government reform, and "women's issues." This selection technique, which provided a range of activists from a broad cross section of occupations, yielded 744 men and 656 women, thereby making the "activist" subsample smaller than the other three groups.

We employed standard mail survey protocol in conducting the study. Eligible candidates received an initial letter explaining the study and a copy of the questionnaire. Three days later, they received a follow-up postcard. Two weeks later, we sent a follow-up letter with another copy of the questionnaire. We supplemented this third piece of correspondence with an e-mail message when possible (for roughly half the lawyers, educators, and political activists). Four months later, we sent all men and women from whom we had not received a survey another copy of the questionnaire. The final contact was made the following month, when we sent, via e-mail, a link to an online version of the survey. The survey was conducted from July 2001 to August 2002.[1]

---

[1] In light of calls for increased public service and community engagement following the events of September 11, 2001, we compared attitudes toward running for office between individuals who returned the questionnaire before versus after the terrorist attacks. We uncovered no differences in political ambition or interest in seeking public office.

From the original sample of 6,800 individuals, 554 surveys were either undeliverable or returned because the individual was no longer employed in the position. From the 6,246 remaining members of the sample, we received responses from 3,765 individuals (1,969 men and 1,796 women). After taking into account respondents who left the majority of the questionnaire incomplete, we were left with 3,614 completed surveys, for a usable response rate of 58 percent, which is higher than that of typical elite sample mail surveys, and substantially greater than the expected response rate of 40 percent (Johnson, Joslyn, and Reynolds 2001).[2]

Six months after collecting the data, we sent a summary of the results to all respondents. We asked individuals to return an enclosed postcard indicating whether we could contact them for a follow-up interview. Of the 3,765 respondents who participated in the study, 1,219 agreed to be interviewed and 374 refused. We did not hear from the remaining sample members. After stratifying by sex and occupation, we randomly selected 100 men and 100 women for phone interviews, which we conducted in July and August 2003. The interviews ranged from 30 minutes to an hour and a half in length.

In early 2008, we completed the second wave of the panel study. Through extensive Internet searches and phone calls, we obtained current address information for 2,976 members (82 percent) of the original sample of respondents who completed the questionnaire in 2001. After employing standard mail survey protocol, we heard from 2,060 men and women, 2,036 of whom completed the questionnaire. This represents a 75 percent response rate for the second wave of the panel.[3] Controlling for sex, race, and profession, individuals who expressed some degree of political ambition in 2001 were no more likely than respondents who had never considered a candidacy to complete the 2008 survey (regression results not shown). I supplemented the 2008 survey data with phone interviews of a random sample of 50 male and 50 female survey respondents. The interviews were conducted in July and August 2008, and ranged from 30 minutes to an hour in length.

---

[2] Response rates within the four subsamples were: lawyers – 68%; business leaders – 45%; educators – 61%; political activists – 68%. Nonresponse is probably inversely correlated with interest in running for political office, but does not differ between women and men.

[3] Response rates for the 2008 survey varied less by profession than was the case in 2001: lawyers – 77%; business leaders – 59%; educators – 71%; political activists – 73%. High response rates for the second wave are to be expected, since each respondent had already demonstrated a propensity to complete the questionnaire. These rates take into account 205 undeliverable surveys.

The First Wave Survey (2001)

Below is a copy of the questionnaire completed by the members of the candidate eligibility pool sample. We modified some questions for the political activist subsample and asked for elaboration regarding their levels of political activity and issue advocacy.

*   *   *   *   *   *   *   *   *   *   *   *

Instructions

Thank you very much for participating in this survey. All of your answers are confidential. Please answer the questions to the best of your ability and then enclose the survey in the addressed, stamped envelope. If you would like a copy of the results, then please write your address on the back of the return envelope. Thank you.

Part I – We would like to begin by asking you about your political attitudes and the ways you participate politically.

1. **Please mark your level of agreement with the following statements:**

	Strongly Disagree	Disagree	Neither Disagree nor Agree	Agree	Strongly Agree
Taxes are too high.	○	○	○	○	○
More gun control laws should be passed.	○	○	○	○	○
Abortion should always be legal in the first trimester.	○	○	○	○	○
The U.S. should move toward universal health care.	○	○	○	○	○
The government should take a more active role combating sexual harassment in the workplace.	○	○	○	○	○
Government pays attention to people when making decisions.	○	○	○	○	○
It is just as easy for a woman to be elected to a high-level public office as a man.	○	○	○	○	○
Waging a war against terrorism is the single most important goal the federal government should pursue in the next 10 years.	○	○	○	○	○
Most men are better suited emotionally for politics than are most women.	○	○	○	○	○
Within the corporate and business world, it is still more difficult for women to climb the career ladder.	○	○	○	○	○
Feminism has had a positive impact on social and political life in the United States.	○	○	○	○	○
Congress should enact hate crime legislation.	○	○	○	○	○

2. How would you describe your party affiliation?
   ○ Democrat
   ○ Republican
   ○ Independent
   ○ Other

3. How would you describe your political philosophy?
   ○ Liberal
   ○ Moderate
   ○ Conservative

4. How closely do you follow national politics?
   ○ Very Closely
   ○ Closely
   ○ Somewhat Closely
   ○ Not Closely

5. How closely do you follow politics in your community?
   ○ Very Closely
   ○ Closely
   ○ Somewhat Closely
   ○ Not Closely

6. Many people do not engage in many political or community activities. In which, if any, of the following activities have you engaged in the past year?

	Yes	No
Voted in the 2000 presidential election	○	○
Wrote a letter to a newspaper	○	○
Joined or paid dues to a political interest group	○	○
Contacted an elected official (by phone, email, letter, etc.)	○	○
Contributed money to a campaign	○	○
Volunteered for a political candidate	○	○
Joined a group in the community to address a local issue	○	○
Volunteered on a community project	○	○
Attended a city council or school board meeting	○	○
Served on the board of a nonprofit organization	○	○

7. When you think about politics, how important are the following issues to you when you are considering how to vote and whether to participate politically?

	Not At All Important	Not Very Important	Important	Very Important
Abortion	O	O	O	O
Education	O	O	O	O
Health Care	O	O	O	O
Environment	O	O	O	O
Economy	O	O	O	O
Guns	O	O	O	O
Crime	O	O	O	O
Gay Rights	O	O	O	O
Foreign Policy	O	O	O	O

8. Do you consider yourself a feminist?
   - O Yes
   - O No

9. Off the top of your head, do you recall the name of your member of the U.S. House of Representatives?
   - O Unsure
   - O Name: _____

10. Off the top of your head, do you recall the names of your U.S. senators?

    1. O Unsure   O Name: _____
    2. O Unsure   O Name: _____

11. Which statement best captures how you feel about people who run for political office?
    - O Most people who run for office are very well intentioned and genuinely hope to improve society.
    - O Most people who run for office are generally interested in their own fame and power.

12. **If you felt strongly about a government action or policy, how likely would you be to engage in each of the following political activities?**

	Very Unlikely	Unlikely	Likely	Very Likely
Give money to a political candidate who favors your position	○	○	○	○
Volunteer for a candidate or group that favors your position	○	○	○	○
Organize people in the community to work on the issue	○	○	○	○
Directly lobby or contact government officials	○	○	○	○
Run for public office	○	○	○	○

Part II – The next series of questions deal with your attitudes toward running for office. We realize that most citizens have never thought about running, but your answers are still very important.

1. **Which of the following options do you think is the most effective way for you to get government to address a political issue?**
   ○ Run for office and become a policymaker
   ○ Form a grassroots organization to lobby government
   ○ Make monetary contributions to appropriate political leaders
   ○ Support a candidate who shares your views

2. **Generally speaking, do you think most elected officials are qualified for the positions they hold?**
   ○ Yes
   ○ No

3. **Have you ever held elective public office?**
   ○ Yes: What office[s]: _____
   ○ No
      If no, have you ever run for public office?
      ○ Yes: What office[s]: _____
      ○ No

4. **If you have never run for office, have you ever thought about running for office?**
   - ○ Yes, I have seriously considered it.
   - ○ Yes, it has crossed my mind.
   - ○ No, I have not thought about it.

5. **If you have ever thought about running for office, have you ever taken any of the following steps?**

	Yes	No
Discussed running with party leaders	○	○
Discussed running with friends and family	○	○
Discussed running with community leaders	○	○
Solicited or discussed financial contributions with potential supporters	○	○
Investigated how to place your name on the ballot	○	○

6. **Regardless of your interest in running for office, have any of the following individuals ever suggested that you run for office?**

	Yes	No
An official from a political party	○	○
A co-worker or business associate	○	○
An elected official	○	○
A friend or acquaintance	○	○
A spouse or partner	○	○
A member of your family	○	○
A non-elected political activist	○	○
Other; specify: _____	○	○

7. **Would you be more likely to consider running for office if:**

	No	Possibly	Yes
Someone from work suggested you run?	○	○	○
Someone from your political party or community suggested you run?	○	○	○
You had more free time?	○	○	○
A friend suggested you run?	○	○	○
You had more impressive professional credentials?	○	○	○
A spouse/partner suggested you run?	○	○	○
You were more financially secure?	○	○	○
You had fewer family responsibilities?	○	○	○
There were issues you were more passionate about?	○	○	○
You knew there was a lot of support for your candidacy?	○	○	○
You had previous experience working on a campaign?	○	○	○
You had more experience with public speaking?	○	○	○
Campaigns were publicly financed?	○	○	○

8. **Please assess how important you think it is that candidates for public office have the following experiences in their backgrounds:**

	Not Important	Somewhat Important	Important	Very Important
Having worked in business	○	○	○	○
Having expertise on policy issues	○	○	○	○
Having a law degree	○	○	○	○
Having campaign experience	○	○	○	○
Having public speaking experience	○	○	○	○

9. Overall, how qualified do you feel you are to run for public office?
   ○ Very Qualified
   ○ Qualified
   ○ Somewhat Qualified
   ○ Not at All Qualified

10. If you were to become a candidate for public office, how would you feel about engaging in the following aspects of a campaign?

	So negative, it would deter me from running			
		Negative		
	Positive			
	Very Positive			
Attending fundraising functions	○	○	○	○
Dealing with party officials	○	○	○	○
Going door-to-door to meet constituents	○	○	○	○
Dealing with members of the press	○	○	○	○
The amount of time it takes to run for office	○	○	○	○

11. We would now like to ask you about your interest in specific public offices.

	1) If you were to run for office, which one would you likely seek first? (check one)	2) What offices might you ever be interested in running for? (check all that apply)
School Board	○	○
Mayor	○	○
State Legislator	○	○
Member of the U.S. House of Representatives	○	○
U.S. Senator	○	○
President	○	○
City, County, or Town Council	○	○
Governor	○	○
Statewide Office (i.e., Attorney General)	○	○
I would never run for any office	○	○
I have held elected office	○	○

12. **If you were to become a candidate for public office, how likely do you think it is that you would win your first campaign?**
    o Very Likely
    o Likely
    o Unlikely
    o Very Unlikely

13. **Which best characterizes your attitudes toward running for office in the future?**
    o It is something I definitely would like to undertake in the future.
    o It is something I might undertake if the opportunity presented itself.
    o I would not rule it out forever, but I currently have no interest.
    o It is something I would absolutely never do.
    o I currently hold elected office.

14. **How have the recent attacks in New York and Washington, DC affected your attitudes about running for public office?**
    o They make me more likely to run.
    o They make me less likely to run.
    o They do not change my attitude.

Part III – Finally, we would like to ask you some questions about your background and family life.

1. **What is your sex?**   o Female   o Male

2. **What is your age?** _____

3. **What is your race?**
    o White
    o Black
    o Asian
    o Hispanic/Latino
    o Native American
    o Other (please specify): _____

4. **In what type of area do you live?**
    o Major City
    o Suburb
    o Small Town
    o Rural Area

5. What is your city and state of residence?

_____

6. What is your current occupation?

_____

7. What is your level of education?
   - ○ Never Completed High School
   - ○ High School Graduate
   - ○ Attended Some College (no degree attained)
   - ○ Completed College (B.A. or B.S. degree)
   - ○ Attended Some Graduate School (no degree attained)
   - ○ Completed Graduate Degree (check all that apply):
       - ○ M.B.A. ○ M.P.A. ○ J.D. ○ M.A. ○ Ph.D. ○ M.D.

8. In what category were your personal and household income last year? (check one for each column)

	Household income	Personal income
under $ 25,000	○	○
$ 25,000–$ 50,000	○	○
$ 50,001–$ 75,000	○	○
$ 75,001–$ 100,000	○	○
$ 100,001–$ 200,000	○	○
over $ 200,000	○	○

9. What is your marital status?
   - ○ Single
   - ○ Unmarried, Living as a Couple
   - ○ Married
   - ○ Widowed
   - ○ Separated
   - ○ Divorced

10. If you are married or live with a partner and your spouse or partner considered running for elective office, how supportive would you be?
    - ○ Very Supportive
    - ○ Somewhat Supportive
    - ○ Not Very Supportive

11. **If you are married or live with a partner, which statement below best describes the division of labor on household tasks, such as cleaning, laundry, and cooking?**
    - ○ I am responsible for all household tasks.
    - ○ I am responsible for more of the household tasks than my spouse/partner.
    - ○ The division of labor in my household is evenly divided.
    - ○ My spouse/partner takes care of more of the household tasks than I do.
    - ○ My spouse/partner is responsible for all household tasks.
    - ○ Other arrangements; describe: _____

12. **Do you have children?**
    - ○ Yes
    - ○ No

	Yes	No
If yes, do they live with you?	○	○
If yes, do you have children under the age of 6 living at home?	○	○
If you do not have children, do you plan to start a family in the future?	○	○

13. **If you have children, which statement best characterizes your child care arrangements?**
    - ○ I am the primary caretaker of the children.
    - ○ I have more child care responsibilities than my spouse/partner.
    - ○ My spouse/partner and I share child care responsibilities completely equally.
    - ○ My spouse/partner has more child care responsibilities than I do.
    - ○ My spouse/partner is the primary caretaker of the children.
    - ○ Other arrangements; describe:_____

14. **When you were in high school or college, did you ever run for office, such as class representative or president?**
    - ○ Yes
    - ○ No

15. **When you were growing up, how frequently did your parents discuss politics with you?**
    - ○ Frequently
    - ○ Occasionally
    - ○ Seldom
    - ○ Never

16. When you were growing up, was your father or mother more likely to discuss politics with you?
    ○ Mother
    ○ Father
    ○ Both spoke equally
    ○ Neither

17. When you were growing up, how frequently did your parents suggest that, someday, you should run for office?
    ○ Frequently
    ○ Occasionally
    ○ Seldom
    ○ Never

18. Did either of your parents ever run for elective office?
    ○ Yes, both parents
    ○ Yes, my father
    ○ Yes, my mother
    ○ No

19. Please answer these questions regarding levels of concern about politics in your past.

	Not at All Concerned	Somewhat Concerned	Very Concerned
How concerned were the students in your high school about current events and politics?	○	○	○
When you were in high school, how concerned were you about current events and politics?	○	○	○
When you were growing up, how concerned were your parents about current events and politics?	○	○	○
How concerned were the students at your college or university about current events and politics?	○	○	○
When you were in college, how concerned were you about current events and politics?	○	○	○

20. **When you were growing up, what description best characterizes the arrangements in your household?**
    - ○ I grew up in a household where my father was the primary bread-winner and my mother was the primary caretaker of the household.
    - ○ I grew up in a two-career household where my parents shared household duties evenly.
    - ○ I grew up in a two-career household where my mother was responsible for most household duties.
    - ○ I grew up in a two-career household where my father was responsible for most household duties.
    - ○ I grew up in a single parent household with my mother.
    - ○ I grew up in a single parent household with my father.
    - ○ Other

21. **In thinking about your own life, how important are the following goals and accomplishments?**

	Not at All Important	Not Very Important	Important	Very Important
Earning a great deal of money	○	○	○	○
Rising to the top of my profession	○	○	○	○
Making my community a better place to live	○	○	○	○
Devoting time to my children	○	○	○	○
Playing a big part in charitable endeavors	○	○	○	○
Devotion to my religion	○	○	○	○
Other: _____				

Thank you very much for participating in this survey. If you would like to offer additional comments about your attitudes toward politics, or your political aspirations, then please feel free to enclose an additional page of comments.

APPENDIX C

The Second Wave Survey (2008)

Below is a copy of the questionnaire completed by the members of the candidate eligibility pool sample in the second wave of the study.

*　　*　　*　　*　　*　　*　　*　　*　　*　　*　　*　　*

Instructions

Thank you very much for participating in our survey once again. All of your answers are confidential. Please answer the questions to the best of your ability and then enclose the survey in the addressed, stamped envelope. If you would like a copy of the results, then please write your address on the back of the return envelope. Thank you.

Part I – We would like to begin by asking you about your political attitudes and experiences.

1. Many people do not engage in many political or community activities. In the past year, did you . . . ?

	Yes	No
Vote in the 2006 elections	o	o
Write or email a letter to a newspaper about a political issue	o	o
Join or renew membership in a political organization	o	o
Contact an elected official (by phone, e-mail, letter, etc.)	o	o
Contribute money to a candidate or political cause	o	o
Volunteer for a community project	o	o

2. How closely do you follow national politics?
   o Very Closely
   o Closely
   o Somewhat Closely
   o Not Closely

3. How closely do you follow politics in your community?
   o Very Closely
   o Closely
   o Somewhat Closely
   o Not Closely

4. How do you characterize the political leanings of the city or town where you live?
   o Heavily Democratic
   o Leans Democratic
   o Roughly Equal Balance
   o Leans Republican
   o Heavily Republican

5. How do you characterize the political leanings of the state where you live?
   o Heavily Democratic
   o Leans Democratic
   o Roughly Equal Balance
   o Leans Republican
   o Heavily Republican

6. **How would you describe your party affiliation?**
   - ○ Strong Democrat
   - ○ Democrat
   - ○ Independent, Leaning Democrat
   - ○ Independent
   - ○ Independent, Leaning Republican
   - ○ Republican
   - ○ Strong Republican

7. **How would you describe your political views?**
   - ○ Liberal
   - ○ Moderate
   - ○ Conservative

8. **Which classification best describes you?**
   - ○ Strong Feminist
   - ○ Feminist
   - ○ Not a Feminist
   - ○ Anti-Feminist

9. **In general, how competitive are elections for local offices in the area where you live?**
   - ○ Very Competitive
   - ○ Competitive
   - ○ Somewhat Competitive
   - ○ Not at All Competitive
   - ○ I Don't Know

10. **In general, how competitive are congressional elections in the area where you live?**
    - ○ Very Competitive
    - ○ Competitive
    - ○ Somewhat Competitive
    - ○ Not at All Competitive
    - ○ I Don't Know

11. **Either professionally, or outside of work, have you ever done any of the following things?**

	Yes	No
Engaged in regular public speaking	○	○
Conducted significant research on a public policy issue	○	○
Solicited funds for an organization, interest group, or cause	○	○
Run an organization, business, or foundation	○	○
Organized an event for a large group	○	○

12. **Thinking about your news habits, how often do you . . . ?**

	Every Day	A Few Times a Week	A Few Times a Month	Rarely/Never
Read a print or online newspaper	○	○	○	○
Watch local television news	○	○	○	○
Listen to political talk radio	○	○	○	○
Watch C-SPAN	○	○	○	○
Watch the Fox News Channel	○	○	○	○
Watch CNN or MSNBC	○	○	○	○
Read political websites	○	○	○	○

13. **Are you at all inspired by any of the following contemporary political leaders? (check all that apply)**
    - ○ John McCain
    - ○ Rudy Giuliani
    - ○ Hillary Clinton
    - ○ Bill Clinton
    - ○ Condoleezza Rice
    - ○ Mitt Romney
    - ○ Nancy Pelosi
    - ○ Barack Obama
    - ○ George W. Bush
    - ○ John Edwards
    - ○ Al Gore
    - ○ Bill Richardson

14. **Throughout the course of your life, have you ever . . . ?**

	Yes	No
Worked or volunteered for a candidate	○	○
Attended a city council or school board meeting	○	○
Attended a political party meeting, convention, or event	○	○
Observed or attended a state legislative committee meeting or floor session	○	○
Interacted with elected officials as part of your job	○	○
Interacted with elected officials socially	○	○
Had an elected official as a family member or friend	○	○
Served on the board of a nonprofit organization or foundation	○	○

15. **Please mark your level of agreement with the following statements:**

	Strongly Disagree	Disagree	Neither Disagree nor Agree	Agree	Strongly Agree
Government pays attention to people when making decisions.	○	○	○	○	○
It is just as easy for women to be elected to high-level office as men.	○	○	○	○	○
It is just as easy for a black person to be elected to high-level office as a white person.	○	○	○	○	○
Within the corporate and business world, it is still more difficult for women to climb the career ladder	○	○	○	○	○
Within the corporate and business world, it is still more difficult for a black person to climb the career ladder.	○	○	○	○	○
When women run for public office, it is more difficult for them to raise money than it is for men.	○	○	○	○	○

Part II – The next series of questions concerns whether you have ever considered running for office.

1. **Do you hold or have you ever held elective public office?**
   ○ Yes

   What office[s]?_____
   What year[s] did you serve?_____

   ○ No
   If no, have you ever run for public office?
   ○ Yes

   What office[s]?_____
   What year[s]?_____

   ○ No

2. **If you have never run for office, have you ever thought about running for office?**
   - ○ Yes, I have seriously considered it.
   - ○ Yes, it has crossed my mind.
   - ○ No, I have not thought about it (please skip to Part III).

3. **How often do you think about running for office?**
   - ○ It is always in the back of my mind
   - ○ At least once a year
   - ○ Sporadically, over the years
   - ○ It has been many years since I last thought about it

4. **To the best of your recollection, how old were you when you first thought about running for office?**_____

5. **Have you ever taken any of the following steps that often precede a run for office?**

	Yes	No
Discussed running with party leaders or elected officials	○	○
Discussed running with friends and family	○	○
Discussed running with community leaders	○	○
Solicited or discussed financial contributions with potential supporters	○	○
Investigated how to place your name on the ballot	○	○

Part III – Most citizens have never thought about running for office. But we're interested in your impressions and experiences even if you're not interested in these things.

1. **Overall, how qualified do you feel you are to run for public office?**
   - ○ Very Qualified
   - ○ Qualified
   - ○ Somewhat Qualified
   - ○ Not at All Qualified

2. **Overall, how qualified do you feel you are to do the job of an elected official?**
   - ○ Very Qualified
   - ○ Qualified
   - ○ Somewhat Qualified
   - ○ Not at All Qualified

3. Would you be more interested in public office if you were appointed, rather than had to engage in a campaign?
   - ○ Yes
   - ○ No

4. Has anyone been particularly persistent or influential in trying to get you to run for office?
   - ○ Yes
   - ○ No

   If yes, was this person a man or woman?
   ○ Man ○ Woman
   What was this person's relationship to you?_____

5. Regardless of your interest in running for office, have any of the following ever suggested it to you?

	More than 5 Times	3–5 Times	Once or Twice	Never
A friend or acquaintance	○	○	○	○
A co-worker or business associate	○	○	○	○
An elected official	○	○	○	○
An official from a political party	○	○	○	○
A spouse or partner	○	○	○	○
A member of your family	○	○	○	○
A non-elected political activist	○	○	○	○
A women's organization	○	○	○	○
Someone from your church, synagogue, mosque, etc.	○	○	○	○

6. Have any of the following individuals ever discouraged you or tried to talk you out of running for office?

	Yes	No
A friend or acquaintance	○	○
A co-worker or business associate	○	○
An elected official	○	○
An official from a political party	○	○
A spouse or partner	○	○
A member of your family	○	○
A non-elected political activist	○	○

7. **In thinking about your qualifications to run for office, do any of the following apply to you? (check all that apply)**
   o I know a lot about public policy issues.
   o I have relevant professional experience.
   o I am a good public speaker.
   o I have connections to the political system.
   o I have or could raise enough money.
   o I am a good self-promoter.
   o My politics are too far out of the mainstream.
   o I don't like to make deals to get things done.

8. **Turning to your interest in specific public offices...**

	1) If you were to run for office, which one would you seek first? (check one)	2) What offices might you ever be interested in running for? (check all that apply)
School Board	o	o
Mayor	o	o
City, County, or Town Council	o	o
State Legislator	o	o
Governor	o	o
Statewide Office (i.e., Attorney General, Secretary of State)	o	o
Member of the U.S. House of Representatives	o	o
U.S. Senator	o	o
President	o	o
Judge	o	o
District Attorney	o	o

9. **Would any of the following resources make you more interested in running for office? (check all that apply)**
   o Manuals and articles on campaigns and elections
   o Interviews with political operatives and elected officials
   o Webcasts on organizing, fundraising, and media skills
   o Training programs sponsored by political organizations

10. Lots of people have a negative view of what is entailed in running for office. How would you feel about...?

	Comfortable	Wouldn't Bother Me	Negative	So Negative, It Would Deter Me from Running
Spending less time with family	O	O	O	O
Loss of privacy	O	O	O	O
Less time for personal interests	O	O	O	O
Hindering professional goals	O	O	O	O

11. If you were to run for public office, how would you feel about engaging in the following aspects of a campaign?

	Comfortable	Wouldn't Bother Me	Negative	So Negative, It Would Deter Me from Running
Soliciting campaign contributions	O	O	O	O
Dealing with party officials	O	O	O	O
Going door-to-door to meet constituents	O	O	O	O
Dealing with members of the press	O	O	O	O
Potentially having to engage in or endure a negative campaign	O	O	O	O

12. How often do you attend religious services?
   - O At least weekly
   - O Monthly
   - O Seldom
   - O Never

13. If you were to run for public office, how likely do you think it is that you would win your first campaign?
   - O Very Likely
   - O Likely
   - O Unlikely
   - O Very Unlikely

14. **In thinking about your qualifications to run for office, do any of the following apply to you? (check all that apply)**
    - ○ I don't have thick enough skin.
    - ○ I have a lot of skeletons in my closet.
    - ○ I worry about how a campaign would affect my family.
    - ○ I am too old.
    - ○ I am the wrong gender.
    - ○ I am the wrong race/ethnicity.

Part IV – Finally, we would like to ask you some questions about your background and family life.

1. **What is your sex?**   ○ Female ○ Male

2. **What is your age?** _____

3. **What was your undergraduate major?**_____

4. **Did you attend a single-sex high school?**
    - ○ Yes
    - ○ No

5. **Did you attend an all-women's college?**
    - ○ Yes
    - ○ No

6. **What is your religious affiliation?**_____

7. **In what category were your personal and household income last year? (check one for each column)**

	Household income	Personal income
under $ 25,000	○	○
$ 25,000–$ 50,000	○	○
$ 50,001–$ 75,000	○	○
$ 75,001–$ 100,000	○	○
$ 100,001–$ 200,000	○	○
over $ 200,000	○	○

8. **What is your marital status?**
    - ○ Single
    - ○ Unmarried, Living as a Couple
    - ○ Married/Civil Union
    - ○ Separated
    - ○ Divorced
    - ○ Widowed

9. **If you are married or live with a partner, which of the following statements best describes the division of labor on household tasks (cleaning, laundry, and cooking)?**
   - ○ I am responsible for all household tasks.
   - ○ I am responsible for more of the household tasks than my spouse/partner.
   - ○ The division of labor in my household is evenly divided.
   - ○ My spouse/partner takes care of more of the household tasks than I do.
   - ○ My spouse/partner is responsible for all household tasks.
   - ○ Other arrangements; describe: _____

10. **How many hours each week do you spend on these household tasks?**

11. **Do you have children?**
    - ○ Yes
    - ○ No (skip to #16)

12. **Do you have children living with you?**
    - ○ Yes
    - ○ No

13. **Do you have children under age 6 living with you?**
    - ○ Yes
    - ○ No

14. **Which statement best characterizes your child care, or characterized it when your children lived at home?**
    - ○ I am the primary caretaker of the children.
    - ○ I have more child care responsibilities than my spouse/partner.
    - ○ My spouse/partner and I share child care responsibilities completely equally.
    - ○ My spouse/partner has more child care responsibilities than I do.
    - ○ My spouse/partner is the primary caretaker of the children.
    - ○ Other arrangements; describe:_____

15. **When your children were (are) young, what were (are) your professional responsibilities?**
    - ○ I work(ed) full time.
    - ○ I work(ed) full time, but scaled back my responsibilities.
    - ○ I work(ed) part time.
    - ○ I am taking (took) a number of years off.

16. Since our last survey in 2001, have you ... ?

	Yes	No
Become more interested in politics	o	o
Become more cynical about politics	o	o
Become more concerned about global warming	o	o
Begun following foreign affairs more closely	o	o
Developed animosity toward the Bush administration	o	o
Become frustrated with the Democrats in Congress	o	o
Known someone sent to Afghanistan or Iraq	o	o

17. **Which statement best characterizes your attitudes toward running for office in the future?**
    o I definitely would like to do it in the future.
    o I might do it if the opportunity presented itself.
    o I would not rule it out forever, but I have no interest now.
    o It is something I would absolutely never do.

18. **In the last six years, have you ... ?**

	Yes	No
Had or adopted a child	o	o
Undergone a career change	o	o
Retired	o	o
Moved to a different town, city, state	o	o
Increased your religious devotion	o	o
Had children move out of the house	o	o
Had to care of a sick or aging parent	o	o
Taken on more responsibilities at work	o	o
Dealt with a serious personal or family illness	o	o

Thank you very much for participating in this survey. If you would like to offer additional comments about your attitudes toward politics, then please feel free to enclose an additional page of comments.

APPENDIX D

The First Wave Interview Questionnaire

Below is an outline of the topics addressed during the phone interviews we conducted. These conversations were free flowing, so the exact wording of each question varied.

Introduction: Thank you for agreeing to take the time to be interviewed. Most of the questions I'm going to ask deal with your attitudes about running for office. I want to emphasize that we're interested in your opinions and attitudes, even if you tend not to be very interested in politics.

Part I – Running for Public Office:

1. Have you ever thought about running for any public office – that is, any office at the local, state, or federal level; has it ever even crossed your mind?

    If they have considered it:
    - Is this something that you think about often? (Depending on the level of specificity in the answer, ask about the level of office.)
    - What makes you think you might want to do this? What's your motivation for wanting to get involved? Can you remember when you first realized that running for office was something that you might want to do?
    - Have you thought about it recently?

    If yes:
    - When was the most recent time you've thought about it?
    - Why did or didn't you decide to run?

- Do you think that, at some point in the future, you will run? Why is this or isn't this something you think you'll do?

If yes:
- What level of office(s) do you think you'd seek?
- Why this office and not others?
- Do you think you would win? Why?
- Would you be willing to run even if you thought your likelihood of winning was quite low? If yes, why?

If they have already run for or held office:
- What office? Why did you decide to seek that particular office?
- When?
- Did you win?
- Could you tell me a little bit about the campaign and the specific race you were involved in? Was it a close race, for example? Were there any aspects of the campaign that were particularly difficult? Surprising?

If they have never considered it:
- Are you interested in politics?
- Do you follow politics in your community? At the national level?
- When you say you've never considered running, does that mean it's something you could never see yourself doing? Why not?
- And this holds for all levels of office?

If they indicate that they could imagine running at some point in the future:
- What level of office(s) do you think you'd seek?
- Why this office and not others?
- Do you think you would win? Why?
- Would you be willing to run even if you thought your likelihood of winning was quite low? If yes, why?

2. Is there anything that might make you more likely to run for office?
   - What type of circumstances or scenarios can you imagine might make you more likely?
   - What position(s) do you think you'd be more likely to seek?
   - What do you think are the most unappealing aspects about running?

3. Has anyone ever suggested or encouraged you to run for office?

   If yes:
   - Who? What were their relations to you? Family and friends versus party leaders, elected officials, colleagues, community activists?
   - For what office?
   - How many different times would you say someone has recommended that you run for office?
   - How important is this kind of support to you in your deciding whether to enter a race?
   - Whose support do you think is most important?
   - So, overall, do you feel like you'd have a lot of support?

   If no:
   - Would receiving support or encouragement make you more receptive to considering a run?
   - Whose support do you think is most important?

4. Do you think you are qualified to hold public office?

   If yes:
   - Why? What experiences and qualifications do you think position you to be a credible candidate?
   - What about high-level office, like Congress? Do you think you are qualified for a position like that?
   - What do you think are the most important qualifications/credentials in public officials and candidates?

   If no:
   - Why not? What experience are you missing?
   - What do you think are the most important qualities and/or credentials in officeholders and candidates?

5. Lots of people say that, in order to enter the political arena, you need to have thick skin. Do you think this is an accurate assessment?

   If yes:
   - Do you think you have what it takes to endure a possibly negative campaign and months of public scrutiny?

   If no:
   - Then how would you characterize the kinds of people who decide to run for office?

6. Others say that, in order to enter politics, you need to have a lot of confidence or ego strength. Do you think this is an accurate assessment?

If yes:
   • Do you think you have these kinds of personality traits that seem necessary?

If no:
   • Then how would you characterize the kinds of people who decide to run for office?

Part II – Political Culture: I'd now like to turn to a few questions about the political environment you live in.

1. Do you live in an area that tends to be liberal or conservative? Democrat or Republican? Very religious? Traditional? Urban, suburban, or rural?

2. Are your political views generally in sync with those in your community or out of sync? Do you think this plays a role in whether you'd ever be interested in running for local level office? How so?

3. Are you involved with your political party? At the local level? Statewide?

4. You might not know this, but are the political parties in your community strong? Do you know if they tend to recruit candidates, even for city council-type positions?

Part III – Professional and Life Goals: Now I'd like to spend a couple of minutes talking about your career goals.

1. Are you still working as a lawyer [or whatever]?
   If yes:
   • How long have you been working in your current profession?
   • Do you feel you still have a lot to accomplish within your profession? Like what?
   • How hard would it be for you to leave your profession and move on to something else if the opportunity presented itself?
   • If you had greater financial security, would you be more likely to consider leaving your current profession?
   • What other career ambitions do you have?

If no:
- When did you leave and what are you currently doing?
- How long have you been working in your current profession?
- Do you feel you still have a lot to accomplish within your profession? Like what?
- How hard would it be for you to leave your profession and move on to something else if the opportunity presented itself?
- If you had greater financial security, would you be more likely to consider leaving your current profession?
- What other career ambitions do you have?

2. Do you think that your current professional status affects your likelihood of running for office? That is, would your current job allow you the time necessary to campaign, fundraise, engage in the kinds of activities required to run?

3. Have you had any mentors help you achieve your professional success?
   If yes:
   - Who? What was the relation (mother, father, professor, supervisor, elected official)?
   - What was this person's sex?

Part IV – Perceptions of a Gendered Environment: Finally, I would like to ask you about some of the gender dynamics you may have witnessed in your professional life.

- Do you think that it is harder for women than men to succeed in your professional environment? Have you ever seen any patterns of sexism?
- Within your work environment, have you ever noticed differences in the levels of confidence men and women exude?
- Within your professional environment, have you ever identified differences in the ways that household responsibilities and/or children affect women and men?

The Second Wave Interview Questionnaire

Below is an outline of the topics addressed during the 2008 phone interviews. These conversations were free flowing, so the exact wording of each question varied.

Introduction: Thank you for agreeing to take the time to be interviewed. Most of the questions I'm going to ask deal with your attitudes about running for office. I want to emphasize that we're interested in your opinions and attitudes even if you tend not to be very interested in politics.

Part I – Running for Public Office:

1. Have you run for public office?

    If yes:
    - What office? Why did you decide to seek that particular office?
    - How did you come to the decision to run? Was there a specific trigger? Can you remember the day you decided to run?
    - When did you run?
    - Did you win?
    - Could you tell me a little bit about the campaign and the specific race you were involved in? Was it a close race, for example? Were there any aspects of the campaign that were particularly difficult? Surprising?

    If no:
    - Have you ever thought about running for any public office? Has it ever even crossed your mind?

If yes (ask the following questions based on the extent to which it seems as though it is something they think about with some degree of regularity or seriousness):
- How often do you think about this?
- When was the most recent time you've thought about it?
- Why did or didn't you decide to run?
- For what office(s)?
- What are you thinking about exactly?
- What makes you think you might want to do this? What's your motivation for wanting to get involved?

If they have never considered it:
- Really, never?
- Are you interested in politics? Do you follow politics in your community? At the national level?
- When you say you've never considered running, does that mean it's something you could never see yourself doing? Why not?

2. Do you think that, at some point in the future, you might be interested in running for office, or even possibly do it?
   - Is there anything that might make you more likely to run for office? What type of circumstances or scenarios can you imagine might make you more likely?
   - What do you think are the most unappealing aspects about running?

3. Looking back over the last seven or eight years, would you say you're more or less interested in running for office?
   - Are there any personal circumstances in your life that you think contribute to why you're more or less interested in running for office?
   - What about professionally? Are there any changes in your career that make it easier or more difficult to run for office? Does your current job allow you the time necessary to campaign, fundraise, engage in the kinds of activities required to run?
   - What about the current political climate? Has current politics made you more or less likely to think about running for office?
   - Have you become more or less cynical about politics? Why the change? Do you think that's a reason you're more or less likely to get involved?

4. I am interested to hear what you think about some of the most prominent people on the political scene right now. What do you think about

Bush, McCain, Hillary Clinton, Obama? Do any of them make you want to get involved in politics (because you love or hate them)? Has any of them made you think more or less about running for office? Does anyone else in politics have that effect on you?

Part II – Recruitment and Qualifications:
Let me now ask you just a couple of questions about your views of candidates, in general, and what kind of candidate you might be. Also, I'm interested in whether anyone has suggested to you that you run for office.

1. Has anyone ever suggested or encouraged you to run for office?

    If no:
    - Really? Not even family members, or friends, or maybe a colleague?

    If yes:
    - Who? What were their relations to you? Family and friends versus party leaders, elected officials, colleagues, community activists?
    - For what office?
    - When was the last time that someone suggested that you should run? (*if it's been within the last 10 years or so, then ask why they think they were recruited and by whom*)
    - How many different times would you say someone has recommended that you run for office?
    - Whose support do you think is most important to you on a personal level?
    - Whose support do you think is most important to winning the race?

2. Do you think you are qualified to hold public office?

    If yes:
    - Why? What experiences and qualifications do you think position you to be a credible candidate?
    - What about high-level office, like Congress? Do you think you are qualified for a position like that?
    - What do you think are the most important qualifications or credentials in public officials and candidates?
    - Do you think you have what it takes to endure a possibly negative campaign and months of public scrutiny?

- Are there any experiences or credentials that you think you might be missing?

If no:
  - Why not? What experience are you missing?
  - What do you think are the most important qualities or credentials in office holders and candidates?

3. Looking back over the course of the last seven or eight years, do you feel like you've become more or less qualified to run for office? Why?

Part III – Political Culture:
I'd now like to turn to a few questions about the political environment you live in.

1. Can you describe just briefly the area where you live?
   - Is it liberal or conservative? Democrat or Republican?
   - Very religious? Traditional?
   - Urban, suburban, or rural?
   - How long have you lived here?

2. Are your political views generally in sync with those in your community or out of sync? Or don't you really know? Do you think this plays a role in whether you'd ever be interested in running for local-level office? How so?

3. Are you involved at all politically in your community or in your state? With your political party?

4. How competitive are the elections where you live?
   - Are there usually a lot of candidates running?
   - Are the margins of victory usually close?
   - Do you have a sense of how much money people spend on campaigns for local or state-level offices in your area?
   - Are there lots of primary elections, too?
   - Have candidates you've supported in the past generally won or lost their races?

5. Would you say that there's a fair degree of diversity among the candidates who run for office where you live? By diversity, I mean, do women run? What about racial and ethnic minorities? Young people who are sort of new to the political scene?

Part IV – Summary Questions (alternate questions):
Thanks so much for your time. I'd just like to ask you one final question.

- As a woman, do you think running for office would pose greater challenges to you than it would if you were a man? How so or why not?
- When it comes down to it, what is the single greatest impediment to you ever running for office?
- When it comes down to it, what would it take for you to throw your hat into the ring and run for office?
- If you wanted to run for office – whether it be a local, state, or federal position – do you think you have the political connections to turn that interest into an actual campaign? Do you think you need those political connections?

APPENDIX F

Coding of Variables

The following chart describes the variables included in the multivariate results presented and discussed throughout the book. Although many of these variables are referenced in more than one chapter, each is noted under the chapter in which it first appears.

Variable	Range	Mean	Standard Deviation	Coding
CHAPTER 3 – "Political Ambition in the Candidate Eligibility Pool"				
Considered running for elective office	0, 1	0.51	0.50	Indicates whether respondent ever considered running for local, state, or federal level office (1) or not (0).
Change in interest in running for office (3-point scale)	−1 − 1	−0.08	0.60	Indicates whether respondent, between the two waves of the study, lost interest in running for office (−1), maintained the same level of interest (0), or gained interest in running for office (1).

Variable	Range	Mean	Standard Deviation	Coding
Change in interest in running for office (5-point scale)	− 2 − 2	− 0.07	0.50	Indicates respondent's level of movement in political ambition between the two waves of the study. The maximum loss in ambition is − 2 steps on the 5-point continuum; the maximum gain in ambition is + 2 steps on the scale.
Size of congressional delegation	1 − 52	17.20	14.68	Indicates the total number of seats in the state's congressional delegation.
Size of state political opportunity structure	2.31 − 212	20.84	29.15	Indicates the total number of seats in the state legislature divided by the size of the congressional delegation (which serves as a proxy for state population).
Size of local political opportunity structure	10 − 2,759	220.59	256.04	Indicates the Census Bureau's count of the total number of "government units" in the state, divided by the size of the congressional delegation.
Term limits	0, 1	0.30	0.46	Indicates whether the state has term limits for members serving in the state legislature (1) or not (0).
Part-time legislature	0, 1	0.29	0.45	Indicates whether the state legislature is part time (0) or full time (1).
Legislative salary	0 − 99,000	36,849	29,344	Indicates the salary earned by members of the state legislature.

Variable	Range	Mean	Standard Deviation	Coding
Democrat	0, 1	0.45	0.50	Indicates whether respondent self-identifies as a Democrat (1) or not (0).
Republican	0, 1	0.30	0.46	Indicates whether respondent self-identifies as a Republican (1) or not (0).
Percent Democratic presidential vote share	28.3 – 90.5	50.65	8.78	Indicates the proportion of the vote share Al Gore won in the state in the 2000 presidential election.
Party congruence with House delegation	0, 1	0.67	0.47	Indicates party congruence between the respondent and the congressional delegation.
Party congruence with state legislature	0, 1	0.78	0.41	Indicates party congruence between the respondent and state legislature.*
Change in state's Democratic presidential vote share	−5.8 – 3.9	−1.83	1.94	Difference in John Kerry's 2004 and Al Gore's 2000 vote share in respondent's state. Positive numbers indicate an increase in a state's Democratic presidential vote share.
Moved	0, 1	0.14	0.35	Indicates whether, between the two waves of the study, respondent moved (1) or not (0).
Became incongruent with political landscape	0, 1	0.22	0.41	Indicates whether respondent currently perceives living in a political climate that is incongruent with his or her party identification and political ideology.

* Democrats with Democratic or "mixed" state legislatures, Republicans with Republican or "mixed" state legislatures, and independents coded 1. Everyone else coded 0. The results do not change when Democrats with Democratic legislatures and Republicans with Republican legislatures are coded as congruent (1) and everyone else is coded as incongruent (0).

Variable	Range	Mean	Standard Deviation	Coding
CHAPTER 4 – "Barack Obama and 18 Million Cracks in the Glass Ceiling: Sex, Race, and Political Ambition"				
Sex (female)	0, 1	0.47	0.50	Indicates whether respondent is a woman (1) or a man (0).
Black	0, 1	0.09	0.29	Indicates whether respondent is African American (1) or not (0).
Latino/a	0, 1	0.05	0.22	Indicates whether respondent is Latino/a (1) or not (0).
Political knowledge	0 – 3	2.43	0.98	Indicates how many of respondent's members of Congress (House of Representatives and Senate) he or she can name.
Political interest	2 – 8	5.53	1.66	Indicates how closely respondent follows local and national news. Ranges from not closely (2) to very closely (8).
Political efficacy	1 – 5	2.79	1.00	Indicates whether respondent agrees that government officials pay attention to people like him or her. Ranges from strongly disagrees (1) to strongly agrees (5).

Variable	Range	Mean	Standard Deviation	Coding
Political participation	0 – 9	5.49	2.31	Indicates level of respondent's political participation (over the course of the past year) based on the following activities: voted, contacted an elected official, joined or paid dues to an interest group, wrote a letter to a newspaper, contributed money to a campaign, volunteered for a candidate, volunteered on a community project, attended a political meeting, served on the board of a nonprofit organization. Lower numbers indicate lower levels of political engagement.

CHAPTER 5 – "You Could be President Someday! Early Socialization, the Role of Family, and Political Ambition"

Variable	Range	Mean	Standard Deviation	Coding
"Political" household	2 – 8	3.77	1.06	Indicates "how frequently [respondent] discussed politics with parents when growing up" and "how often parents encouraged [him/her] to run for office someday." Higher numbers indicate a more "political" household.
Parent ran for office	0, 1	0.14	0.35	Indicates whether either of respondent's parents ever ran for office (1) or not (0).

Variable	Range	Mean	Standard Deviation	Coding
Ran for office as a student	0, 1	0.55	0.50	Indicates whether respondent ran for office in high school and/or college (1) or not (0).
Married	0, 1	0.75	0.44	Indicates whether respondent is married (1) or not (0).
Children	0, 1	0.76	0.43	Indicates whether respondent has children (1) or not (0).
Children under age 6 living at home	0, 1	0.14	0.35	Indicates whether respondent has children under the age of 6 living at home (1) or not (0).
Responsible for majority of household tasks	0 – 2	1.00	0.61	Indicates whether respondent is responsible for less than half (0), half (1), or the majority (2) of the household tasks.
Responsible for majority of child care	0, 1	0.11	0.32	Indicates whether respondent is responsible for the majority of the child care tasks (1) or not (0; which includes respondents who have no children).
Encouraged to run for office by a family member	0, 1	0.26	0.44	Indicates whether a family member ever encouraged respondent to run for office (1) or not (0).
Encouraged to run for office by a spouse/partner	0, 1	0.20	0.40	Indicates whether a spouse/partner ever encouraged respondent to run for office (1) or not (0).
Newly married	0, 1	0.07	0.26	Indicates whether, between the two waves of the study, respondent married (1) or not (0).

Variable	Range	Mean	Standard Deviation	Coding
No longer married	0, 1	0.06	0.23	Indicates whether, between the two waves of the study, respondent separated, divorced, or became widowed (1) or not (0).
Had or adopted a child	0, 1	0.31	0.46	Indicates whether, between the two waves of the study, respondent had a child (1) or not (0).
Had child move out of the house	0, 1	0.31	0.46	Indicates whether, between the two waves of the study, respondent's child(ren) moved out of the house (1) or not (0).
Dealt with a personal or family illness	0, 1	0.56	0.50	Indicates whether, between the two waves of the study, respondent dealt with a personal or family illness (1) or not (0).
Cared for an aging or sick parent	0, 1	0.35	0.48	Indicates whether, between the two waves of the study, respondent cared for an aging or sick parent (1) or not (0).
Recently encouraged to run for office by a family member	0, 1	0.13	0.34	Indicates whether, between the two waves of the study, respondent was encouraged to run for office by a family member (1) or not (0).
Recently encouraged to run for office by a spouse/partner	0, 1	0.10	0.30	Indicates whether, between the two waves of the study, respondent was encouraged to run for office by a spouse/partner (1) or not (0).

Variable	Range	Mean	Standard Deviation	Coding
CHAPTER 6 – "On-the-Job Training: Professional Circumstances and the Decision to Run for Office"				
Income	1 – 6	4.58	1.21	Indicates respondent's annual household income. Ranges from under $25,000 (1) to more than $200,000 (6).
Self-assessed qualifications to run for office	1 – 4	2.52	1.03	Indicates respondent's level of self-perceived qualifications to run for elective office. Ranges from "not at all qualified (1) to "very qualified" (4).
Underwent a career change	0, 1	0.17	0.38	Indicates whether, between the two waves of the study, respondent changed jobs (1) or not (0).
Took on more responsibilities at work	0, 1	0.56	0.50	Indicates whether, between the two waves of the study, respondent took on more responsibilities at work (1) or not (0).
Retired	0, 1	0.09	0.29	Indicates whether, between the two waves of the study, respondent retired from his or her job (1) or not (0).

Variable	Range	Mean	Standard Deviation	Coding
Change in household income	−4 – 4	0.25	0.74	Difference in respondent's income, in intervals, between the two waves of the study. Positive numbers indicate higher income in 2008 than in 2001. Negative numbers indicate lower income in 2008 than in 2001.
Change in political involvement	−9 – 7	0.10	1.79	Difference in number of the following political acts respondent participated in during 2007, compared with 2000: voted (in 2006), contacted elected official, joined or paid dues to an interest group, wrote letter to a newspaper, contributed money to a campaign, volunteered for a candidate, volunteered on a community project, attended a political meeting, served on board of a nonprofit organization. Negative numbers indicate lower levels of political engagement in 2008 than in 2001.
Change in self-assessed qualifications to run for office	−3 – 3	0.24	0.87	Indicates change in respondent's level of self-perceived qualifications to run for elective office. Ranges from "not at all qualified" (1) to "very qualified" (4) for each point in time. Negative numbers indicate lower levels of self-perceived qualifications in 2008 than in 2001.

Variable	Range	Mean	Standard Deviation	Coding
CHAPTER 7 – "You Think I Should Run for Office? Political Parties, Political Recruitment, and Political Ambition"				
Recruited to run by an electoral gatekeeper	0, 1	0.49	0.50	Indicates whether party official, nonelected activist, or elected official ever encouraged the respondent to run for office (1) or not (0).
Worked or volunteered on a campaign	0, 1	0.65	0.48	Indicates whether respondent worked or volunteered for a candidate or campaign (1) or not (0).
Attended a political meeting	0, 1	0.79	0.41	Indicates whether respondent attended a school board, city council, or local political meeting (1) or not (0).
Served on a nonprofit board	0, 1	0.71	0.46	Indicates whether respondent served on the board of any organization or foundation (1) or not (0).
Attended political party meeting or event	0, 1	0.64	0.48	Indicates whether respondent attended any party meeting or event (1) or not (0).
Interacted with elected officials at work	0, 1	0.66	0.47	Indicates whether respondent interacts with elected officials as part of his or her job (1) or not (0).
Contact with women's organization(s)	0, 1	0.15	0.35	Indicates whether respondent has had contact with a women's organization (1) or not (0).

Variable	Range	Mean	Standard Deviation	Coding
Began following foreign affairs more closely	0, 1	0.63	0.48	Indicates whether, between the two waves of the study, respondent began following foreign affairs more closely (1) or not (0).
Animosity toward the Bush administration	0, 1	0.69	0.46	Indicates whether, between the two waves of the study, respondent increased animosity toward Bush (1) or not (0).
Frustration with Democrats in Congress	0, 1	0.60	0.49	Indicates whether, between the two waves of the study, respondent grew increasingly frustrated with the Democrats in Congress (1) or not (0).
Number of political leaders considered inspiring	0 – 12	3.00	2.10	Indicates how many of the following the respondent considers "inspirational": George Bush, Bill Clinton, Hillary Clinton, John Edwards, Rudy Giuliani, Al Gore, John McCain, Barack Obama, Nancy Pelosi, Condoleezza Rice, Bill Richardson, Mitt Romney.
Age	22 – 88	48.47	11.02	Indicates respondent's age.
Change in political interest	−6 – 5	0.17	1.34	Indicates change in how closely respondent follows local and national news. Ranges from not closely (2) to very closely (8) at each point in time. Negative numbers indicate lower levels of political interest in 2008 than in 2001.

Variable	Range	Mean	Standard Deviation	Coding
Became more cynical about politics and the political system	0, 1	0.62	0.48	Indicates whether respondent, between the two waves of the study, became more cynical about politics and the political process (1) or not (0).
Recruited recently to run for office by a political actor	0, 1	0.23	0.42	Indicates whether, between the two waves of the study, respondent was recruited by at least one elected official, party leader, or political activist (1) or not (0).
CHAPTER 8 – "Biting the Bullet: Deciding to Run for Office"				
Ran for elective office	0, 1	0.09	0.29	Indicates whether respondent ever sought local, state, or federal level office (1) or not (0).

Works Cited

Aberbach, Joel D., Robert D. Putnam, and Bert A. Rockman. 1981. *Bureaucrats and Politicians in Western Democracies*. Cambridge, MA: Harvard University Press.

Abney, F. Glen. 1974. "Factors Related to Negro Turnout in Mississippi." *Journal of Politics* 36(4):1057–63.

Abney, Glen and John D. Hutcheson. 1981. "Race, Representation, and Trust: Changes in Attitudes after the Election of a Black Mayor." *Public Opinion Quarterly* 45(1):91–101.

Aldrich, John H. 2000. "Southern Parties in the State and Nation." *Journal of Politics* 62(3):643–70.

Alejano-Steele, AnnJanette. 1997. "Early Career Issues: Let the Juggling Begin." In *Dilemmas of a Double Life: Women Balancing Careers and Relationships*, ed. N.B. Kaltreider. Northvale, NJ: Jason Aronson.

Alford, John. 2008. "Twin Studies, Molecular Genetics, Politics, and Tolerance: A Response to Beckwith and Morris." *Perspectives on Politics* 6(4):793–97.

——, Carolyn L. Funk, and John R. Hibbing. 2005. "Are Political Orientations Genetically Transmitted?" *American Political Science Review* 99(2):153–67.

Almond, Gabriel Abraham and Sidney Verba. 1963. *The Civic Culture: Political Attitudes and Democracy in Five Nations*. Princeton, NJ: Princeton University Press.

Amundsen, Kirsten. 1971. *The Silenced Majority: Women and American Democracy*. Englewood Cliffs, NJ: Prentice Hall.

Andolina, Molly W., Krista Jenkins, Cliff Zukin, and Scott Keeter. 2003. "Habits from Home, Lessons from School: Influences on Youth Civic Engagement." *PS: Political Science & Politics* 36(2):275–80.

Apter, Teri. 1993. *Working Women Don't Have Wives: Professional Success in the 1990s*. New York, NY: St. Martin's Press.

Astin, Helen S. and Carole Leland. 1991. *Women of Influence, Women of Vision: A Cross-Generational Study of Leadership and Social Change.* San Francisco, CA: Jossey-Bass.

Atkeson, Lonna Rae. 2003. "Not All Cues Are Created Equal: The Conditional Impact of Female Candidates on Political Engagement." *Journal of Politics* 65(4):1040–61.

_____ and Nancy Carrillo. 2007. "More is Better: The Influence of Collective Female Descriptive Representation on External Efficacy." *Politics & Gender* 3(1):79–101.

Bachrach, Peter. 1967. *The Theory of Democratic Elitism: A Critique.* Boston, MA: Little, Brown and Company.

Banerji, Shilpa. 2006. "AAUP: Women Professors Lag in Tenure, Salary." *Diverse Issues in Higher Education,* 26 October.

Barber, James D. 1965. *The Lawmakers: Recruitment and Adaptation to Legislative Life.* New Haven, CT: Yale University Press.

Barone, Michael and Richard E. Cohen. 2008. *Almanac of American Politics.* Washington, DC: National Journal.

Barreto, Matt and Matthew Streb. 2007. "Barn Burners and Burn Out: The Effects of Competitive Elections on Efficacy and Trust." Paper presented at the annual meeting of the Midwest Political Science Association, Chicago, April 12.

Baxter, Sandra and Marjorie Lansing. 1983. *Women and Politics: The Visible Minority.* Ann Arbor, MI: University of Michigan Press.

Beck, Paul Allen and M. Kent Jennings. 1982. "Pathways to Participation." *American Political Science Review* 76(1):94–108.

Beckwith, Jon and Corey A. Morris. 2008. "Twin Studies of Political Behavior: Untenable Assumptions?" *Perspectives on Politics* 6(4):785–91.

Beloff, Halla. 1992. "Mother, Father and Me: Our IQ." *Psychologist* 5(1): 309–11.

Bergmann, Barbara. 1986. *The Economic Emergence of Women.* New York, NY: Basic Books.

Berkman, Michael B. 1994. "State Legislators in Congress: Strategic Politicians, Professional Legislatures, and the Party Nexus." *American Journal of Political Science* 38(4):1025–55.

_____ and Robert E. O'Connor. 1993. "Do Women Legislators Matter?" *American Politics Quarterly* 21(1):102–24.

Bernstein, Robert. 1986. "Why Are There So Few Women in the House?" *Western Political Quarterly* 39(1): 155–64.

Beyer, Sylvia and Edward M. Bowden. 1997. "Gender Differences in Self-Perceptions: Convergent Evidence from Three Measures of Accuracy and Bias." *Personality and Social Psychology Bulletin* 23(2):157–72.

Black, Gordon S. 1972. "A Theory of Political Ambition: Career Choices and the Role of Structural Incentives." *American Political Science Review* 66(1):144–59.

Bledsoe, Timothy and Mary Herring. 1990. "Victims of Circumstances: Women in Pursuit of Political Office." *American Political Science Review* 84(1):213–23.

Blumstein, Philip and Pepper Schwartz. 1991. "Money and Ideology: Their Impact on Power and the Division of Household Labor." In *Gender, Family, and the Economy: The Triple Overlap*, ed. R. L. Blumberg. Newbury Park, CA: Sage Publications.

Bobo, Lawrence and Frank Gilliam. 1990. "Race, Sociopolitical Participation, and Black Empowerment." *American Political Science Review* 84(2):377–93.

Bowles, Hannah Riley, Linda C. Babcock, and Kathleen McGinn. 2005. "Constraints and Triggers: Situational Mechanics of Gender in Negotiation." *Journal of Personality and Social Psychology* 89(6):951–65.

Boxer, Barbara. 1994. *Politics and the New Revolution of Women in America*. Washington, DC: National Press Books.

Brader, Ted. 2006. *Campaigning for Hearts and Minds: How Emotional Appeals in Political Ads Work*. Chicago, IL: University of Chicago Press.

Brownlow, Sheila, Rebecca Whitener, and Janet M. Rupert. 1998. "I'll Take Gender Differences for $1000! Domain-Specific Intellectual Success on 'Jeopardy'." *Sex Roles: A Journal of Research* 38(3):269–86.

Brudnick, Ida A., R. Eric Petersen, Patrick J. Purcell, Mildred Amer, Matthew Eric Glassman, Jennifer E. Manning, Michael L. Koempel, and Judy Schneider. 2010. *Congressional Pay and Perks: Salaries, Pensions and Retirement, Franking, Travel, and Other Benefits for U.S. Senators and Representatives*. Alexandria, VA: TheCapitol.Net, Inc.

Bullock, Charles, S.A. MacManus, F.E. Atkins, L.J. Hoffman, and A. Newmark. 1999. "Winning in My Own Backyard: County Government, School Board Positions Steadily More Attractive to Women Candidates." In *Women in Politics: Outsiders or Insiders?*, 3rd ed., ed. L. D. Whitaker. Upper Saddle River, NJ: Prentice Hall.

Bureau of the Census. 1992. *1992 Census of Governments*. Washington, DC: Department of Commerce.

Burns, Nancy, Kay Lehman Schlozman, and Sidney Verba. 2001. *The Private Roots of Public Action: Gender, Equality, and Political Participation*. Cambridge, MA: Harvard University Press.

Burrell, Barbara. 1996. *A Woman's Place Is in the House: Campaigning for Congress in the Feminist Era*. Ann Arbor, MI: University of Michigan Press.

Bylsma, Wayne H. and Brenda Major. 1992. "Two Routes to Eliminating Gender Differences in Personal Entitlement: Social Comparisons and Performance Evaluations." *Psychology of Women Quarterly* 16(2):193–200.

Byrnes, James, David C. Miller, and William D. Schafer. 1999. "Gender Differences in Risk-Taking: A Meta-Analysis." *Psychological Bulletin* 125(3):367–83.

Cain, Bruce E. and Thad Kousser. 2004. *Adapting to Term Limits: Recent Experiences and New Directions*. San Francisco, CA: Public Policy Institute of California.

Campbell, Angus, Philip E. Converse, Warren E. Miller, and Donald E. Stokes. 1960. *The American Voter*. New York, NY: Wiley.

Campbell, David E. and Christina Wolbrecht. 2006. "See Jane Run: Women Politicians as Role Models for Adolescents." *Journal of Politics* 68(2):233–247.

Canon, David T. 1990. *Actors, Athletes, and Astronauts: Political Amateurs in the United States Congress.* Chicago, IL: University of Chicago Press.

———. 1999. *Race, Redistricting, and Representation: The Unintended Consequences of Black Majority Districts.* Chicago, IL: University of Chicago Press.

———. 1993. "Sacrificial Lambs or Strategic Politicians? Political Amateurs in the U.S. Elections." *American Journal of Political Science* 37(4):1119–41.

Carroll, Susan J. 1994. *Women as Candidates in American Politics,* 2nd ed. Bloomington, IN: Indiana University Press.

———, Debra L. Dodson, and Ruth B. Mandel. 1991. *The Impact of Women in Public Office: An Overview.* New Brunswick, NJ: Eagleton Institute of Politics' Center for American Women and Politics.

——— and Krista Jenkins. 2003. "Increasing Diversity or More of the Same? Term Limits and the Representation of Women, Minorities, and Minority Women in State Legislatures." In *Contemporary Patterns of Politics, Praxis, and Culture,* ed. G. A. Persons. New Brunswick, NJ: Transaction Publishers.

——— and Wendy S. Strimling. 1983. *Women's Routes to Elective Office: A Comparison with Men's.* New Brunswick, NJ: Center for the American Woman and Politics.

Carsey, Thomas M. and Geoffrey C. Layman. 2006. "Changing Sides or Changing Minds? Party Identification and Policy Preferences in the American Electorate." *American Journal of Political Science* 50(2):464–77.

Casellas, Jason P. 2009. "The Institutional and Demographic Determinants of Latino Representation." *Legislative Studies Quarterly* 34(3):399–426.

Center for American Women and Politics (CAWP). 2001. "Women State Legislators: Past, Present, and Future." New Brunswick: Eagleton Institute of Politics.

———. 2008. "Gender Differences in Voter Turnout." http://www.cawp.rutgers.edu/fast_facts/voters/turnout.php (July 15, 2009).

———. 2010a. "Women and Elective Office." http://www.cawp.rutgers.edu/fast_facts/levels_of_office/documents/elective.pdf (July 18, 2010).

———. 2010b. "Women in State Legislatures." http://www.cawp.rutgers.edu/fast_facts/levels_of_office/documents/stleg.pdf (September 26, 2010).

Chaney, Carol and Barbara Sinclair. 1994. "Women and the 1992 House Elections." In *The Year of the Woman,* eds. E. A. Cook, S. Thomas, and C. Wilcox. Boulder, CO: Westview Press.

Citrin, Jack and Donald Philip Green. 1986. "Presidential Leadership and the Resurgence of Trust in Government." *British Journal of Political Science* 16(4):431–53.

———, Donald P. Green, and David O. Sears. 1990. "White Reactions to Black Candidates: When Does Race Matter?" *Public Opinion Quarterly* 54(1):74–96.

Clark, Janet. 1994. "Getting There: Women in Political Office." In *Different Roles, Different Voice,* eds. M. Githens, P. Norris, and J. Lovenduski. New York, NY: Harper-Collins.

Clawson, Rosalee A. and Zoe M. Oxley. 2008. *Public Opinion: Democratic Ideals, Democratic Practice,* Washington, DC: Congressional Quarterly.

Clinton, Bill. 2004. *My Life.* New York: Alfred A. Knopf.

Clinton, Hillary Rodham. 2003. *Living History*. New York: Simon and Schuster.

Cohen, Cathy J. and Michael C. Dawson. 1993. "Neighborhood Poverty and African American Politics." *American Political Science Review* 87(2):286–302.

Cohen, Jeff. 2006. *Cable News Confidential: My Misadventures in Corporate Media*. Sausalito, CA: PoliPointPress.

Coltrane, Scott. 2000. "Research on Household Labor: Modeling and Measuring the Social Embeddedness of Routine Family Work." *Journal of Marriage and the Family* 62(4):1208–33.

Conway, M. Margaret. 1991. *Political Participation in the United States*, 2nd ed. Washington, DC: Congressional Quarterly.

_____, David W. Ahern, and Gertrude A. Steuernagel. 2004. *Women and Political Participation: Cultural Change in the Political Arena*, 2nd ed. Washington, DC: Congressional Quarterly.

Cook, Elizabeth Adell. 1998. "Voter Reaction to Women Candidates." In *Women and Elective Office*, eds. S. Thomas and C. Wilcox. New York, NY: Oxford University Press.

Cook, Timothy E. and Paul Gronke. 2005. "The Skeptical American: Revisiting the Meanings of Trust in Government and Confidence in Institutions." *Journal of Politics* 67(3):784–803.

Cose, Ellis. 1994. *The Rage of a Privileged Class*. New York, NY: HarperCollins.

Costantini, Edmond. 1990. "Political Women and Political Ambition: Closing the Gender Gap." *American Journal of Political Science* 34(3):741–70.

Craig, Barbara Hinkson and David M. O'Brien. 1993. *Abortion and American Politics*. Chatham, UK: Chatham House.

Darcy, Robert, Charles D. Hadley, and Jason F. Kirksey. 1993. "Electoral Systems and the Representation of Black Women in American State Legislatures." *Women & Politics* 13(2):73–89.

_____, Susan Welch, and Janet Clark. 1994. *Women, Elections, and Representation*, 2nd ed. Lincoln, NE: University of Nebraska Press.

Deckman, Melissa. 2007. "Gender Differences in the Decision to Run for School Board." *American Politics Research* 35(4):541–63.

Diamond, Irene. 1977. *Sex Roles in the Statehouse*. New Haven, CT: Yale University Press.

Dolan, Kathleen. 2006. "Symbolic Mobilization? The Impact of Candidate Sex in American Elections." *American Politics Research* 34(6):687–704.

_____. 2004. *Voting for Women: How the Public Evaluates Women Candidates*. Boulder, CO: Westview Press.

_____. 1998. "Voting for Women in the 'Year of the Woman,'" *American Journal of Political Science* 42(1):272–93.

_____ and Lynne E. Ford. 1997. "Change and Continuity Among Women State Legislators: Evidence from Three Decades." *Political Research Quarterly* 50(1):137–51.

Dolbeare, Cushing N. and Anne J. Stone. 1990. "Women and Affordable Housing." In *The American Woman*, ed. S. Rix. New York, NY: Norton.

Druckman, James, Martin J. Kifer, and Michael Parkin. 2009. "Campaign Communication in U.S. Congressional Elections." *American Political Science Review* 103(3):343–66.

Duerst-Lahti, Georgia. 1998. "The Bottleneck, Women as Candidates." In *Women and Elective Office*, eds. S. Thomas and C. Wilcox. New York, NY: Oxford University Press.

Ehrenhalt, Alan. 1991. *United States of Ambition: Politicians, Power, and the Pursuit of Office*. New York: Times Books.

Ellison, Christopher G. and Bruce London. 1992. "Social and Political Participation of Black Americans: Compensatory and Ethnic Community Perspectives Revisited." *Social Forces* 70(3):681–701.

Enloe, Cynthia. 2004. *The Curious Feminist*. Berkeley, CA: University of California.

Eulau, Heinz and Kenneth Prewitt. 1973. *Labyrinths of Democracy: Adaptations, Linkages, Representation, and Policies in Urban Politics*. Indianapolis, IN: Bobbs-Merrill Company.

Falkenheim, Jacquelina C. and Mark K. Feigener. 2008. "2007 Records Fifth Consecutive Annual Increase in U.S. Doctoral Awards." November, NSF 09–307. Arlington, VA: National Science Foundation.

Fiber, Pamela and Richard L. Fox. 2005. "A Tougher Road for Women: Assessing the Role of Gender in Congressional Elections." In *Gender and American Politics*, ed. S. Tolleson-Rinehart and J. Josephson. New York NY: M. E. Sharpe.

Fields, Cheryl D. 2007. "A Scant Presence: Black and Latino Faculty at Research Institutions." *Diverse: Issues in Higher Education*, July 12, http://diverseeducation.com/article/8425/ (accessed September 12, 2010).

Fishel, Jeff. 1971. "Ambition and the Political Vocation: Congressional Challengers in American Politics." *Journal of Politics* 33(1):25–56.

Fisher, Samuel H. and Rebekah Herrick. 2002. "Whistle While You Work: Job Satisfaction and Retirement from the U.S. House." *Legislative Studies Quarterly* 27(3):445–57.

Flammang, Janet. 1997. *Women's Political Voice: How Women Are Transforming the Practice and Study of Politics*. Philadelphia, PA: Temple University Press.

Flanigan, William H. and Nancy H. Zingale. 2002. *Political Behavior of the American Electorate*, 10th ed. Washington, DC: Congressional Quarterly.

Fowler, Erika Franklin and Travis N. Ridout. 2010. "Advertising Trends in 2010." *The Forum* 8(4): Article 4. Accessed at http://astrid-online.com/Comunicazi/Studi–ric/Fowler_Ridout_The-Forum_4_2010.pdf (February 26, 2011).

Fowler, Linda L. 1993. *Candidates, Congress, and the American Democracy*. Ann Arbor, MI: University of Michigan.

———. 1996. "Who Runs for Congress?" *PS: Political Science and Politics* 29(3):430–4.

——— and Jennifer L. Lawless. 2009. "Looking for Sex in All the Wrong Places: Press Coverage and the Electoral Fortunes of Gubernatorial Candidates." *Perspectives on Politics* 7(3):519–37.

——— and Robert McClure. 1989. *Political Ambition*. New Haven, CT: Yale University Press.

Fowlkes, Diane L., Jerry Perkins, and Sue Tolleson-Rinehart. 1979. "Gender Roles and Party Roles." *American Political Science Review* 73(3):772–80.

Fox, Richard L. 2010. "Congressional Elections: Women's Candidacies and the Road to Gender Parity." In *Gender and Elections*, 2nd ed., eds. S. Carroll and R. Fox. New York, NY: Cambridge University Press.

_____. 1997. *Gender Dynamics in Congressional Elections*. Thousand Oaks: Sage.

_____ and Jennifer L. Lawless. 2003. "Family Structure, Sex-Role Socialization, and the Decision to Run for Office." *Women & Politics* 24(4):19–48.

_____ and _____. 2011. "Gendered Perceptions and Political Candidacies: A Central Barrier to Women's Equality in Electoral Politics." *American Journal of Political Science* 55(1): 59–73.

_____ and _____. 2010. "If Only They'd Ask: Gender, Recruitment, and Political Ambition." *Journal of Politics* 72(2):310–26.

_____ and _____. 2005. "To Run or Not to Run for Office: Explaining Nascent Political Ambition." *American Journal of Political Science* 49(3):642–59.

_____, _____, and Courtney Feeley. 2001. "Gender and the Decision to Run for Office." *Legislative Studies Quarterly* 26(3):411–35.

_____ and Zoe Oxley. 2003. "Gender Stereotyping in State Executive Elections: Candidate Selection and Success." *Journal of Politics* 65(3):833–50.

_____, Robert Van Sickel, and Thomas Steiger. 2007. *Tabloid Justice: Criminal Justice in an Age of Media Frenzy*, 2nd ed. Boulder, CO: Lynne Rienner.

Franklin, Benjamin. 1787. "Madison Debates, July 26." Available through the Yale University Law School's Avalon Project, http://avalon.law.yale.edu/18th_century/debates_726.asp (accessed July 13, 2010).

Frederick, Brian. 2009. "Are Female House Members Still More Liberal in a Polarized Era? The Conditional Nature of the Relationship Between Descriptive and Substantive Representation." *Congress & the Presidency* 36(2):181–202.

Freedman, Estelle. 2002. *No Turning Back*. New York, NY: Ballantine Books.

Freeman, Jo. 2000. *A Room at a Time: How Women Entered Party Politics*. Lanham, MA: Rowman and Littlefield.

Fulton, Sarah A., Cherie D. Maestas, L. Sandy Maisel and Walter J. Stone. 2006. "The Sense of a Woman: Gender, Ambition and the Decision to Run for Congress." *Political Research Quarterly* 59(2):235–48.

Furnham, Adrian and Richard Rawles. 1995. "Sex Differences in the Estimation of Intelligence." *Journal of Social Behavior and Personality* 10:741–8.

Gaddie, Ronald Keith. 2004. *Born to Run: Origins of the Political Career*. Lanham, MD: Rowman and Littlefield.

_____ and Charles S. Bullock. 2000. *Elections to Open Seats in the U.S. House: Where the Action Is*. Lanham, MD: Rowman and Littlefield.

Galinsky, Ellen and James T. Bond. 1996. "Work and Family: The Experiences of Mothers and Fathers in the U.S. Labor Force." In *The American Woman, 1996–1997*, eds. C. Costello and B. K. Krimgold. New York, NY: W. W. Norton.

Gamble, Katrina L. 2007. "Black Political Representation: An Examination of Legislative Activity Within U.S. House Committees." *Legislative Studies Quarterly* 32(3):421–47.

Gartner, Scott Sigmund and Gary M. Segura. 2008. "All Politics are Still Local: The Iraq War and the 2006 Midterm Elections." *PS: Political Science and Politics* 41(1):95–100.

Gay, Claudine. 2001. "The Effect of Black Congressional Representation on Participation." *American Political Science Review* 95(3):589–602.

———. 2002. "Spirals of Trust? The Effect of Descriptive Representation on the Relationship between Citizens and Their Government." *American Journal of Political Science* 46(4):717–32.

Gerrity, Jessica C., Tracy Osborn, and Jeanette Morehouse Mendez. 2007. "Women and Representation: A Different View of the District?" *Politics & Gender* 3(2):179–200.

Githens, Marianne. 2003. "Accounting for Women's Political Involvement: The Perennial Problem of Recruitment." In *Women and American Politics*, ed. S. Carroll. New York, NY: Oxford University Press.

——— and Jewel L. Prestage. 1977. *A Portrait of Marginality: The Political Behavior of the American Woman*. New York, NY: Longman.

Gneezy, Uri, Muriel Niederle, and Aldo Rustichini. 2003. "Performance in Competitive Environments: Gender Differences." *Quarterly Journal of Economics* 118(3):1049–74.

Golden, Catherine. 1996. *Campaign Manager: Running and Winning*. Ashland, OR: Oak Street Press.

Goodliffe, Jay. 2001. "The Effect of War Chests on Challenger Entry in U.S. House Elections." *American Journal of Political Science* 45(4):830–44.

Goren, Paul. 2005. "Party Identification and Core Political Values." *American Journal of Political Science* 49(4):881–96.

Graber, Doris A. 2010. *Mass Media and American Politics*, 8th ed. Washington, DC: CQ Press.

Gray, Virginia, Russell L. Hanson, and Herbert Jacob. 2000. *Politics in the American States: A Comparative Analysis*. Washington, DC: Congressional Quarterly.

Griffin, John D. and Brian Newman. 2007. "The Unequal Representation of Latinos and Whites." *Journal of Politics* 69(4):1032–46.

Grose, Christian R. 2005. "Disentangling Constituency and Legislator Effects in Representation: Black Legislators or Black Districts?" *Social Science Quarterly* 86(2):427–43.

Guterbock, Thomas M. and Bruce London. 1983. "Race, Political Orientation, and Participation: An Empirical Test of Four Competing Theories." *American Sociological Review* 48(4):439–53.

Haider-Markel, Donald P. 2007. "Representation and Backlash: The Positive and Negative Influence of Descriptive Representation." *Legislative Studies Quarterly* 32(1):107–33.

———, Mark R. Joslyn, and Chad J. Kniss. 2000. "Minority Group Interests and Political Representation: Gay Elected Officials in the Policy Process." *Journal of Politics* 62(2):568–77.

Hain, Paul L. and James E. Pierson. 1975. "Lawyers and Politics Revised: Structural Advantages of Lawyer-Politicians." *American Journal of Political Science* 19(1):41–51.

Hajnal, Zoltan L. 2007. *Changing White Attitudes toward Black Political Leadership*. New York, NY: Cambridge University Press.

Hamilton, Alexander. 1787. "The Federalist Number 21: Other Defects of the Present Constitution." In *The Federalist Papers*, ed. C. Rossiter. New York, NY: New American Library, 1961.

Hamilton, Charles V. 1986. "Social Policy and the Welfare of Black Americans: From Rights to Resources." *Political Science Quarterly* 101(2):239–55.

Hansen, Susan B. 1997. "Talking About Politics: Gender and Contextual Effects on Political Proselytizing." *Journal of Politics* 59(1):73–103.

Hart, Daniel, Thomas M. Donnelly, James Youniss, and Robert Atkins. 2007. "High School Community Service as a Predictor of Adult Voting and Volunteering." *American Education Research Journal* 44(1):197–219.

Hayes, Danny. 2011. "When Gender and Party Collide: Stereotyping in Candidate Trait Attribution." *Politics & Gender* 7(2):133–65.

Haynie, Kerry L. 2001. *African American Legislators in the American States*. New York, NY: Columbia University Press.

Hess, F. 2002. *School Boards at the Dawn of the 21st Century*. Alexandria, VA: American School Boards Association.

Hess, Robert D., Judith Torney-Purta, and Jaan Valsiner. 2006. *The Development of Political Attitudes in Children*. Edison, NJ: Transaction Publishers.

Hetherington, Mark. 2005. *Why Trust Matters: Declining Political Trust and the Demise of American Liberalism*. Princeton, NJ: Princeton University Press.

Highton, Benjamin. 2004. "White Voters and African American Candidates for Congress." *Political Behavior* 26(1):1–25.

Hill, David. 1981. "Political Culture and Female Political Representation." *Journal of Politics* 43(1):159–68.

Hill, Kim Quaile and Jan E. Leighley. 1992. "The Policy Consequences of Class Bias in State Electorates." *American Journal of Political Science* 36(2):351–65.

Hirlinger, Michael W. 1992. "Citizen-Initiated Contacting of Local Government Officials: A Multivariate Explanation." *Journal of Politics* 54(2):553–64.

Hochschild, Arlie. 1989. *The Second Shift*. New York: Avon.

Hochschild, Jennifer. 1995. *Facing up to the American Dream*. Princeton, NJ: Princeton University Press.

Hopkins, Daniel J. 2009. "No More Wilder Effect, Never a Whitman Effect: When and Why Polls Mislead about Black and Female Candidates." *Journal of Politics* 71(3):769–781.

Hsiao, Cheng. 2003. *Analysis of Panel Data*, 2nd ed. New York, NY: Cambridge University Press.

———. 2007. "Panel Data Analysis – Advantages and Challenges." *TEST* 16(1):1–22.

Huber, Gregory A. and John S. Lapinski. 2006. "The Race Card Revisited: Assessing Racial Priming in Policy Contests." *American Journal of Political Science* 50(2):421–40.

Huckshorn, Robert J. and Robert C. Spencer. 1971. *The Politics of Defeat: Campaigning for Congress*. Amherst, MA: University of Massachusetts Press.

Iyengar, Shanto and Jennifer A. McGrady. 2006. *Media Politics: A Citizen's Guide*. New York, NY: W. W. Norton.

Jacobson, Gary C. 2001. *The Politics of Congressional Elections*, 5th ed. Boston, MA: Allyn and Bacon.

Jamieson, Kathleen Hall. 1995. *Beyond the Double Bind*. New York, NY: Oxford University Press.

───── and Joseph N. Capella. 2008. *Echo Chamber: Rush Limbaugh and the Conservative Media Establishment*. New York, NY: Oxford University Books.

Jennings, M. Kent. 2006. "The Gender Gap in Attitudes and Beliefs about the Place of Women in American Politics Life: A Longitudinal, Cross-Generational Analysis." *Politics & Gender* 2(2):193–219.

───── and Barbara G. Farah. 1981. "Social Roles and Political Resources: An Over-Time Study of Men and Women in Party Elites." *American Journal of Political Science* 25(3):462–82.

───── and Gregory B. Markus. 1984. "Partisan Orientations over the Long Haul: Results from the Three-Wave Political Socialization Panel Study." *American Political Science Review* 78(4):1000–18.

───── and Richard G. Niemi. 1981. *Generations and Politics: A Panel Study of Young Adults and Their Parents*. Princeton, NJ: Princeton University Press.

Jewell, Malcolm E. and Sarah M. Morehouse. 2001. *Political Parties and Elections in American States*, 4th ed. Washington, DC: Congressional Quarterly.

Johnson, Janet B., Richard A. Joslyn and H. T. Reynolds. 2001. *Political Science Research Methods*, 4th ed. Washington, DC: Congressional Quarterly.

Jones, Charles E. and Michael L. Clemons. 1993. "A Model of Racial Crossover Voting: An Assessment of the Wilder Victory." In *Dilemmas of Black Politics: Issues of Leadership and Strategy*, ed. G. A. Persons. New York, NY: Harper Collins.

Kahn, Kim Fridkin. 1996. *The Political Consequences of Being a Woman*. New York, NY: Columbia University Press.

Kamber, Victor. 2003. *Poison Politics: Are Negative Campaigns Destroying Democracy?* New York, NY: Basic Books.

Kathlene, Lyn, Susan E. Clarke, and Barbara A. Fox. 1991. "Ways Women Politicians Are Making a Difference." In *Reshaping the Agenda: Women in State Legislatures*, eds. D. Dodson and S. Carroll. New Brunswick, NJ: Eagleton Institute of Politics' Center for American Women and Politics.

Kazee, Thomas A. 1980. "The Decision to Run for the U.S. Congress: Challenger Attitudes in the 1970s." *Legislative Studies Quarterly* 5(1): 79–100.

─────. 1994. "The Emergence of Congressional Candidates." In *Who Runs for Congress? Ambition, Context, and Candidate Emergence*, ed. Thomas Kazee. Washington, DC: Congressional Quarterly.

Keele, Luke. 2007. "Social Capital and the Dynamics of Trust in Government." *American Journal of Political Science* 51(2):241–54.

Kennedy, Edward M. 2009. *True Compass: A Memoir*. New York, NY: Hachette Book Group.

Kerr, Brinck and Will Miller. 1997. "Latino Representation, It's Direct and Indirect." *American Journal of Political Science* 41(3):1066–71.

King, David C. 1997. "The Polarization of American Parties and the Mistrust of Government." In *Why People Don't Trust Government*, eds. Joseph S. Nye, Jr., Philip D. Zelikow, and David C. King. Cambridge, MA: Harvard University Press.

Kling, Kristen C., Janet Hyde, Carolin Showers, and Brenda N. Buswell. 1999. "Gender Differences in Self-Esteem: A Meta-Analysis." *Psychological Bulletin* 125(4):470–500.

Koch, Jeffrey W. 2000. "Do Citizens Apply Gender Stereotypes to Infer Candidates' Ideological Orientations?" *Journal of Politics* 62(2):414–29.

Kousser, Thad. 2005. *Term Limits and the Dismantling of State Legislative Professionalism*. New York, NY: Cambridge University Press.

Kunin, Madeleine. 2008. *Pearls, Politics, and Power: How Women Can Win and Lead*. White River Junction, VT: Chelsea Green Publishing.

Lane, Robert Edwards. 1959. *Political Life: Why People Get Involved in Politics*. Glencoe, IL: Free Press.

Lasswell, Harold. 1948. *Power and Personality*. Stanford, CA: Stanford University Press.

Lawless, Jennifer L. 2004a. "Politics of Presence: Women in the House and Symbolic Representation." *Political Research Quarterly* 57(1):81–99.

———. 2009. "Sexism and Gender Bias in Election 2008: A More Complex Path for Women in Politics." *Politics & Gender* 5(1):70–80.

———. 2004b. "Women, War, and Winning Elections: Gender Stereotyping in the Post September 11th Era." *Political Research Quarterly* 53(3):479–90.

——— and Richard L. Fox. 2010. *It Still Takes A Candidate: Why Women Don't Run for Office*. New York, NY: Cambridge University Press.

——— and ———. 2005. *It Takes A Candidate: Why Women Don't Run for Office*, New York, NY: Cambridge University Press.

——— and ———. 2001. "Political Participation of the Urban Poor." *Social Problems* 48(3):265–82.

——— and Kathryn Pearson. 2008. "The Primary Reason for Women's Under-Representation: Re-Evaluating the Conventional Wisdom." *Journal of Politics* 70(1):67–82.

——— and Sean M. Theriault. 2005. "Will She Stay or Will She Go? Career Ceilings and Women's Retirement from the U.S. Congress." *Legislative Studies Quarterly* 30(4):581–96.

Lee, Marcia Manning. 1976. "Why So Few Women Hold Public Office: Democracy and Sexual Roles." *Political Science Quarterly* 91:297–314.

Levine, Martin D. and Mark S. Hyde. 1977. "Incumbency and the Theory of Political Ambition: A Rational Choice Model." *Journal of Politics* 39(4):959–83.

London, Bruce and Michael W. Giles. 1987. "Black Participation: Compensation or Ethnic Identification." *Journal of Black Studies* 18(1):20–44.

Lublin, David. 1997. *The Paradox of Representation*. Princeton, NJ: Princeton University Press.

Maestas, Cherie. 2003. "The Incentive to Listen: Progressive Ambition, Resources, and Opinion Monitoring Among State Legislators." *Journal of Politics* 65(2):439–56.

———. 2000. "Professional Legislatures and Ambitious Politicians: Policy Responsiveness of Individuals and Institutions." *Legislative Studies Quarterly* 25(4):663–90.

———, Lonna Rae Atkeson, Thomas Croom, and Lisa A. Bryant. 2008. "Shifting the Blame: Federalism, Media, and Public Assignment of Blame Following Hurricane Katrina." *Publius* 38(4):609–32.

———, Sarah Fulton, L. Sandy Maisel, and Walter J. Stone. 2006. "When to Risk It? Institutions, Ambitions, and the Decision to Run for the U.S. House." *American Political Science Review* 100(2):195–208.

———, L. Sandy Maisel, and Walter J. Stone. 2005. "National Party Efforts to Recruit State Legislators to Run for the U.S. House." *Legislative Studies Quarterly* 30(2):277–300.

Maisel, L. Sandy and Walter J. Stone. 1997. "Determinants of Candidate Emergence in U.S. House Elections: An Exploratory Study." *Legislative Studies Quarterly* 22(1):79–96.

——— and ———. 1998. "The Politics of Government-Funded Research: Notes from the Experience of the Candidate Emergence Study." *PS: Political Science & Politics* 31(4):811–7.

Malbin, Michael J., Norman J. Ornstein, and Thomas E. Mann. 2008. *Vital Statistics on Congress 2008*. Washington, DC: Brookings Institution.

Mansbridge, Jane. 1999. "Should Blacks Represent Blacks and Women Represent Women? A Contingent 'Yes'." *Journal of Politics* 61(3):628–57.

Mark, David. 2006. *Going Dirty: The Art of Negative Campaigning*. Lanham, MD: Rowman and Littlefield.

Mason, Mary Ann and Mark Goulden. 2002. "Do Babies Matter? The Effect of Family Formation of the Lifelong Careers of Academic Men and Women." *Academe* 88(6):21–7.

Masuoka, Natalie. 2008. "Defining the Group: Latino Identity and Political Participation." *American Politics Research* 36(1):33–61.

Matthews, Donald R. 1984. "Legislative Recruitment and Legislative Careers." *Legislative Studies Quarterly* 9(4):547–85.

——— and James W. Prothro. 1966. *Negroes in the New Southern Politics*. New York, NY: Harcourt Brace.

Mayhew, David. 1974. *The Electoral Connection*. New Haven, CT: Yale University Press.

McDermott, Monika L. 1998. "Race and Gender Cues in Low-Information Elections." *Political Research Quarterly* 51(4):895–918.

———. 1997. "Voting Cues in Low-Information Elections: Candidate Gender as a Social Information Variable in Contemporary US Elections." *American Journal of Political Science* 41(1):270–83.

McGlen, Nancy E., Karen O'Connor, Laura Van Assendelft, and Wendy Gunther-Canada. 2005. *Women, Politics, and American Society*, 4th ed. New York, NY: Longman.

McIntosh, Hugh, Daniel Hart, and James Youniss. 2007. "The Influence of Family Political Discussion on Youth Civic Development: Which Parent Qualities Matter?" *PS: Political Science & Politics* 40(3):495–99.

Mendelberg, Tali. 2001. *The Race Card: Campaign Strategy, Implicit Messages, and the Norm of Equality*. Princeton, NJ: Princeton University Press.

Miller, Anita. 1994. *The Complete Transcripts of the Clarence Thomas–Anita Hill Hearings: October 11, 12, 13, 1991*. Chicago, IL: Academy Chicago Publishers.

Minta, Michael. 2009. "Legislative Oversight and Substantive Representation of Black and Latino Interests in Congress." *Legislative Studies Quarterly* 34(2):193–218.

Moncrief, Gary F., Peverill Squire, and Malcolm E. Jewell. 2001. *Who Runs for the Legislature?* Upper Saddle River, NJ: Prentice Hall.

Moore, Michael K. and John R. Hibbing. 1992. "Is Serving in Congress Fun Again? Voluntary Retirement from the House Since the 1970s." *American Journal of Political Science* 36(3):824–8.

Myrdal, Alva. 1968. *Nation and Family*. Cambridge, MA: Massachusetts Institute of Technology.

National Association for Law Placement Foundation. 2010. "Women and Minorities in Law Firms by Race and Ethnicity." http://www.nalp.org/race_ethn_jan2010 (accessed September 12, 2010).

National Conference of State Legislatures. 2010a. "2010 Legislator Compensation Data." http://www.ncsl.org/default.aspx?tabid=20117 (accessed July 13, 2010).

———. 2010b. "2010 Legislative Session Calendar." http://www.ncsl.org/?tabid=18630 (accessed July 13, 2010).

———. 2010c. "Population and Size of the Legislature." http://www.ncsl.org/Default.aspx?TabId=13527 (accessed July 13, 2010).

National League of Cities. 2010. "The Number of Local Governments in the U.S." http://www.nlc.org/about_cities/cities_101/142.aspx (accessed July 13, 2010).

Nechemias, Carol. 1987. "Changes in the Election of Women to U.S. State Legislative Seats." *Legislative Studies Quarterly* 12(1):125–42.

Niederle, Muriel and Lise Vesterlund. 2007. "Do Women Shy Away from Competition? Do Men Compete Too Much?" *Quarterly Journal of Economics* 122(3):1067–1101.

——— and ———. 2010. "Explaining the Gender Gap in Math Test Scores: The Role of Competition." *Journal of Economic Perspectives* 24(2): 129–44.

Niemi, Richard G. 1974. *How Family Members Perceive Each Other: Political and Social Attitudes in Two Generations*. New Haven, CT: Yale University Press.

Niven, David. 1998. *The Missing Majority: The Recruitment of Women as State Legislative Candidates*. Westport, CT: Praeger.

———. 2006. "Throwing Your Hat Out of the Ring: Negative Recruitment and the Gender Imbalance in State Legislative Candidacy." *Politics & Gender* 2(4):473–89.

Nixon, David L. and Robert Darcy. 1996. "Special Elections and the Growth of Women's Representation in the House of Representatives." *Women & Politics* 16 (Winter):96–107.

Norrander, Barbara and Clyde Wilcox. 2008. "The Gender Gap in Ideology." *Political Behavior* 30(4):503–23.

Okin, Susan Moller. 1989. *Justice, Gender, and the Family*. New York, NY: Basic Books.

Olsen, Marvin E. 1970. "Social and Political Participation of Blacks." *American Sociological Review* 35(4): 682–97.

Orum, Anthony M. 1966. "A Reappraisal of the Social and Political Participation of Negroes." *American Journal of Sociology* 72(1):32–46.

Owen, Diana and Jack Dennis. 1988. "Gender Differences in the Politicization of American Children." *Women & Politics* 8(Summer):23–43.

Paine, Thomas. 1776. "Of Monarchy and Hereditary Succession." *Common Sense*. Philadelphia, PA: W. and T. Bradford.

Pajares, Frank. 2002. "Gender and Perceived Self-Efficacy in Self-Regulated Learning." *Theory Into Practice* 41(2):116–25.

Palin, Sarah. 2009. *Going Rogue: An American Life*. New York, NY: Harper-Collins Publishers.

Palmer, Barbara and Dennis Simon. 2008. *Breaking the Political Glass Ceiling: Women and Congressional Elections*, 2nd ed. New York, NY: Routledge.

Pantoja, Adrian D. and Gary M. Segura. 2003. "Does Ethnicity Matter? Descriptive Representation in Legislatures and Political Alienation Among Latinos." *Social Science Quarterly* 84(2):441–60.

Paolino, Phillip. 1995. "Group-Salient Issues and Group Representation: Support for Women Candidates in the 1992 Senate Elections." *American Journal of Political Science* 39(2):294–313.

Pasek, Josh, Lauren Feldman, Daniel Romer, and Kathleen Hall Jamieson. 2008. "Schools as Incubators of Democratic Participation: Building Long-Term Political Efficacy with Civic Education." *Applied Developmental Science* 12(1):26–37.

Pitkin, Hanna F. 1967. *The Concept of Representation*. Berkeley, CA: University of California Press.

Piven, Frances Fox and Richard Cloward. 1997. *The Breaking of the American Social Compact*. New York: New York Press.

Philpot, Tasha S. and Hanes Walton. 2007. "One of Our Own: Black Female Candidates and the Voters Who Support Them." *American Journal of Political Science* 51(1):49–62.

Piliawsky, Monte. 1989. "Racial Politics in the 1988 Presidential Election." *The Black Scholar* 20:1–11.

Plutzer, Eric and John F. Zipp. 1996. "Gender Identity and Voting for Women Candidates." *Public Opinion Quarterly* 60(1):30–57.

Preuhs, Robert R. 2006. "The Conditional Effects of Minority Descriptive Representation: Black Legislators and Policy Influence in the American States." *Journal of Politics* 68(3):585–99.

Prewitt, Kenneth. 1970a. "Political Ambitions, Volunteerism, and Electoral Accountability." *American Political Science Review* 64(1):5–17.

_____. 1970b. *The Recruitment of Political Leaders: A Study of Citizen Politicians.* Indianapolis, IN: Bobbs-Merrill.

Prinz, Timothy S. 1993. "The Career Paths of Elected Politicians: A Review and Prospectus." In *Ambition and Beyond: Career Paths of American Politicians,* eds. S. Williams and E. Lascher. Berkeley, CA: Institute of Governmental Studies.

Rausch, John D., Mark Rozell, and Harry L. Wilson. 1999. "When Women Lose: A Case Study of Media Coverage of Two Gubernatorial Campaigns." *Women & Politics* 20(4):1–22.

Renshon, Stanley A. 1975. "Temporal Orientations and Political Life: The Psychology of Political Impatience." *British Journal of Political Science* 7(2):262–72.

Roberts, T. 1991. "Gender and the Influences of Evaluation on Self-Assessment in Achievement Settings." *Psychological Bulletin* 109(2):297–308.

Rohde, David W. 1979. "Risk-Bearing and Progressive Ambition: The Case of the U.S. House of Representatives." *American Journal of Political Science* 23(1):1–26.

Rule, Wilma. 1990. "Why More Women Are State Legislators: A Research Note." *Western Political Quarterly* 43(2).437–48.

_____. 1981. "Why Women Don't Run: The Critical Contextual Factors in Women's Legislative Recruitment." *Western Political Quarterly* 34 (March): 60–77.

Sabato, Larry J. 2000. *Feeding Frenzy: Attack Journalism and American Politics.* Baltimore, MD: New Lanahan Editions in Political Science.

Saint-Germain, Michelle A. 1989. "Does Their Difference Make a Difference? The Impact of Women on Public Policy in the Arizona State Legislature." *Social Science Quarterly* 70(4):956–68.

Sanbonmatsu, Kira. 2006. *Where Women Run: Gender and Party in the American States.* Ann Arbor, MI: University of Michigan Press.

Sanchez, Gabriel R. 2006. "The Role of Group Consciousness in Political Participation Among Latinos in the United States." *American Politics Research* 34(4):427–50.

Sapiro, Virginia. 1982. "Private Costs of Public Commitments or Public Costs of Private Commitments? Family Roles versus Political Ambition." *American Journal of Political Science* 26(2):265–79.

Schleicher, David. 2007. "Why Is There No Partisan Competition in City Council Elections: The Role of Election Law." *Journal of Law and Politics* 23(4):419–73.

Schlesinger, Joseph A. 1966. *Ambition and Politics: Political Careers in the United States.* Chicago, IL: Rand NcNally.

Schwindt-Bayer, Leslie A. and Renato Corbetta. 2004. "Gender Turnover and Roll-Call Voting in the U.S. House of Representatives." *Legislative Studies Quarterly* 29(2):215–29.

Schwindt-Bayer, Leslie A. and William Mishler. 2005. "An Integrated Model of Women's Representation." *Journal of Politics* 67(2):407–28.

Seligman, Lester G., Michael R. King, Chong Lim Kim, and Roland E. Smith. 1974. *Patterns of Recruitment: A State Chooses Its Lawmakers.* New York, NY: Rand McNally.

Shaw, Catherine. 2004. *The Campaign Manager: Running and Winning Local Elections,* 3rd ed. Boulder, CO: Westview.

Shingles, Richard D. 1981. "Black Consciousness and Political Participation: The Missing Link." *American Political Science Review* 75(1):76–91.

Simon, Stefanie and Crystal L. Hoyt. 2008. "Exploring the Gender Gap in Support for a Woman for President." *Analyses of Social Issues and Public Policy* 8(1):157–81.

Smith, Eric R.A.N. and Richard L. Fox. 2001. "A Research Note: The Electoral Fortunes of Women Candidates for Congress." *Political Research Quarterly* 54(1):205–21.

Sonenshein, Raphael J. 1990. "Can Black Candidates Win Statewide Elections?" *Political Science Quarterly* 105(2):219–41.

Soule, John W. 1969. "Future Political Ambitions and the Behavior of Incumbent State Legislators." *Midwest Journal of Political Science* 13(3):439–54.

Squire, Peverill. 1988. "Career Opportunities and Membership Stability in Legislatures." *Legislative Studies Quarterly* 13(1):65–80.

———. 2000. "Uncontested Seats in State Legislative Elections." *Legislative Studies Quarterly* 25(1):131–46.

Stoker, Laura and M. Kent Jennings. 1995. "Life-Cycle Transitions and Political Participation: The Case of Marriage." *American Political Science Review* 89(2):421–33.

Stokes, Atiya Kai. 2003. "Latino Group Consciousness and Political Participation." *American Politics Research* 31(4):361–78.

Stokes-Brown, Atiya Kai. 2006. "Racial Identity and Latino Vote Choice." *American Politics Research* 34(5):627–52.

Stone, Pauline Terrelonge. 1980. "Ambition Theory and the Black Politician." *Western Political Quarterly* 33(1):94–107.

Stone, Walter J. and L. Sandy Maisel. 2003. "The Not-So-Simple Calculus of Winning: Potential U.S. House Candidates' Nominations and General Election Prospects." *Journal of Politics* 65(4):951–77.

———, ———, and Cherie D. Maestas. 2004. "Quality Counts: Extending the Strategic Competition Model of Incumbent Deterrence." *American Journal of Political Science* 48(3):479–95.

Studlar, Donley T. and Susan Welch. 1990. "Multi-Member Districts and the Representation of Women: Evidence from Britain and the United States." *Journal of Politics* 52(2):391–412.

Sutter, Daniel. 2006. "Media Scrutiny and the Quality of Public Officials." *Public Choice* 129(1–2):25–40.

Swain, Carol M. 1995. *Black Faces, Black Interests: The Representation of African Americans in Congress.* Cambridge, MA: Harvard University Press.

Swers, Michele L. 1998. "Are Congresswomen More Likely to Vote for Women's Issue Bills Than Their Male Colleagues?" *Legislative Studies Quarterly* 23(3):435–48.

———. 2002. *The Difference Women Make*. Chicago, IL: University of Chicago Press.

Swinerton, E. Nelson. 1968. "Ambition and American State Executives." *Midwest Journal of Political Science* 12(4):538–49.

Swint, Kerwin C. 2006. *Mudslingers: The Top 25 Negative Political Campaigns of All Time Countdown from No. 25 to No. 1*. Westport, CT: Greenwood.

Teixeira, Ruy A. 1992. *The Disappearing American Voter*. Washington, DC: Brookings Institution.

Terkildsen, Nayda. 1993. "When White Voters Evaluate Black Candidates: The Processing Implications of Candidate Skin Color, Prejudice, and Self-Monitoring." *American Journal of Political Science* 37(4):1032–53.

Theriault, Sean M. 1998. "Moving Up or Moving Out: Career Ceilings and Congressional Retirement." *Legislative Studies Quarterly* 23(3):419–33.

Thomas, Sue. 1994. *How Women Legislate*. New York, NY: Oxford University Press.

———. 1998. "Introduction: Women and Elective Office: Past, Present, and Future." In *Women and Elective Office*, eds. S. Thomas and C. Wilcox. New York, NY: Oxford University Press.

———. 2002. "The Personal is the Political: Antecedents of Gendered Choices of Elected Representatives." *Sex Roles* 47(7–8):343–53.

——— and Susan Welch. 1991. "The Impact of Gender on Activities and Priorities of State Legislators." *Western Political Quarterly* 44(2):445–56.

Thompson, Fred. 2010. *Teaching a Pig to Dance: A Memoir of Growing Up and Second Chances*. New York, NY: Random House.

Treier, Shawn and D. Sunshine Hillygus. 2009. "The Nature of Political Ideology in the Contemporary Electorate." *Public Opinion Quarterly* 73(4):679–703.

Trounstine, Jessica and Melody E. Valdini. 2008. "The Context Matters: The Effects of Single-Member versus At-Large Districts on City Council Diversity." *American Journal of Political Science* 52(3):554–69.

United States Census Bureau. 2010. "State and County Quick Facts." http://quickfacts.census.gov/qfd/states/00000.html (July 18, 2010).

Valentino, Nicholas. 1999. "Crime and the Priming of Racial Attitudes During Evaluations of the President." *Public Opinion Quarterly* 63(3):293–320.

Verba, Sidney, Key Lehman Schlozman, and Henry E. Brady. 1995. *Voice and Equality: Civic Voluntarism in American Politics*. Cambridge, MA: Harvard University Press.

——— and Norman H. Nie. 1972. *Participation in America: Political Democracy and Social Equality*. New York, NY: Harper and Row.

Welch, Susan. 1978. "Recruitment of Women to Office." *Western Political Quarterly* 31(2):372–80.

——— and Albert K. Karnig. 1979. "Correlates of Female Office Holding in City Politics." *Journal of Politics* 41(2):478–91.

Whitaker, Lois Duke. 2008. *Voting the Gender Gap*. Champaign, IL: University of Illinois Press.

Wigfield, Allan, Jacquelynne S. Eccles, and Paul R. Pintrich. 1996. "Development Between the Ages of 11 and 25." In *Handbook of Educational Psychology*, eds. D.C. Berliner and R.C. Calfee. New York, NY: Macmillan.

Wilcox, Clyde. 1994. "Why Was 1992 the 'Year of the Woman?' Explaining Women's Gains in 1992." In *The Year of the Woman: Myths and Realities*, eds. E. A. Cook, S. Thomas, and C. Wilcox. Boulder, CO: Westview Press.

Wilson, James Q. 1962. *The Amateur Democrat.* Chicago, IL: University of Chicago Press.

Wilson, William J. 1991. "Public Policy Research and the Truly Disadvantaged." In *The Urban Underclass*, eds. C. Jencks and P.E. Peterson. Washington, DC: Brookings.

Witt, Linda, Karen Paget, and Glenna Matthews. 1994. *Running as a Woman.* New York, NY: Free Press.

Wolfinger, Nicholas H. and Raymond E. Wolfinger. 2008. "Family Structure and Voter Turnout." *Social Forces* 86(4):1513–28.

Index